D1586995

MUSSOORIE
AND
LANDOUR

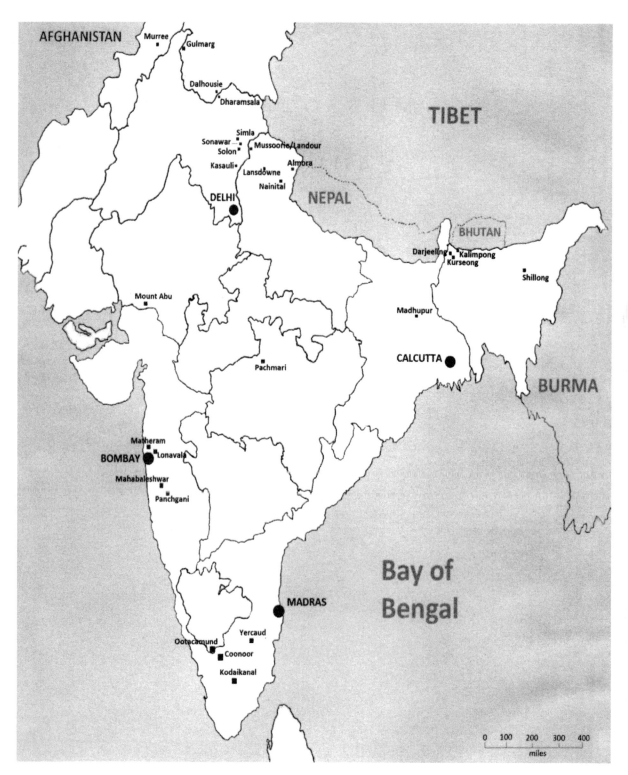

A pre-Independence map of India with all the major hill stations.

MUSSOORIE AND LANDOUR

~Footprints of the Past~

VIRGIL MIEDEMA
STEPHANIE SPAID MIEDEMA

RUPA

Published by
Rupa Publications India Pvt. Ltd 2014
7/16, Ansari Road, Daryaganj
New Delhi 110002

Sales Centres:
Allahabad Bengaluru Chennai
Hyderabad Jaipur Kathmandu
Kolkata Mumbai

ISBN: 978-81-291-2434-0

10 9 8 7 6 5 4 3 2 1

The moral right of the authors has been asserted.

Printed at Thomson Press India Ltd., Faridabad

To Barbara and Allison
and
to our many friends in Mussoorie and Landour

.

CONTENTS

FOREWORD

First impressions count. And our first impression of Mussoorie got ever higher as we made our steady way 7,000 feet up the hill to it.

One winter weekend about ten years ago, my wife Clare and I caught the overnight train from Delhi to Dehra Dun. We arrived at 8.00 a.m., had breakfast and took a taxi up, up and still further up the 15-mile switchback road to Mussoorie. As the slope got steeper, we twisted and turned and corkscrewed and double-backed and triple-backed. If we'd been attached to a rope, we would literally have tied ourselves in knots.

We passed dozens of tea stalls perched perilously on the edge of precipitous drops and eventually reached Mussoorie, feeling a little nauseated. But as we opened the car doors, we stepped out into a fresher, more invigorating world. It wasn't just the climate—you'd expect a keen winter chill at 7,000 feet (2,133 metres). It was more that the town, straddling its long ridge, had a relaxed holiday feel. The houses, hotels and shops, clinging to their hillsides, were waiting to be enjoyed; which, as this staggeringly well-researched book shows, is precisely what 'the pleasure capital of the Raj' was created for.

I'll come clean here. Virgil Miedema is an old friend and he was travelling with us. We had been staying with him and his family in Delhi and he insisted we should come with him to Mussoorie. He had discovered the place a few years before, and it had instantly joined Darjeeling and Nainital as a favourite hill station. All, of course, were once thoroughly, tweedily British—cherished retreats for the Raj, where servants of the Empire escaped from the summer heat of the plains and unwound in high-altitude recreations of home counties' cosiness.

Over subsequent years, we made several more trips together. The three of us share an interest in British India, which runs as a main theme through this book. Reminders of it soon became our focus in Mussoorie. True, we enjoyed the town's cluttered, touristy bazaars, where crowds throng. The stalls and shops reminded us Brits of an old-fashioned English seaside promenade; 'a bit raffish', as Ruskin Bond, the town's celebrated resident author, once described it to me.

Bond actually lives along a narrow ridge from Mussoorie, in the quieter settlement of Landour. Its own bazaars have a more authentic feel, and we paid many a visit to Mr Prakash the grocer for his wonderful plum jam and fruit cakes, his home-made cheese and cheese from Sikkim, and his marmalade made in Bhutan: food from the mountains.

For all the ready pleasures of the bazaars, though, it was the relics of 'British days', as older Indians say, that really captivated us. We explored the old Victorian churches, particularly primrose-yellow Christ Church, built in 1836 as, in the evocative words of a bishop of the day, 'the first church raised amidst the eternal snows of Upper India'. Inside were memorials charged with the pathos of short lives in foreign lands (Georgianna Compton, died in 1862, aged twenty-one) and with the pride of longer lives usefully spent. Here was a 'sterling character' who had given 'faithful service'; there 'a kind loyal friend'; further along a person of 'watchful care'. Monkeys clattered over the corrugated iron roof.

We wandered round the ghostly Savoy Hotel, once one of the great Indian hotels, gay with fancy-dress balls, but, ten years ago, forlorn and all but deserted. The wind whistled across the ballroom; moth-eaten stags' heads drooped from the walls; the dining room had bare floorboards (though, since then, it has been completely renovated). Down the hill, with clouds creeping slowly along the valleys, we toured cemeteries where mossy obelisks mark the graves of many of the people mentioned in this book.

We visited Hamer's Chemist, with its original Edwardian fittings, and the ice rink, where Gilbert and Sullivan echoed from the loudspeakers. We had lunch at the Carlton Plaisance Hotel. In the grate was a wood fire; on the floor a bearskin rug, its head caught in eternal roar.

And we browsed the dusty shelves of the town's library, a time capsule of British middlebrow taste with its ancient scuffed novels by Vicki Baum, Warwick Deeping and Ruby M. Ayres. May Edginton's *The Sun Will Shine* had a flurry of date stamps shortly after publication in 1938, but had sat on the shelves, unissued, from 1945 to 1980.

All this may sound a touch melancholy, but Virgil's enthusiasm made it strangely exhilarating, particularly with the snow-topped Himalayas looming—an icy luminescent blue—behind the town. This was, I decided, an oddly back-to-front resort. Its main attractions look out over the plains; the spectacular mountain views are almost private, hidden at the back, with wood smoke drifting around the deodars as mists rise in a sky streaked pink, gold and orange.

The plains' panorama, however, is magical at night, with vast skies, twinkling stars merging into the twinkling lights of Dehra Dun far below, and the silence disturbed only by distant barking dogs.

One slightly surreal afternoon, we visited a grand old house full of sepia photographs of Mussoorie-ites long gone, drank tea out of china cups and nibbled sandwiches with their crusts trimmed. An almost-elderly resident bent my ear. 'Education is not what it was,' he lamented, 'one is no longer taught how to bag a partridge or land a trout.'

All this is Virgil Miedema's Mussoorie. His and his daughter Stephanie's love for it comes over on every page of their book. The town was, as they write, 'an out-of-India place for the British'. And, of course, for Anglophile and Indophile Americans.

Stephen McClarence
Travel writer (*The Times* and *Daily Telegraph,* London)

Joseph Vail Barrows (b.1886–d.1972) and Nora Doreen Searle (b.1902–d.1937), departing in a rickshaw after their 23 August 1932 wedding at Christ Church. Joseph was a Presbyterian minister from New Wilmington, Pennsylvania (USA), who had been sent to the Punjab to work among villagers. Nora was born in India, her father Colonel Charles Thomas Arnaud Searle being a British army officer. In a letter to her grandfather announcing her engagement, Nora had written, 'We will have to ride away in a double rickshaw, as no motors can come to Mussoorie, but Mr. Fazl-ud Din, one of my language teachers, will see if he can get hold of some rajah's nice rickshaw with liveried coolies!'

Mr Fazl-ud Din apparently succeeded to some extent, as the rickshaw bears a crest, but alas, the coolies standing by were not very well-liveried. This 1932 photo is juxtaposed with a 2009 view of the Christ Church parsonage in the background.

(Kind courtesy of Mrs Dorothy Durling, USA, granddaughter of Reverend and Mrs Barrows)

PREFACE

Our attachment to Mussoorie goes back to the mid 1990s, when friends working at Woodstock, an international school located in Landour, encouraged us to visit the hill station. We were living in New Delhi then, and Mussoorie soon became our bolthole from the dizzying pace—and searing heat—of the capital city. Our affection for this Himalayan resort continued to grow over the years as our visits increased. This book is a result of our enduring fascination and association with the town, combined with an amateur's interest in history.

In the latter half of the nineteenth century, Mussoorie and the Landour Cantonment and its adjoining bazaar were quite distinct from each other. Today, Mussoorie and Landour have merged, but each still has its own character. Mussoorie is often said to be 'for the tourists', as it is chock-a-block with small hotels, restaurants and bric-a-brac shops selling everything from walking sticks—something from the town's earliest days—to faux jewellery, monkey caps, ice-cream cones and popcorn. During the 'Season', which now seems to extend throughout the year, thanks to improved transportation and a vibrant Indian middle class, Mussoorie takes on a carnival atmosphere.

Landour, on the other hand, has retained much of its quiet hillside aura. More than anything else, this is due to the fact that about two-thirds of Landour consists of cantonment or military property, with protected forests and strict limits on building. Other major portions of Landour, such as the Survey of India and school properties, are also well-protected. Lower Landour boasts a small but lively bazaar that serves the needs of local residents. As one proceeds further up the hillside, shops give way to bungalows and forests. Thus, many of the attractions that first drew Frederick Young and his compatriots to Landour are still there, high above Mussoorie.

This pictorial and narrative history of the Station focuses on the colonial era, covering the period from 1823 when the two Fredericks, Frederick Young and Frederick Shore, built their 'shooting box' on Camel's Back to 1947, when India gained independence. However, some later historical events, like the Dalai Lama's presence in Mussoorie in the late 1950s, are also touched upon here. Throughout the book, we have attempted to link the past to the present in order to give the modern reader a sense of 'what happened next'. The postscript offers a few more observations about the early post-Independence period and today's Mussoorie. In the various chapters, which grew in number as research continued, we have tried to show a progression in Mussoorie's development, without slavishly following a strict timeline.

The earliest colonizers to enter the area, as well as the later Victorians, built Mussoorie between 1823 to 1901, with significant growth after the '1857 Mutiny' or First War of Independence. The Edwardians enjoyed the salubrious clime of the Station in the early twentieth century, even though the sun was already lowering in the Imperial sky. From the 1920s until the beginning of the Second World War, Mussoorie saw a less prosperous period, as travel back and forth to Britain became easier and affordable for many of those who otherwise would have gone to the hills during the hot weather. However, the Second World War itself ended such travel. During the 1940s and early 1950s Mussoorie experienced a revival, fuelled by soldiers and other expatriates and, importantly, by Indian royalty who were also restricted in their travel during the war and, after it, didn't wish to go to depressed Europe in the early 1950s. In the 1960s, Mussoorie saw another downturn that lasted until a rapidly growing Indian middle class came to see the Station in the same light as the British rulers had; that is, as a getaway. This trend continues unabated, as attested by scores of visitors today who weave their way through the crowded Mall with its festive atmosphere.

Yet, amidst the crowds and the many changes, physical remnants of the past remain scattered along the ridge lines, from the Botanical Gardens in the west to the 'haunted house' in the east. We have tried to touch on each of these and locate them in various contexts covering lifestyles, holiday-making and just 'getting on' in the early years.

In doing so, we came across interesting bits of information and local lore that may be new to readers, even to those who are quite familiar with the Station. Just how many houses did Frederick Young, the 'founder' of the Station, have in Mussoorie and Landour? And why in the early years was his Mullingar House nicknamed Mulliagoes? Why did Everest buy his Park Estate sight unseen? Who was the famous preacher and linguist who made Mussoorie his home and after whom a local church is named? How did Mussoorie become linked—in rather unlikely ways—to Afghanistan, and all the three Anglo–Afghan Wars that spanned the nineteenth and twentieth centuries? British royalty rarely made it to Mussoorie, so what was the Princess of Wales doing in the Station on an unplanned visit in 1906? Where is the pictorial or other evidence to show that Indians were kept off the Mall in Mussoorie in the British days? The waterfalls around Mussoorie were mostly named after early residents but the name ascribed to Kempty Falls, a popular tourist site, does not represent any resident of the bygone days. From where did the Falls derive its name? Which is the oldest 'English' school in the Himalayas? Were pianos only tuned in Mussoorie, or was there more to this 'entertainment industry'? How was it that the residents of Mussoorie enjoyed electricity well before their counterparts in other major cities on the plains? And, finally, is it possible to put to rest why Woodstock School is still nicknamed the 'Company School'?

It is all local history at its best!

In telling the tale of Mussoorie, we have relied heavily on early guidebooks. We doff our hats to these contributors of yore: John Northan (*Guide to Masuri, Landaur, Dehra Dun and the Hills North of Dehra*, 1884), Robert Hawthorn (*The Beacon's Guide to Mussoorie*, 1890), F. Bodycot (*Guide to Mussoorie with Notes on Adjacent Districts and Routes into the Interior*, 1907), T. Kinney (*The Echo Guide to Mussoorie*, 1908), and C. Williams[1] (*A Mussoorie Miscellany*, 1936). For some of the early post-Independence information that is scattered throughout the book, we have partially relied on R.N. Singh (*Guide to Mussoorie*, 1969).

We wish to express our gratitude for the assistance given by many people. In Mussoorie itself, numerous individuals gave valuable interview time, answered many of our questions and provided important leads and much encouragement. These include Hugh and Colleen Gantzer; local historian Gopal Bhardwaj; Lillian Skinner Singh and Sylvia Skinner Mahindroo of Sikander Hall; Arthur and Dagma Houghton and the late Myrtle Tindale of Woodlands Estate in Landour; Sunil Arora of the famous Cambridge Bookstore; Dr Rita Leavell; Martand Singh of the House of Kapurthala; and Swatantra Kumar, proprietor of the (former) Mela Ram & Sons photography shop, and his most capable staff who took some excellent modern-day photographs. We are especially indebted to Alok Jain, Uttarakhand finance secretary, who advised us throughout this project and was a source of great encouragement.

On the ecclesiastical side, our thanks go to Father Peter Rawat, Reverend G. Cornelius, Reverend Erik Templeton and Reverend Anita Templeton, all in Mussoorie; and to Sister Françoise Barras of the Religious of Jesus and Mary in Rome. Information about the various boarding schools was kindly provided by several staff members at these institutions, notably Monica Roberts, Steve Alter and

---

[1]C. Williams's nom de plume was 'The Rambler'.

Judy Crider at Woodstock School, Leslie Tindale and Lynette Cashmore at Wynberg Allen, Sister Anita at Waverley and Brother Christopher Dawes at St George's.

Special thanks must go to Tarjeed Singh, better known in Mussoorie as Winkie, who, along with his staff, has offered us on several occasions the warmest of hospitality at his All Seasons Guest House, besides providing important information for this book, particularly about St George's School, his beloved alma mater.

We appreciate the efforts of Anita Jacob and Joyoti Roy, archivists at the fabulous Alkazi Collection of Photography, New Delhi, who arranged for copies of nineteenth-century photographs, and to Cate Whitcomb, Jack Hinz and Anuradha and Alok Jain for their hospitality.

We deeply thank Peter Tiller and Marilyn Metz in the UK for their friendship over many years, and for their warm and unstinting hospitality on our many visits to London and the British Library. At the library, we were ably assisted by Dr Jennifer Howe and Mike Moloney. Also of particular assistance in the UK were Dr Rosie Llewellyn-Jones, former secretary of the British Association of Cemeteries in South Asia (the association made up of members whom someone recently called 'ancestor worshippers'); Sonia and John Harriyott, and Jennifer and Andrew Warren in Cambridge; David Swain at the Oriental Club; the late Michael Stokes in Kent, who generously shared his fabulous Mussoorie postcard collection, and his wife Prue; Sue Farrington; Hugh Ashley Rayner in Bath for his friendship and for kindly sharing pictures and valuable information; Bob Williams, Gerald Eates, Bob Francis, William Lethorn, Ian Morshead and Timothy George for lending valuable reference material; and, last but not the least, Stephen McClarence and Clare Jenkins for their constant encouragement and for sharing their friendship and love of India.

In Ireland, special thanks must go to Adrian Stevenson and George Mills, both descendants of George Young (brother of Gardiner Young who was Frederick Young's father), who provided information on Frederick Young's place of burial and details of his remaining estate. Jennifer Murphy, library assistant at the Representative Church Body (Church of Ireland) recommended Justin Homan Martin of Dublin to help search Young's gravesite. He and Miss Jennifer M.J. Kavanagh kindly managed the photographs of Young's grave. And a final Irish thanks to Bernie Deasy, keeper of Patrician Brotherhood records at Delany Archive, Carlow College.

Bob Francis in Australia provided a wealth of information on the Mussoorie of his day and answered numerous questions. Bob's family lived in the Station from the early 1920s to 1962.

Both Eric Frazier at the Library of Congress Rare Book and Special Collections Division and Jeffery Bridges at the Prints and Photographs Division were extremely helpful in accessing valuable material. Of particular importance was bringing to our attention the fascinating collection of Mussoorie photographs taken by an American couple, Mr and Mrs. Samuel Alexander Hill, who were residing at the Charleville Hotel during the 1888 Season. The Hills were friends of Rudyard Kipling and he captioned the pictures, some of which appear in this book, published for the first time. Susan Meinheit, the library's Tibetan specialist, was also very helpful in accessing information about the Dalai Lama's time in Mussoorie. Jere Daniell, retired Dartmouth College professor and our neighbour and friend, offered many helpful suggestions. Bruce Keelan, Peter Haynal, Dennis Dean Tidwell and Bert Haloviak kindly provided information on the well-remembered Seventh Day Adventists' Vincent Hill School. Carl Dutto did a wonderful job of tracking down information on Paoli Solaroli and John Dixon in Hawaii applied his talented hand in sketching Bassett Hall for us. Others in the United States who provided assistance include Omar Khan, Dorothy Durling, Verena Rybicki and Steve Van Rooy.

A few explanatory notes on the text may be useful. 'The Station' is the term we have used when referring to both Mussoorie *and* Landour. 'Cantonment' refers only to the army-owned part of Landour, not the (lower) bazaar. We have tried to standardize place names, but have not meddled with the original—and highly erratic—spellings found in direct quotes. Some readers may find the numerous quotations onerous, but we have chosen to use them at regular intervals rather than paraphrase, as we feel it gives a good sense of the period and styles of writing. Some of the notes and references found at the end of the chapters are quite detailed, which we hope will give the keenest readers additional information that clarifies and expands on the text. The Station's schools and houses of worship are given stand-alone chapters in light of their physical prominence and historical importance in the Station, while other institutions are covered collectively in the chapter entitled 'Community Life in the Clouds'.

It was a joy to have access to so many historic pictures and lithographs of the Station, only a fraction of which we could use in this book. We trust we have selected wisely.

Virgil Miedema and Stephanie Spaid Miedema

Hanover, New Hampshire (USA)

May 2014

CHRONOLOGY

1786	Frederick Young, founder of Mussoorie and Landour, born in Ireland
1802	Frederick Young arrives in India
1803	James Skinner raises a regiment of irregular cavalry, Skinner's Horse
1805	Battle of Trafalgar (British defeat of French and Spanish fleets)
1811	Hyder Young Hearsey 'buys' the Dun from the raja of Garhwal, Sudarshan Shah
1813	East India Company's monopoly abolished
1814	British declare war against the Nepalese
1815	British victory over Nepalese; Sirmur Battalion raised by Frederick Young
	British defeat of Napoleon (Battle of Waterloo)
1816	Treaty of Sugauli signed, Dun and hills to the north annexed to British India
1820	Death of King George III and accession of George IV
1823	Frederick Young and Frederick John Shore build shooting box on 'Masuri' ridge
1825	Frederick Young marries Jeanette Bird
1825	Frederick Young builds Mullingar House
1827	Landour Depot for convalescing soldiers established (success for Young)
1828	Sixteen houses in the Station (Mussoorie and Landour)
	Death of Captain Charles Farrington (oldest gravesite in the Station)
1830	Old Brewery established
	Death of King George IV and accession of William IV to the British throne
1833	Frederick Young named political agent to the Dun
	George Everest arrives at his Park Estate in Mussoorie
1834	Mussoorie Seminary established (first school in Station)
	Slavery officially abolished in the British Empire
1836	Foundation stone of Christ Church laid
1837	Death of King William IV and accession of Victoria to the British throne
	Frederick ('Pahari') Wilson invalided to Landour, to return later as timber tycoon
1840	St Paul's Church, Landour, established
	Amir Dost Mohammad Khan surrendered to British and brought to Mussoorie
1841	Himalaya Club founded
	St Peter's Catholic Church, Landour, established
1842	Frederick Young leaves Mussoorie and the Dun, assigned to Bundelkhand
	Amir Dost Mohammad Khan leaves Mussoorie and returns to power in Kabul
	F.O. Wells undertakes settlement of lands in the Station ('Well's Settlement')
	Municipal Committee formed (later becomes Board)
	The Hills, the Station's first newspaper, begins publishing
1843	George Everest leaves Mussoorie

	Municipal Library established
1845	Waverley Convent School opens
1852	Mrs Frederick (Jeanette Bird) Young dies in Dinapore
1852	Maharaja Duleep Singh in Mussoorie for the Season at Castle Hill Estate
1853	Maharaja Duleep Singh again in Mussoorie for the Season
	St George's College established
1854	Frederick Young returns to Ireland (Crimean War is raging)
	Lodge Dalhousie (Masonic Lodge) constituted
	Protestant Girls' School opens in Caineville House (Woodstock School)
1856	End of Crimean War; some invalid soldiers to Mussoorie
1857	First War of Independence (the 'Mutiny') begins
1858	Sovereignty of India invested in the Queen, ending East India Company rule
1862	Colonel Norman undertakes another settlement of lands ('Norman Guarantee')
1864	Caineville House School opens
	John George Lang, Australian-born author, dies and is buried in Mussoorie
1865	Peak XV at Latitude North 27° 59' 16.7" and 29,002 feet above sea level named 'Mount Everest'
1867	Crown Brewery opens in Barlowganj
1868	Landour Union Church established
1870	Alfred, duke of Edinburgh, visits Mussoorie, first English royal family member ever to visit
1871	Mussoorie Volunteer Rifle Corps raised
1876	Hindustani Church established
1877	Victoria proclaimed empress of India at Delhi Durbar
	The Charleville Hotel opens
1880	Amir Mohammad Yaqub Khan brought to Mussoorie by British
1884	About 480 houses in the Station (340 European and 140 Indian)
	Philander Smith Institute for Boys opens in Mullingar House
	Duke and duchess of Connaught visit Mussoorie
1887	Sind–Punjab Railway School opens (Oak Grove School)
1888	Christian Training School and Orphanage opens (Wynberg Allen School)
	Woodlands School opens
1897	Military hands over Landour Bazaar to the municipality
1900	St Mary's Cottage Hospital established (first hospital in the Station)
	Mussoorie Seminary (Maddock's School) closes
	Mansumrat Dass named as the first Indian to municipal board
1901	Death of Queen Victoria and accession of Edward VII
1902	Savoy Hotel opens
1903	Mussoorie municipal boundaries revised to cover 19 square miles

	St Emilian's Church established (Sacred Heart Church)
	Kellogg Church established
	Chateau de Kapurthala completed
1904	Happy Valley Club opens
1905	Philander Smith Institute moves to Nainital
1906	Princess of Wales visits Mussoorie
1909	Electricity comes to Mussoorie and Landour
	'Electric pictures' (the cinema) arrive
1910	Telephones come to Mussoorie
1911	Vincent Hill School opens
1912	Eighty private homes in Landour
1914	British Empire enters First World War
1918	End of First World War
1920	Negotiations between Afghanistan and the British open in Mussoorie
	First motor car enters Mussoorie
1922	Hampton Court Preparatory Boys' School opens
1923	Dumbarnie Homes and Orphanage opens (now site of Manava Bharati School)
	Amir Mohammad Yaqub Khan dies in Dehra Dun
1924	Cantonments Act limited new construction and felling of trees in Landour Depot
1931	Landour Community Hospital established
1936	Death of King George V; abdication of Edward VIII; accession of George VI
1939	Second World War begins
1945	Second World War ends
1947	Partition and independence of India

Colonel Frederick Young, first commandant of the Sirmoor Rifles,
political agent of the Dun and the founder of Mussoorie and Landour.
Young first arrived in India in 1802 as a sixteen-year-old military cadet from Ireland.
(Courtesy of Library of Congress)

1

JOHNNY RAW FROM THE BOGS

Through all the changing scenes of life…
~ *From an Irish hymn by Nicholas Brady and Nahum Tate, 1698* ~

The early histories of Indian hill stations are deeply entwined with the rise and fall of the British Colonial Empire, and with the lives of its military and civilian officers who lived far from the British Isles. The particular history of Mussoorie-the-Station and Landour-the-Cantonment begins with one of these satraps of Empire, a young man by the name of Frederick Young.

Frederick Young of Ireland is often described as the 'discoverer' of Mussoorie in much of today's promotional material. However, when he came upon the scene in 1814, there was no Mussoorie hill station, and so his 'discovery' was more to do with breaking ground for a hunting lodge in the hills north of the Dun Valley. At the time of Young's discovery, the area we know today as Mussoorie was all forested, hillsides and ridges, beautiful, cool and excellent for shikar (hunting). Over the early years of the nineteenth century, Young, the military man, emerged as the overseer and avid promoter of Dehra Dun, the founder of Mussoorie and the Landour cantonment, political agent and, as described in 1836 by the bishop of Calcutta, '...the King in fact of the Dhoon...'[1]

Young was born in Greencastle near Moville on the Inishowen Peninsula, in the far north of Ireland's County Donegal, on 30 November 1786. His parents were Reverend Gardiner and Mrs Catherine Young. Young's Presbyterian ancestors had arrived in the County from Devonshire, southwest England, during the 1630s as tenants of the marquis of Donegal.[2]

One of several children, Young was named after his godfather Frederick Harvey, who was the bishop of Derry and a cousin. Years later, Frederick Young would pass on his name to his godson, Frederick Sleigh Roberts (b.1832–d.1914), who later became known to the world as Field Marshal Lord Roberts of Kandahar.

Young's adoring daughter, Louisa, a survivor of the 1857 'Mutiny' or First War of Independence, wrote when she was ninety years old:

> Frederick was fortunate in obtaining a cadetship in the East India Company – a rare piece of good fortune in those days, for selections were made with much care. Latin, Greek, mathematics, and foreign languages did not count for much, but a straight shot and good manners went far! The candidates, so far as one could judge from family and surroundings, had to give promise of being men – and, particularly, gentlemen.[3]

The story goes that before Young's departure, a ghostly visitation apparently foretold his good luck. Young's daughter records his leave-taking from his large family, including a visit to cousins at Shanes Castle, where he was said to have seen a ghost of an old woman who allegedly appeared only once or twice in a generation. Those 'honoured' with such a visitation were believed to be blessed with good luck and a safe homecoming. In the event, his life in India was, indeed, filled with much good fortune and a safe return. Young left India for the final time in 1854, after fifty-two years filled with extraordinary and dramatic events.

At the very beginning of his career, as with all soldiers who joined the British Army, Young was asked: 'Are you willing to die for king and country?' The young soldier's answer was an emphatic 'I am!'[4] And with that, in 1800, fourteen-year-old Young started his journey as a cadet in the 2nd Native Infantry. He sailed for the first time to India from Portsmouth in February 1802, an experience he described many years later in a letter home, calling himself '...a regular Johnny Raw from the bogs.'[5]

Upon arrival in Calcutta, the young ensign was sent for training, as customary, to the Old College of Baraset[6], and is said to have served for a short period at Balasore[7] (now Baleshwar, Odisha state). By the time Ensign Young was seventeen years old, he was serving under General Lake in the so-called Central India Campaign[8], during which time he acquired a deep '...love and admiration...' for Lord Lake. Young distinguished himself in the campaign, as evidenced by his adventures while volunteering at the Battle of Bharatpur:

> On some ladder or bridge, no doubt struggling for precedence in the crowd, Frederick Young fell from a considerable height into the ditch below him. Here he was quickly covered up by all sorts of dreadful debris. It took him a considerable time to extricate himself and crawl out of his uncomfortable position. He had been given up as lost when he finally appeared among his comrades, a miserable object, covered with mud and blood, but quite uninjured![9]

Recognized for such pluck and courage, by 1810, Young was serving in Calcutta as aide-de-camp (ADC) to Colonel Robert Rollo Gillespie and, in this capacity, he accompanied Gillespie on an expeditionary force to Java. The French, with whom the British were at war in Europe, had overrun Holland and claimed the Dutch possessions in the Far East as their own. The Far East Campaign was bloody but successful for the British and in late 1813 Gillespie—now General Sir Robert Rollo Gillespie—and his ADC returned to India. Frederick Young had been '...blown up and much burnt but not dangerously...' at Jogjakarta. At the time, Young was twenty-seven years old and, indeed, his luck was holding.

But it was not so for Young's commander, Rollo Gillespie, the colourful Ulsterman whose achievements included taking the Dutch city of Batavia (now Jakarta, the capital of Indonesia), deposing the sultan of Sumatra and purportedly even killing a tiger running amok on the Bangalore racecourse. Exactly one year after the Far East Campaign, on 31 October 1814, General Gillespie was shot through the heart

3

at Kalunga[10] in the Dun Valley and died in Young's arms, just 89 feet (27 metres) from the palisade.[11]

Gillespie's death occurred whilst he was leading a second attempt to take the Kalunga Fort, which was held by the Nepalese, who had been occupying the Dun since 1803. For some twenty years, the Nepalese had been expanding their western territories—perhaps taking advantage of a rather relaxed British policy vis-à-vis their expansionism—and it was Lord Minto (Sir Gilbert Elliot), the then governor general, who decided that Nepalese '...aggression, illegal occupation, tyrannical rule and corruption' must come to an end. The local hill rajas who had sought refuge in East India Company territory[12] encouraged Lord Minto in this effort. Thus, a military operation against the Nepalese was planned, with Gillespie in charge of the third division or column of 10,500 men and twenty pieces of ordnance.[13]

The first and second attacks against Kalunga Fort were bloody and ended in failure for the British. However, the surrounded Nepalese garrison, under the command of General Bal Bahadur Thapa, had also suffered a great deal at the hands of the British and, miserably short of supplies and with their water supply cut off, the remaining survivors slipped away from the fort under cover of darkness on a night in late November 1814. The British razed an empty Kalunga Fort to the ground. Thus ended the so-called 'Battle of Nalapani'.

To this day, the Kalunga War Memorial, erected along what is now the Sahasradhara (Thousand Streams) Road—previously called Sulphur Springs Road—on the edge of the Dun Valley, stands as a British tribute to Nepalese soldiers, whom they had come to greatly admire. Restored in 2006 by the Archaeological Survey of India, it is said to be the only war memorial in the world erected by the British to honour their foe, the Gurkhas.[14]

With the fall of the Kalunga Fort, the Dun was secure for the British. But the war, formally declared by the new Governor General Lord Moira (Francis Rawdon-Hastings) on 1 November 1814, the day after Gillespie was killed, was not over.

The division of which Young was a part, now under the command of Major General Gabriel Martindall, headed towards Nahan, and it was at the Battle of Jaithak that Lieutenant Young's luck seemed to be running out. Along with some fellow officers, he was captured by the Nepalese.

It is not known how long Young was held by the Nepalese and some historians question if he ever was a prisoner.[15] However, the *List of the Officers of the Bengal Army* states clearly that Young was '...taken prisoner during [the] Nepal War' (see

The Kalunga War Memorial of the Nepal War of 1814–1815, as it appeared in 1877. It is said to be the only war memorial the British ever erected that recognizes their losses as well as those of their enemy. The ultimately victorious British came out of this war with great respect for the fighting men of Nepal, leading to the incorporation of Gurkha regiments into the Indo–British armies, which continues to this day. The memorial on Sahasradhara Road in Dehra Dun has recently been renovated.

(Courtesy of the National Army Museum, London)

Appendix A for details on Young's life). His daughter certainly believed he had been a prisoner, for she writes:

> ...I know that he was treated with every mark of honour as a brave foe and that he usefully employed the time. He became intimately conversant with their [Nepali] language; he studied their religion, their prejudices, their manners and customs, and gained their steady admiration and even friendship as a man among men.[16]

In the meantime, the war continued. But finally, it was David Ochterlony, as head of the second division on the Western Front, who succeeded in routing the Nepalese at the Battle of Dionthal[17] (near Shimla) and, later, at the Battle of Makwanpur (south of Kathmandu). Finally, faced with an invasion of the Kathmandu Valley, the

Nepalese sued for peace. The Treaty of Sugauli, ratified on 4 March 1816, ended the British East India Company's war against the Nepalese.[18]

This conflict had long-lasting impact. In immediate terms, Ochterlony, of course, got his kudos. He received the thanks of both Houses of Parliament back in Britain, became the first officer in the British East India Company army to be awarded the GCB[19], was reinstated Resident at Delhi where he lived a sumptuous lifestyle and, in what was supposed to have been a lasting tribute, the company built a memorial to him on the Maidan in Calcutta.[20]

But much more important than Ochterlony's fate was that the British came out of this Anglo–Nepalese War with a profound and lasting respect for the martial skills of those '…little hill men', who had fought so valiantly against them. Now a lieutenant, Young was prominent among those who shared this view, remembering what he had experienced on the battlefield and, possibly, as a prisoner. His daughter recorded that when Young was imprisoned, some Nepalese soldiers said to him '…We could serve under men like you.'[21] Whatever the context, this sentiment was not lost on the lieutenant.

After the war, Young was put in charge of Nepalese prisoners of war in Saharanpur (now in Uttar Pradesh state). When the company asked what should be done with them, he said:

> Give me authority first to release the prisoners to tell them they are free men. Then I will ask them to volunteer for the Company's service. If they do – and I am sure that many will – I undertake to raise a body of soldiers who will not disgrace you, or the country, or myself.

So, within the year (1815), the first unit of Gurkha soldiers was enlisted for service in the army of the East India Company. Young was always proud to say, '…I went there [to Saharanpur] one man and I came out 3,000.'[22] Thus began the Sirmur Battalion with Frederick Young as its first commander.

Indeed, his luck had not deserted him.

It must be noted here that the major impact of the Anglo–Nepalese War of 1814–15—even more profound than the long and illustrious history of the Nepalese martial race and its continuing and honoured place in British and Indian military history—was the geo-political outcome. The war altered forever the map of northern India. By forcing the Nepalese back to the Sarda (Mahakali) River, which still forms the western border between Nepal and India, Ochterlony's British and Indian troops had secured Garhwal, Kumaon and the Dun Valley for British India and, ultimately, for independent India. In an ironic modern-day turn of history, the Calcutta memorial to Ochterlony—a man who succeeded in leading the charge which considerably enlarged the map of India—does not now primarily remember him, as the memorial was re-dedicated as the Shaheed Minar or Martyrs' Column, in honour of Indian freedom fighters.

With the annexation of the Dun and the hills to the north, the district was placed under the care of R. Grindall, the collector of Saharanpur, with day-to-day affairs looked after by an assistant collector. Thomas Palin Calvert (b.1789–d.1817), who was the first to hold this post, was succeeded by Frederick John Shore as joint magistrate and superintendent of revenues for the Dun. In 1825, the district was put under the commissioner of Kumaon and in 1829, it was re-transferred and placed under a collector or magistrate styled the 'superintendent of the Dun'.

But well before this time, the policing of the area was in the hands of Frederick Young and his Sirmur Battalion, and it was Young who emerged as the leading protagonist of the Dun in these early years of local British rule.

Promoted to colonel, this larger-than-life figure was seemingly everywhere in and around the Dun. These were his halcyon days. The sobriquet 'king of the Doon' really seemed to fit, and Young's 'reign' lasted from 1815 until 1842.

Young's reputation for bravery and leadership had, according to his friends, allowed him to '...ask for anything' he wanted from Calcutta and, of course, he had been given the responsibility of the Sirmur Battalion. In the Dun, he soon became not only commander but also judge, magistrate, collector and surveyor involved in land settlements, his official role combining military and civilian responsibilities that was highly unusual even at the time. And he was only in his thirties!

In 1833, Young felt confident enough to ask Calcutta to officially appoint him as political agent to the Dun for the East India Company. His request was approved by Calcutta, and he carried this additional title until 1842 (see Appendix A).

As founder, 'beloved chief'[23] and commandant, he led his men in action in the 3rd Mahratta War (1817) and at Bharatpur (1825).[24] With his soldiers, he subdued the insurgents and dacoits in the Dun and surrounding area. And importantly, Young pushed for and succeeded in establishing the Landour cantonment as a convalescent depot. The cantonment thrives to this day as headquarters of the Ministry of Defence Research and Development Organization's Institute of Technology Management (see Chapter 4).

An early twentieth-century postcard view of Mullingar. The Philander Smith Institute for Boys was located in Frederick Young's Mullingar House from 1884–1905, when it moved to Nainital. The message on the back of the postcard, dated Christmas 1926, reads: 'Dear Cecil, I hope you will have a Merry Xmas & enjoy lots of fun. This is your Daddy's old school. I suppose yours is much bigger? Hope you are getting on nicely. I am having my holidays now and hope to go and see Uncle George & Auntie Flo. With lots of love to you, Mummie and Daddy. Your loving, Auntie Sal.'
(Courtesy of the private collection of the late H. Michael Stokes, United Kingdom)

Impressed with the hunting possibilities and the salubrious climate, Frederick Young and Frederick Shore built a 'shooting box' in 1823 on the slope of what would later be called the 'Camel's Back'. This is assumed to be the first 'house' built in what was to become Mussoorie. But Young soon did better than that. The earliest map of the Station shows that by 1831, he owned three houses there (Mullingar proper and Mullingar Cottage, together called the Mullingar Estate, and the shooting box on Camel's Back). The shooting box is no more; the other two are still atop Mullingar Hill in Landour, but much altered.

In its early days, Mullingar was nicknamed 'Mulliagoes' (a likely cross between 'Mullingar' and 'Potatoes') or the 'Potato Garden', testimony to Young having allegedly planted the first potatoes ever grown in the Himalayas.[25] The Young family occupied Mullingar in the summers and their 'castle' in Dehra Dun during the winter months. Young's houses were settings for the entertaining required of his position. Mullingar, as the property is still commonly called, is today occupied by Tibetans but, sadly, is in a very rundown condition.

THE MANY LIVES OF MULLINGAR

When Frederick Young built Mullingar in 1825 in what was to become Landour, he could not have imagined how much his house would continue to be in demand, even to this day, in its dilapidated state. However, he probably would have been very pleased, for he was considered to be a man of generous hospitality.

Young also could not have imagined the tax advantages that his property would enjoy. Under the famous 'Norman Guarantee' of 1862, the Mullingar Estate, along with five other properties on the eastern edge of Landour, was exempted for many years from taxes, since it straddled both cantonment and municipal lands. This dual placement of property apparently was too complicated for the assessor, Colonel Norman, so he gave the various owners a tax holiday!

Mullingar House was Young's summer home and is said to be the first permanent building constructed in all of Mussoorie and Landour (there was also a Mullingar Cottage on the estate). Young used Mullingar as a centre to entertain the high and mighty of British India. Its reputation for hospitality has far outlived its founder.

Young named his estate 'Mullingar' not after the town of Mullingar, which was and is the administrative centre of County Westmeath in central Ireland, and quite far from Young's birthplace. Rather, he named it after Mullingar, a townland in the civil parish of Donaghmore, in his home County Donegal. Many of the extended Young family members owned and leased land in that townland (a 'townland' being a small territory within a civil parish), and this property was no doubt a source of considerable prosperity for the Young clan.

The Mullingar Estate had a couple of nicknames. In her 1920 book about her father's life, written in her ninetieth year, Louise Jenkins writes about 'Mulliagoes', presumably Mullingar 'crossed' with a potato! She also notes that the house was often known as 'The Potato Garden'. Both these monikers are linked to the tradition that credits Young with growing the first potatoes in the Himalayas.

Young left Mussoorie and the Dun in 1842 but probably held ownership of the house for some time. In February 1847, Mauger (pronounced 'major') Monk said in a letter to his sister on Guernsey, '...I write from my new house, Mullingar, where I hope I am permanently fixed for the next ten years, if it please God to spare my life so long.' Monk died less than two years later, on 9 December 1849 (see Chapter 10).

For several years in the 1860s and in the early part of the 1870s, Mullingar was used by the congregation of the Union Church, before a permanent home for the church was constructed in Kulri, now a landmark in the Station.

By 1884, Northam's Mussoorie guidebook reported that the Mullingar House had by then already gone through several iterations as a hotel:

> For some years, a hotel has been established at Mullingar...during which time it has changed hands several times. First started as the 'Caledonian' by Mr MacFie; secondly, as the 'Imperial', by Messrs Porter and Zinck; it is now metamorphosed into the 'Oriental' by M. F. H. Treherne. It may be conceded to the writer to mention that M. Treherne's managment of the 'Charleville' is a sufficient guarantee that the 'Oriental' will be well and successfully conducted.

However, despite the positive review, Mr Treherne's Oriental Hotel did not last for long, for it is not mentioned with other hotels in Bodycot's 1907 *Guide to Mussoorie.*

Sometime after 1884, Mullingar became the home of the Philander Smith Institute for Boys, founded by the United Methodist Church, USA (see Chapter 5). It remained as such until 1905.

Between 1906–1914, a much-altered Mullingar was the Furlough Home for Soldiers with 300 beds and kept open all year.

In 1914, it became home to Moore's Landour Boarding and Day School, when that school moved from nearby Sunny Bank. When Moore's school folded, its new proprietors ran it as a hotel for Indian guests.

In 1934, Young's former home was remodelled to house British military families during their seasonal visits. From this point onwards, Mullingar took on what is a continuing role as a way station for temporary residents or displaced persons. During the Second World War, Mullingar was said to have been overflowing with convalescing soldiers and refugee Britons from Burma, the Andamans and northeast India. Then, in 1947, Colonel Roderick Minchin of the Indian Army Reserve—a medical doctor and physics teacher at Woodstock School—set up 'headquarters' at Mullingar, where Landour Muslims sought refuge, awaiting a fleet of buses to take them to Pakistan.

After about a decade of disuse during the 1950s, Mullingar again became home to refugees.

In 1959, Prime Minister Jawaharlal Nehru gave refuge to Tibetans escaping Communist rule. Some of the Tibetan refugees who came to Mussoorie gradually gravitated towards Mullingar and since that time have made it their home.

Dating back to as early as the 1930s, Mullingar was owned by Mansa Ram & Sons Bankers, of Landour. However, this bank failed in June 1955 and, in the 1970s, the court-appointed receiver auctioned off Mullingar (and other bank properties). Municipal records indicate that in 1985, Mullingar was 'resumed' by the Military Estate Office (MEO). So, it seems that today, the MEO is notionally the owner, although Tibetans remain in occupation.

Whatever the tangled ownership, Mullingar still stands, after almost 190 years, atop one of the most beautiful spots in the entire area, with multi-hued Buddhist prayer flags as today's contribution to a house that indeed has had a colourful history.

There is a legend that Frederick Young sometimes haunts the Mullingar courtyard on moonlit nights as a ghostly rider, returning even now to his much-loved home in the hills!

The steep road leading to it from the bazaar is still called 'Mullingar Hill'.

Young's famous hospitality—for he '...shared all good things, and the benevolent thought and consideration for all members of the community, irrespective of class or colour...'— was enjoyed by such personages of the day as Sir Charles Medcalfe, a member of the Supreme Council in Calcutta who provisionally succeeded Lord William Bentinck in the governor generalship, and by Lord Combermere, commander-in-chief of the Indian army (1825–1830). But Young's hospitality was not without well-considered forethought!

'...I want nothing for myself, but who knows what might turn up? And what opportunities of serving some of my friends might not arise on some future occasion from his recollecting the name of Young in consequence of attention to his comforts here, and a word from our worthy friend, Sir Charles Metcalfe, on his way through [to] Calcutta to the Vice-Royalty!'[26]

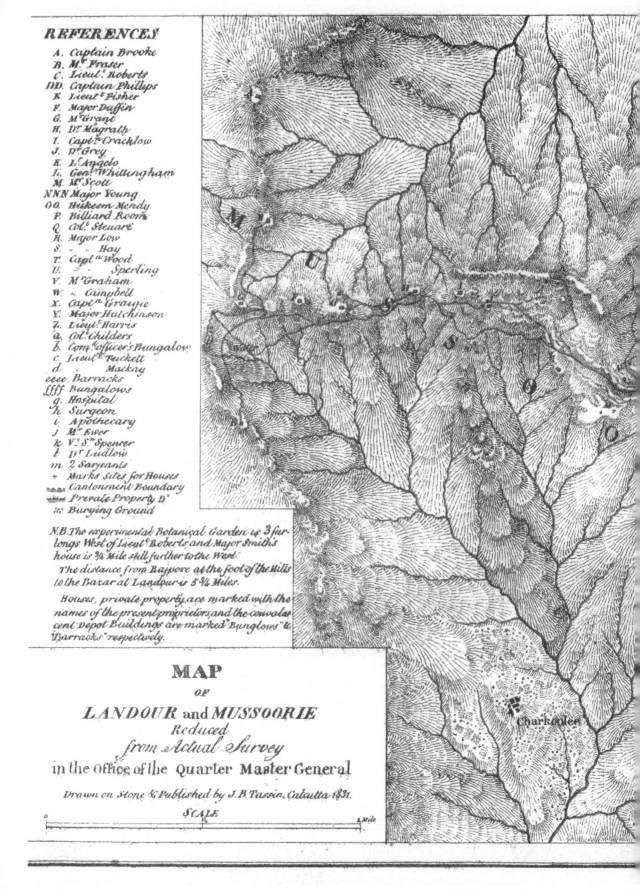

REFERENCES

A. Captain Brooke
B. Mr. Fraser
C. Lieut. Roberts
DD. Captain Phillips
E. Lieut. Fisher
F. Major Duffin
G. Mr. Grant
H. Dr. Magrath
I. Capt. Cracklow
J. Dr. Grey
K. L. Angelo
L. Gen. Whittingham
M. Mr. Scott
NNN Major Young
OO. Hakeem Mendy
P. Billiard Room
Q. Col. Steuart
R. Major Low
S. " Hay
T. Capt. Wood
U. " Sperling
V. Mr. Graham
W. " Campbell
X. Capt. Craigie
Y. Major Hutchinson
Z. Lieut. Harris
a. Col. Childers
b. Com. officer's Bungalow
c. Lieut. Tuckett
d. " Mackay
eeee Barracks
ffff Bungalows
g. Hospital
h. Surgeon
i. Apothecary
j. Mr. Ewer
k. V. S. Spencer
l. Dr. Ludlow
m. 2 Sarjeants
+ Marks Sites for Houses
━━ Cantonment Boundary
━━ Private Property Do.
∷∷ Burying Ground

N.B. The experimental Botanical Garden is 3 furlongs West of Lieut. Roberts, and Major Smith's house is 3/4 Mile still further to the West.

The distance from Rajpore at the foot of the Hills to the Bazar at Landour is 5 3/4 Miles.

Houses, private property, are marked with the names of the present proprietors, and the convalescent Depot Buildings are marked "Bunglows" & "Barracks" respectively.

MAP
OF
LANDOUR and MUSSOORIE
Reduced
from Actual Survey
in the Office of the Quarter Master General

Drawn on Stone & Published by J. B. Tassin, Calcutta 1831.

SCALE

0   1 Mile

Charkodee

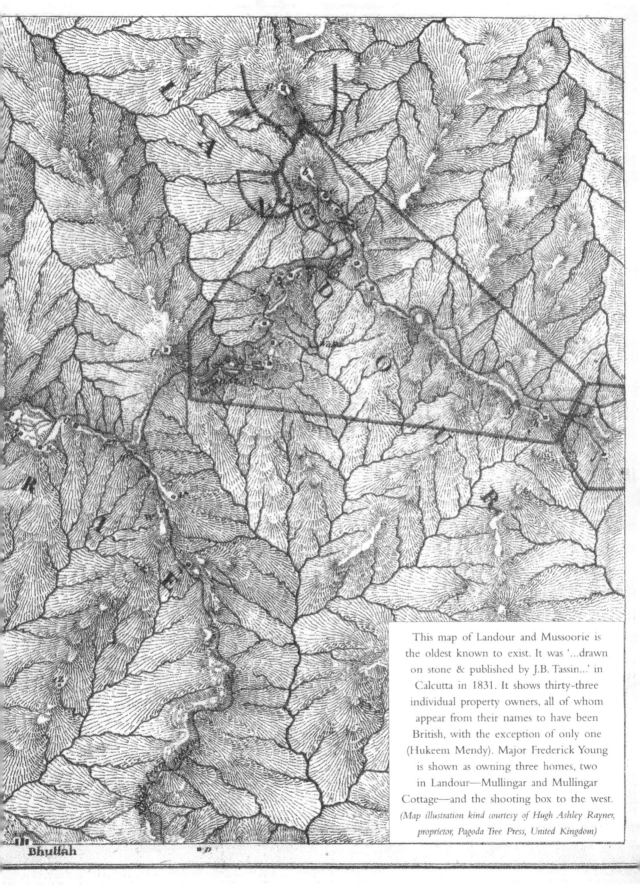

This map of Landour and Mussoorie is the oldest known to exist. It was '...drawn on stone & published by J.B. Tassin...' in Calcutta in 1831. It shows thirty-three individual property owners, all of whom appear from their names to have been British, with the exception of only one (Hukeem Mendy). Major Frederick Young is shown as owning three homes, two in Landour—Mullingar and Mullingar Cottage—and the shooting box to the west. *(Map illustration kind courtesy of Hugh Ashley Rayner, proprietor, Pagoda Tree Press, United Kingdom)*

Bhullah

Frederick Young and his family spent the cold season in their 'castle' in Dehra Dun. Mrs Young was said to have been a splendid horsewoman, this picture depicting her favourite chestnut Arab in the foreground. In this and the Mussoorie house '...the hospitable doors were open wide, and the fame of its generous welcome was spread to the four quarters of John Company's dominions.' The Dehra Dun house was built on what are now the grounds of St Joseph's Academy, off Rajpur Road. The building no longer exists, having been torn down to make way for a new bicentenary administrative building that was inaugurated by the Patrician Brotherhood in 2008.
(*Picture and quote from Jenkins, Louisa Hadow,* General Frederick Young, First Commandant of Sirmur Battalion [2nd Gurkha Rifles], *London: George Routledge & Sons, 1923, p.56 and facing p.84*)

Young was not an aloof political agent, for he was very active in community affairs. He was a founding member of the Himalaya Club in Mussoorie (est. 1841) and its first president. He was a churchman. At the laying of the Christ Church foundation stone in 1836 he read out from a copy the inscription on the stone which, presumably, is still planted somewhere in the ground roundabout the church. He also collected and exported birds and snakes to England in the interest of science. He led the hunt, having imported the first pack of English hounds ever brought to India ('...the sport was free to all...'). He is credited with triggering the economic development of the Dun, long depleted by war, but soon '...the desert blossomed as the rose.' Related to this there is, of course, the potato legacy. Young is also said to have been the first to start cultivating tea in the area (his plantation was apparently taken over later by the government without payment). If this is correct, Young probably got into tea with support and encouragement from Dr Hugh Falconer, the well-known Scottish botanist (and paleontologist) who, during 1832–1842, was the superintendent of the nearby Saharanpur Botanical Garden. Falconer had been commissioned by the government to look into the possibilities of tea cultivation, and was a strong advocate.[27]

In 1825, Frederick married Jeanette, the daughter of Colonel and Mrs John Bird. Bird was posted at the time in Saharanpur. The adoring daughter, Louisa, later described her mother:

> For many[...]years she was the worthy queen and co-ruler of the beautiful valley and its immediate neighbourhood. Widely known as a splendid horsewoman she shared her husband's love of animals.[...] In every way co-operating with her generous husband in all his undertakings and duties and pleasures, she brought happiness and beauty and contentment into his home.[28]

(L) A picture of Frederick Young from an 1839 oil painting by J. Reynolds Gwatkin. At the time of this picture, Young was fifty-three years old. Interestingly, regarding the artist J. Reynolds Gwatkin, there are memorial plaques to two of his children—Robert Lovell Gwatkin and Amy Theophila Lewis, née Gwatkin—on the walls of Christ Church, near Gandhi Chowk (Library Chowk). (R) Frederick married Jeanette when he was thirty-nine years old. They had eight children.
(*Photos from Jenkins, Louisa Hadow,* General Frederick Young, First Commandant of Sirmur Battalion [2nd Gurkha Rifles], *London:George Routledge & Sons, Ltd., 1923, facing p. 160*)

Frederick and Jeanette had eight children, all of whom survived, except a daughter, Eliza, which was certainly a better than average record for this early period of the British in India. The three oldest children (Catherine, Susan and Mary) went home to Ireland with their governess in 1835, where they studied while staying with relatives. In 1839, Louisa, Charles Frederick (the 'heir' who later served in the 50th Regiment of Foot, retiring as a captain in 1869), Hatton and Marion joined them, this time along with their mother, who later returned to India.

But it wasn't only his natural-born children whom Young sent home to Ireland. Describing her father's '...straight and generous character', his daughter Louisa relates that in 1814—eleven years before his marriage—Young essentially adopted the daughter of a native chief (unnamed), who had been orphaned in the then ongoing war against the Gurkhas. In time, 'Mary Dhoon' was sent to Ireland with an English nurse, her education and upbringing entrusted to Young's relatives, presumably at Young's expense. Though feeble and suffering from a spinal complaint, Mary was said to have lived her adult life '...with her own servants and establishment' in Coleraine (Northern Ireland), as a woman of some attainments who drew, painted and did her needlework, sang and played the piano, read and spoke French and Italian. A proper Victorian lady, indeed. She was said to have been a great favourite of Young's wife. Young's daughter adds:

> Certainly no one I knew lived in the same luxurious atmosphere, and whatever destiny had ruled out from her life everything possible had been done to compensate her...how long she lived and where she died, I do not know.[29]

Young stayed on in the Dun and Mussoorie until 1842, when he was again promoted and sent as brigadier general to command the Bundelkhand Agency (now in Madhya Pradesh state). He stayed in Bundelkhand until 1846 when, after forty-four years of service in India, he took to his one and only home back in Ireland. He spent two years there with his family. On his return to India, he was made commander of the Ferozepore Brigade (1848–1849), from whence he went to Dinapore, near Patna, to take up the brigade command there. Young's wife, Jeanette, died in Dinapore in 1852 and is buried there. It was during this period that, given his military experience in the hills, Young was called to the Darjeeling area, where trouble was brewing with the raja of Sikkim.

Throughout these post-Dun years, he travelled much on official duty. Essentially a self-educated man, he is said to have remained well read, up-to-date on current

There are no memorials to General Frederick Young in Mussoorie, Landour or Dehra Dun, although there is still a Young Road in the Dehra Dun Cantonment. (*Photo from authors' private collection*)

affairs and healthy in mind and body. His daughter wrote that rather than taking the typical afternoon nap, he would play billiards. But after nearly thirty years in the Dun, he must have missed his 'hill kingdom' very much indeed.

In 1854, at the age of sixty-eight and after fifty-four years of service with the East India Company, widower Young retired back to Ireland. Having led a physically very active life, he was said to be in much better health then his compatriots who had never left home.

It had been an exciting and active life...and his luck had held, at a time in history when 'two monsoons'[30] was an ominous warning for the British who had come out to the East. But in 1866, twelve years after having returned from India, Young did run into financial difficulty, when the Agra Bank failed and he suffered great financial loss, even having to move into the Albany, a smaller house at Ballybrack, County Kildare, east of Dublin. Yet, fortunately, he still had his East India Company pension.

After a severe fall that caused a fractured thigh, the founder of Mussoorie died '...not complaining', on 22 May 1874, twenty years after leaving India for the last time. He was eighty-seven years old.

Life expectancy for men in Britain at the time was fifty-three years.

General Frederick Young's gravesite in the Deansgrange Cemetery, two miles northwest of Ballybrack, County Kildare, east of Dublin. The inscription reads as follows:

To the Memory of General Frederick Young, late Bengal Army.
Born November 30th, 1786. Died May 22nd, 1874.
Erected in affectionate remembrance of a dearly beloved father by his children.
He giveth his beloved sleep.
(Photo kind courtesy of Justin Homan Martin and Jennifer M.J. Kavanagh, Ireland)

Notes

1. Bateman, Josiah, *The Life of the Right Rev. Daniel Wilson, D.D., Late Lord Bishop of Calcutta and Metropolitan of India.* vol. 2, London: John Murray, 1860: 109.

2. Young's ancestors came to County Donegal as 'planters' and settled on lands in Culdaff leased from the marquis of Donegal and the Protestant bishop of Derry. They prospered as landed gentry. Their family members still live in Culdaff, although their main Culdaff House, built in 1779, was burned during the 1922–1923 Irish Civil War. There is a memorial to

the Young family in the village, opposite the church where members of the family (other than Frederick Young) are interred.

The Young family was part of the 'plantation' of Protestants from England, Scotland and Wales, which began in the 1550s as an effort by the Crown government in Dublin to pacify and anglicize Ireland under English rule and incorporate the native ruling classes into the English aristocracy. The idea (ultimately unrealized, of course) was that Ireland would then become a peaceful and reliable possession, without risk of rebellion or foreign invasion. The plantations changed the demography of Ireland by creating large communities with a British and Protestant identity, effectively opposed to the interests of the earlier inhabitants, who had an Irish and Roman Catholic identity. The physical and economic nature of Irish society also changed as new concepts of ownership, trade and credit were introduced. These changes led to the creation of a British Protestant ruling class in Ireland. The final official plantations took place under Oliver Cromwell during the 1650s, when thousands of former soldiers were settled in Ireland; however, significant migration into Ireland continued well into the eighteenth century, from both Britain and continental Europe. The male line of Gardiner and Catherine Young is now extinct.

3. Jenkins, Louisa Hadow, *General Frederick Young, First Commandant of Sirmur Battalion (2nd Gurkha Rifles)*, London: George Routledge & Sons Ltd, 1923: 3.

4. When Frederick Young joined his country's military, George III was the reigning monarch (1760–1815). George III was succeeded by George IV (1815–1830) and William IV (1830–1837). By the time Young retired back to Ireland in 1854, Queen Victoria was seventeen years into her long reign (1837–1901).

5. Jenkins (1923:80) refers to a letter Young wrote from Landour to his sister Barbara in October 1835. In the nineteenth-century British army, a new recruit was known as 'Johnny Raw'. Rudyard Kipling referred to Johnny Raw in at least one of his poems, 'The Men That Fought at Minden', to humorously emphasize the subservience of raw recruits to officers and other senior soldiers: 'Run an' get the beer, Johnny Raw—Johnny Raw! Ho! run an' get the beer, Johnny Raw!'

6. In his autobiography, Sir John Hearsey (see Chapter 10) wrote, '…The college at Baraset was a most riotous place, and I was not sorry to leave it. In fact, the congregation of such a number of devil-may-care young men at a place only sixteen miles from Calcutta, whither they used to gallop at early night after roll-call, creating disturbances at the different beer shops and inns, was considered a pest to that city; so much so that the Chief Justice at that time at Calcutta said that if any of them were caught by the police and were found guilty, he would hang or transport them' (as contained in Pearse, Hugh, *The Hearseys: Five Generations of an Anglo-Indian Family*, Edinburgh and London: William Blackwood and Sons, 1905:131-132).

7. Balasore, on the coast of Odisha state, was an early trading post for the British, French, Dutch and Danish. It was established as an entrepot by the Danish who sold it to the British. Because of shallow waters, it was later much reduced in importance as a centre of

trade. Today, a Government of India rocket-launching station is located there.

8. Gerard Lake, later 1st Viscount Lake, had taken a leading role in the defeat of the main force of the French incursion at the Battle of Ballinamuck (a small village in County Longford, Ireland), which marked the defeat of the Irish at the close of the 1798 Rebellion. As commander-in-chief of British India, Lord Lake's forces fought against the Houses of Sindhia and Holkar in the Second Anglo–Maratha War in 1803 (the 'Central India Campaign'). Allegedly inspired by the French, the Marathas were attempting to free themselves from British control. Initially defeating the Marathas at Kol (now Aligarh in Uttar Pradesh state), Lake's forces moved on to Delhi and Agra, and won 'a great victory' at the Battle of Laswari (now in Rajasthan state), where the power of Sindhia was broken with the loss of thirty-one disciplined battalions—trained and officered by Frenchmen—and 426 pieces of ordnance. This British victory, followed a few days later by Major General Arthur Wellesley's success at the Battle of Argaon (Maharashtra state), finally compelled Sindhia to come to terms, and a treaty with him was signed in December 1803. At the same time, operations continued against his confederate, Yashwantrao Holkar, who, in late November 1804, was defeated by Lake at the Battle of Farrukhabad (Uttar Pradesh state). But in early 1805, the fortress of Bharatpur (Rajasthan state) held out against four assaults. Frederick Young participated in these assaults, showing great bravery and soldierly skill. Later, Cornwallis, who succeeded Lord Wellesley as governor general of India in July 1805 and, at the same time, superseded Lake as commander-in-chief, resolved to put an end to the war. Later in the same year, after the sudden death of Cornwallis in October, Lake pursued Holkar into the Punjab and compelled him to surrender at Amritsar in December 1805, thus ending the campaign. For his 'matchless energy, ability and valour', Lake received the thanks of the Parliament—wherein he later served—and, in September 1806, he was rewarded by being titled Baron Lake of Delhi and Laswari, and of Aston Clinton in the county of Buckingham. In 1807, he was given the title of Viscount Lake, but when he died in 1808 he was in near penury. (Compiled from various sources)

9. Jenkins, Ibid, p. 20.

10. In historical documents, Kalunga is variously spelled Kalinga, Khalanga or Khaluga. The Kalunga Fort was a typical Gurkha garrison, built on a hill 500 feet (152 metres) high and surrounded by dense undergrowth and a palisade of rough-hewn logs and rocks.

11. General Robert Rollo Gillespie was buried in Meerut (Uttar Pradesh state) in the Christian cemetery near St John's Church in the Cantonment. His tombstone, which still stands, reads:

Vellore. Cornelles [Fort Cornelis, eight miles inland from Batavia]. *Palembang.*

Sir R.R. Gillespie

Djocjocarta,

d. 31ˢᵗ October 1814.

Kalunga.

12. According to F. Bodycot, 'The immediate cause of the Gurkha war was the destruction of a police station in a disputed portion of our frontier territory and the barbarous murder of

the Daroga [police chief] in charge after a gallant defense in which eighteen of his constables were killed and six wounded. Another police station was raided shortly afterwards.' (Bodycot, F. ['compiler'], *Guide to Mussoorie with Notes on Adjacent Districts and Routes into the Interior*, Mussoorie: Mafasilite Printing Works, 1907:25).

13. A total of four divisions or columns set out in this campaign against the Nepalese. The Eastern Front was formed by a division that was ordered against Kathmandu through Butwal and the Sheoraj pargannas (a group of neighbouring villages) and another on the Sikkim border. Both of these divisions failed in their efforts to rout the Nepalese. The Western Front forces, made up of Gillespie's division and another headed by David Ochterlony, which were to penetrate the passes into the Dun Valley, were ultimately successful.

14. The inscriptions on the two Kalunga Memorial pillars in 1877 read: (first pillar) 'To the memory of Major General Sir Robert Rollo Gillespie, K.C.B.; Lieutenant O'Hara, 6th Native Infantry; Lieutenant Gosling, Light Battalion; Ensign Fothergill, 17th Native Infantry; Ensign Ellis, Pioneers, killed 31 October 1814. Captain Campbell, 6th Native Infantry; Lieutenant Luxford, Horse Artillery; Lieutenant Harrington, HM's 53rd Regiment; Lieutenant Cunningham, 13th Native Infantry, killed on 27 November 1814 and of the non-commissioned officers and men who fell at the two assaults.

'On the highest point of the hill above this tomb stood the fort of Kalunga; after two assaults on 31 October and 27 November it was captured by the British troops on 30 November 1814 and completely razed to the ground.

'Troops engaged: Detachments of Horse & Foot Artillery, 100 men of the 8th Royal Irish Light Dragoons who were led to the assault by Sir R.R. Gillespie, HM's 53rd Regiment, 1st Battalion 6th Native Infantry, 1st Battalion 13th Native Infantry, 1st Battalion 17th Native Infantry, 7th light Cavalry, *Ressalah* [cavalry unit] Skinner's Horse.'

(second pillar) 'This is inscribed as a tribute of respect for our gallant adversary Bulbudder [sic, Bal Bahadur Thapa], Commander of the Fort and his brave Ghoorkhas who were afterwards while in the service of Runjeet Singh shot down in their ranks to the last man by Afghan artillery' (from records of the National Army Museum, London).

15. Irish author and historian Turtle Bunbury writes: 'Early histories of the Nepalese War refer to the defeat of Young's Irregulars at Jaithak but there is no mention of his capture in any of the key sources. Even if he had been briefly imprisoned and escaped, there would have been some record of the event, either in official dispatches or in letters written by his friends. Presumably Mrs Jenkins heard the story directly from her father when he was a whiskery old General living back in Ballybrack, County Donegal. Like any good soldier, he might have been inclined to embellish the tale.' (From *Heroes & Villains* [a paper], by Turtle Bunbury, 2009).

The historian John Pemble, author of *The Invasion of Nepal: John Company at War*, makes no mention of Young's imprisonment in his 1971 history of the war. According to Bunbury, Pemble believes that Mrs Jenkins's romantic account of her father's captivity, published in 1923, is pure mythology. 'But it is no less interesting for that', he reasons. 'It demonstrates just how powerfully the Gurkhas appealed to the Western imagination in the 1920s. The Gurkhas' extraordinary heroics during the First World War certainly elevated these tough, wiry men to the status of mythical super-warriors. Of the more than 200,000 Gurkhas who served, approximately 20,000 died and 2,000 received awards for gallantry. So perhaps Mrs Jenkins simply felt a post-war urge to spice up the story of these Himalayan gallants with the "memoirs" of a boy from the hills of Donegal. She clearly knew that her imperial readers would adore a good paternal yarn where her dashing hero would master the language of the enemy and create an unimpeachable bond of devotion between officer and soldier.' (Oxford: Clarendon Press, 1971.)

16. Jenkins, Ibid, p. 49.

17. Dionthal is a ridge that overlooked Malaun Fort (near Shimla, now in Himachal Pradesh state), the main Nepalese stronghold in the area.

18. Recent reports coming out of Nepal say that the Government of Nepal's official copy of the Treaty of Sugauli cannot be found, neither in the national archives nor in the recently taken-over Narayanahiti Palace in Kathmandu.

19. Knight Grand Cross of the Order of the Bath (GCB), a British order of chivalry.

20. Upon his death, David Ochterlony, like Gillespie, was buried in the Cantonment cemetery in Meerut. His tomb also still stands. Interestingly, Ochterlony was born in Boston, Massachusetts, USA (12 February 1758), and educated at the Dummer Charity School in Byfield, Massachusetts, now the Governor's Academy and the oldest operating independent boarding school in the USA. Ochterlony went to India as a cadet in 1777, so it is possible that he never set foot in England or, if so, it would have been for a very short period.

21. Jenkins, Ibid, p. 52.

22. Smith, Lt Col Eric D. *The Story of the Sirmoor Rifles*, Singapore: privately published, 1968:2.

23. Jenkins, Ibid, p. 65.

24. Colonel Young was on the only furlough he ever had during his India career when the First Sikh War took place (1845–1846); this must have been a grave disappointment to him but, at the same time, a joy to learn of his battalion's successes at the decisive Battle of Sobraon. A decade later, after Young had permanently left India, the Sirmur Battalion became famous in Britain as one of the Indian regiments that remained loyal in 1857, fighting alongside the British at the Siege of Delhi. The Sirmur Rifles exist to this day in both the Indian and British armies. The Sirmur Battalion became the 2nd King Edward VII's Own Gurkha Rifles (The Sirmur Rifles), a regiment of the British Indian Army, before being transferred to the British Army on India's Independence, whence it became the 1st Battalion, Royal Gurkha Rifles. The 4th Battalion joined the Indian Army as the 5th Battalion, the 8th Gurkha Rifles (Sirmur Rifles).

25. The earliest known reference to 'potato' in India is from an account by Edward Terry, who was chaplain to Sir Thomas Roe, British ambassador to the court of the Mughal Emperor Jahangir, from 1615 to 1619. However, this may have been the sweet potato. Governor General Warren Hastings promoted (true) potato cultivation during his term, from 1772

to 1785, and by the late eighteenth century to the early nineteenth century, potatoes had sufficiently taken root in the hills and plains of India that different varieties had acquired local names. However, the potato remained a garden vegetable of minor scale during this time and, apparently, was often grown at higher altitudes by British colonizers as a summer crop. So, it is possible, but by no means certain, that Young was indeed the first to bring the potato into the Himalayan foothills. (Information compiled from the Central Potato Research Institute [CPRI], a part of the Indian Council of Agricultural Research [ICAR], Government of India).

26. Jenkins, Ibid, p. 76.
27. Dr Hugh Falconer also had a home in Mussoorie, 'Logie Estate', located near the Municipal Gardens that he also helped to establish. A part of this estate is now a boutique hotel. Logie Estate was undoubtedly named after a well-known property of the same name in Falconer's native place of Forres in northern Scotland. Interestingly, Falconer's years in Saharanpur and Mussoorie corresponded almost exactly with those of George Everest.
28. Jenkins, Ibid, p. 71-72.
29. Jenkins, Ibid, p. 50, 82, 138-140.
30. The term 'two monsoons' refers to what was often an eighteenth- and nineteenth-century reality for Britons that, if only one managed to live through two monsoons in the East, he had a better chance of survival to old age. The term was popularized in modern times by the late Theon Wilkinson who authored a book by the same name, published in London by Duckworth, 1976.

Rajpur Bazaar, 1888. Rajpur was the starting point for the last leg of a trip up to Mussoorie and Landour, until the advent of better roads and motor vehicles. The trip via the Bridle Path was made by walking, riding on horseback or by being carried (daytime trips only) in a jampan or a dandy. In the late 1800s, Rajpur boasted no less than five hotels that offered the wayfarer food and rest before heading to the hills. 'I Built my Soul a Lordly Pleasure House' is how Rudyard Kipling referred to this and other images of the fantastically painted building in this picture.

(Photo by Mr and Mrs S.A. Hill from the Ballade of Photographs, 1888, captioned by Rudyard Kipling, courtesy of the Rare Book and Special Collections Division, Library of Congress)

2

ENTERING THE GATES OF PARADISE

For the hills look down on the burnt plains under,
And the great green mountains are good to see—
Fair to behold and sweet to gain;
They are capped with the snow and cooled with the rain,
Cooled with the tears of the wailing thunder.
~ From Rudyard Kipling's poem Himalaya[1]~

Getting to Mussoorie has never been easier than it is today. Catch the early morning Shatabdi train from New Delhi station, arrive in Dehra Dun about lunchtime, flag a taxi up the hillside and one is easily settled in by teatime. Flying to Jolly Grant Airport makes it even faster.

But travellers of yore did not have it so easy, even though Mussoorie has always been the most accessible of the major hill stations in India, being on an outside spur of the lesser Himalayas.

As early as 1823, Frederick Young and Frederick J. Shore presumably scrambled up goat tracks to their shooting box. But alas, no written descriptions by either Young or Shore of their travelling up in the 1820s to what was to become Mussoorie and Landour seem to have survived.

In Mussoorie's earliest days, getting there was indeed an ordeal, albeit one that travellers generally considered worth the effort, even though sometimes dangerous, in order to escape the heat of the plains and bask in the beauty and cool serenity of the Himalayan foothills.

The most descriptive of the early travelling-up narratives comes from Captain John Luard while he was writing and sketching during his first tour of duty in India (1822–1830):

The hill called Mussoori, has of late years become a most delightful retreat from the hot winds of the plains. It is about seven miles from Deyrah in the Dhoon, and the road is now an excellent one, though still very steep in some parts; but an hour is sufficient for any one mounted upon a Ghoont (a hill pony, so called), to reach the summit of the hill, from the village of Rajepore, which is situated at the foot. It is hardly possible to conceive anything of a similar kind more delightful than the ascent of this hill; at its base the thermometer stands at from 90 to 120 degrees [32° to 49° Celsius]: the climate is gradually changing as the ascent is made, and with it the numerous and beautiful plants and trees continue to vary, through all the changes from a tropical to a temperate climate; and as the hot wind of the plains ceases to be felt, and the cooler breeze of the mountains refreshes the traveller, the eye is delighted with the magnificent prospect below, expanding proportionally as height is gained; and the interest of the scenery increases with the frequent change of direction necessary in the ascent, and the apparently bottomless glens which the road passes, overhanging some of them most fearfully. The first house built on Missourie belonged to Major Young, who commanded a Gourkha corps in the Dhoon,—it was called the Potato Garden, and it was some years before other houses were built; but in 1828, there were fifteen or sixteen; since which they have greatly increased.

The adjoining hill to Missourie is Landour, exceeding the former in height some hundred feet, being upwards of 7,000 feet above the level of the sea [2,313 meters]. The thermometer here seldom exceeds 70 degrees [21° Celsius] in the shade, and during the rains falls to 64 and 65 degrees [17° and 18° Celsius]: in the winter the climate is exceedingly severe, with snow, hail, and very high wind; and the thunderstorms are terrific.[2]

The next year, Captain Charles F. Trower, 33rd Bengal Native Infancy and 3rd Nizam's Cavalry, recorded his 'awe' in response to the natural beauty...but he had trouble with porters.

May 5th [1835] Drove to Rajpur [at] the foot of the hills where we found our horses and rode up. I cannot describe the mingled emotions of awe and delight which thrilled me as I came up, thro[ugh] these magnificent mountains. I have endeavoured to give an idea of the kind of scenery but pen and ink...cannot convey the effect.

A view of Mussoorie from Landour, sketched by Captain John Luard of the 16th Lancers in 1828, when the Landour Cantonment was being established. *(From a volume presented by the artist to his wife in 1838; kind courtesy of their great-great-grandson Captain James Luard, Royal Navy, United Kingdom)*

May 6th Find great difficult in engaging coolies to proceed with us into the interior and across the mountains to Simla. They dread the undertaking and we are obliged to pay exorbitantly to induce them to go. Amused myself walking about and sketched…

May 7th Left Landour about 4.00 pm and commenced our journey into the interior and across to Simla. The ride to one unaccustomed to hill travelling is a nervous undertaking…[3]

A sketch made in Landour in May 1835 by Captain Charles F. Trower of the 33rd Bengal Native
Infantry and the 3rd Nizam's Cavalry. Trower was an excellent amateur artist who left many
pen-and-ink drawings of his travels through India during 1834–1838.
The upper house in this sketch is Mullingar, which was built by Frederick Young in 1825.
The cut-out path shows what today is Mullingar Hill Road. *(Courtesy of British Library)*

In 1838, Emily Eden, sister of the governor general, reported '…going up precipices…',
in order to get to the new sanatorium.[4] In the same year, another Englishwomen,
Fanny Parkes, made her way up from Rajpur in a jampan,

> …an armchair, with a top to it, to shelter you from the sun or rain; four long
> poles affixed to it. Eight of those…hill fellows were harnessed between the poles,
> after their fashion, and they carried me up the hill. My two women went up
> in *dolīs*, a sort of tray for women, in which one person can sit native fashion;
> these trays are hung upon long poles, and carried by Hill-men. The ascent from
> Rajpur is seven miles, climbing almost every yard of the way.[5]

When Emily Eden was travelling in 1838 with her brother, Governor General Lord

Auckland (George Eden), she was shocked to hear this story from the district agent about small European children travelling up to Mussoorie without being accompanied by their parents or other European guardians:

> He [district agent] said a palanquin was brought to his house containing three little children—a little girl nine years old and two smaller brothers. They were going up to Mussoorie, had been travelling three days, and had about a week's more journey. They had not even their names written on a piece of paper, or a note to the magistrates of the district, but were just passed on from one set of bearers to the other....The bearers who brought these children to... [the district agent] said they thought the children were tired, and so they had brought them to an European house for a rest. [The district agent] had them washed and dressed, and fed them and kept them half a day, when he was obliged to send them away for fear they should lose their *dak*. He said they were very shy, and would hardly speak, but he made out their names and gave them notes to other magistrates, and some months afterwards he saw them at school at Mussoorie; but it is an odd way of sending children to school.[6]

No doubt, these would have been children of European parents who were too poor to send their children home to school and who were, perhaps, concerned for their health in the plains. Given the year of 1838, it is unclear where the young girl would have studied in Mussoorie. The boys may have been at the Mussoorie Seminary, which opened in 1835; however, the first European school for girls in Mussoorie—Waverley—only opened in 1845. In any case, it was indeed a strange way of sending off one's children but, at the same time, it suggests that there was great confidence in the system of relay bearers that operated during this period.

Another early account of travelling up to Mussoorie is given by W. Wilson who, in the early 1860s, set out on '...a summer ramble in the Himalayas'. He wrote of his travels under the pseudonym 'Mountaineer'. Starting in Meerut, he headed towards Mussoorie '...in the primitive fashion of palanquin and bearers, which is, as yet, in India the only means of speedy travelling on any but the grand trunk roads...'

> I left Meerut for Mussoorie, one of the hill sanitariums. The distance is one hundred and ten miles [177 kms], and the journey generally occupies thirty-six hours, including stoppages for refreshment at the different *dâk* bungalows. From Mozufernugger, about twenty-four miles [39 kms] out of Meerut, the

snowy mountains could, in the clear light of the early morning, be distinctly seen, and here, at the distance of one hundred and twenty miles [193 kms], I had the first view of these 'habitations of the Deity', as the Hindoo deems them, though in clear weather they are often visible from Meerut. The road was very good to Sharunpore, being thus far on the route to the large military station of Umballa; but from thence it was extremely dusty, and full of deep ruts, which ought not to be the case, considering that it leads to a place which in summer contains more European residents than any station in Upper India. The pass through or over the Sewalie hills, which bound the pretty valley of the Dhoon, was, from Mohun to near the crest of the low range, a distance of six miles [9.7 kms], the bed of a mountain-torrent, strewn thickly over with stones and boulders of all sizes, which must make it at all times rather rough work for wheeled carriages, and in the rains almost impassable. The slight descent into the Dhoon was comparatively good road. The whole way from Kerree to beyond Shorepore, on the approach to, and passage through this low range of hills, some twenty-four miles [39 kms], is through dense jungle, in some places nearly impenetrable, from the high rank grass which nearly buries the trees. Deer, and jungle and pea-fowl, frequently cross the path before the traveller, and once or twice a year, as if to prove they still exist near, a tiger or wild elephant disturbs the tranquil passage of one more unfortunate, or fortunate if he is one of the sterner sex and likes the excitement, than the rest. Half way across the Dhoon, I was put down at the neat little town of Deyrah, at a very nice hotel kept by an Englishman, where I was most comfortably housed for a few days…Deyrah is the winter residence of the invalid officers and others who have made Mussoorie a permanent home, the climate in the cold weather being thought more agreeable than that of the hill station.[7]

'Mountaineer' continues his trip up to Mussoorie:

The drive to Rajpore at the foot of the hill, six miles [9.7 kms], in a buggy from the hotel, and the pony ride from thence to Mussoorie, on a bright spring morning, was something in itself worth a journey from the plains. From Rajpore, a large thriving village, with two hotels, the ascent is about seven miles [11.3 kms], the first half a steady pull in zigzags along the hill side, in some places far too steep for comfortable riding; the other half a little diversified, with here and there a few score yards of level ground, a great relief to both man and beast. The whole was through forest, nowhere very dense, which changed in character as we ascended. The lower part was covered with dwarf trees and bushes, intermingled with gigantic creepers. Before we got half way up, pines, oak, and rhododendron gradually made their appearance, and are the principal trees on the Mussoorie range...

I almost envy the man who has yet to enjoy his first ride up the Mussoorie hill. To the most indifferent it cannot but be interesting. The lateral valley on the left, with its villages and green fields cut in terraces along the hillsides, the varied hue of the forest patches, the ridge above dotted with white mansions, the park-like Dhoon valley below, its encircling range of low wooded hills, and the shadowy plains beyond, gave at each fresh turn a succession of views so novel, and so widely different from the flat plains of India, that the journey seemed too soon over.

Bands of porters were transporting baggage up-hill, some sturdy hill-men from the interior, with their loads strapped to their backs; others, many of them of the gentler sex, appeared to be from the plains, and carried their loads on their heads. Some carried single loads others two, four, or half-a-dozen together; and to one large box, which I was told contained a pianoforte, twenty-four men were attached...The only difficult thing to pass was the piano, which, where I overtook it, took up the entire breadth of the road, and I had to ride behind it some distance till we reached a wider part, where I could pass.

Two annas and a half, or about four pence, is the regulated hire for a single load, or for every porter when more than one are required to a load. The loads are not weighted, and some are more and some less, but fifty-six pounds [25 kilograms] is considered the average...[8]

Thus was the trip up to Mussoorie in the 1860s, about thirty years after the establishment of the Station. But improvements in transport facilities soon changed the mode of travel. And it was the railway that made escape to the hills possible for hitherto unimaginable numbers.

Once the rail line came through as far as Ghaziabad, near Delhi, travellers would de-train there and proceed—uncomfortably—by a doli (litter). And by 1884, when Northam was writing the first-ever 'complete' guide to Mussoorie, the Shahdara-Saharanpur Light Railway (SSLR) was running from the northeastern part of Delhi to Saharanpur[9], and this became the favoured route. From there, the traveller proceeded by gharry, which was a horse-drawn cab of sorts, often in the style of a wheeled palanquin (palki). One had to book his northbound gharry in advance.

> If, during the rush to the hills, the traveller has not pre-engaged his *gharry*, so as to travel northwards during the night, he has little chance of starting until the next morning, and the impatient excursionist has the mortification of seeing gharry after gharry depart hill wards to the lively though unmusical sound of the coachman's bugle. It is an ill-wind that blows nobody good, and one of the several hotels, or the dâk bungalow, will profit by the wayfarer's discomfiture. If nobody takes precedence of him, he may be sent on at midnight, which is the commencement of the dak gharry day.[10]

The price in 1884 for the 49-mile gharry ride from Saharanpur to Rajpur at the foot of the hills was Rs 25 (one inside seat only), plus '...it is advisable to tip the coachman, if he behaves well'. Starting at eight or nine in the evening, one would arrive in Rajpur by about five or six the next morning, with rest stops and pony changes en route. However, day travel was advised in order to enjoy the views, particularly of the Siwalik Range. For the steeper portions in the Siwalik Range, up to the tunnel[11], some of the dak companies changed ponies (tats) for bullocks, which made the going even slower. Elephants, deer, wild boar and even tigers were not uncommon sightings.

Passing through Dehra Dun, the gharry made its way to '...the pretty little plateau at the foot of the Rajpur bazaar'. The coachman would sound his bugle and drive his ponies—usually three or four to a gharry at this higher point—past the grounds of the Viceroy's Bodyguard (now the President's Bodyguard), and into the compound of one of the (by this time) five hotels that offered the wayfarer food and rest.

> The plateau before-mentioned [Rajpur] is one great hostelry for the entertainment of man and beast. There are the Ellenbourough, the Rajpur, and the Prince of Wales, as well as 'Agency Retiring Rooms' and a Resthouse, the latter under native superintendence... They all furnish fair entertainment, and administer to one's comforts with commendable solicitude and at very moderate rates. Having made his choice of a hotel, probably the first matter that strikes the traveller's attention is the necessity for a good tub, which can be had, hot or cold, on the shortest notice.[12]

An 1890s transport advertisement. In the latter half of the nineteenth century, Buckle & Co. was the major provider of transport between Saharanpur, which was the closest railhead, and Mussoorie. Buckle & Co. was dealt a blow when the railway line was put through in 1900 all the way to Dehra Dun. *(From Hawthorne, Robert ['compiler'],* The Beacon's Guide to Mussoorie, *Mussoorie: The Beacon Press, 1890)*

Via the Bridle Path, there were three ways of getting from Rajpur to Mussoorie: walking, riding on horseback or being carried (daytime trips only), in a jampan or a dandy. As Fanny Parkes noted, the jampan resembled a chair, albeit covered with an oilcloth roof and attached to poles. The whole artifact was supported by eight coolies, four at a time, taking their places between the projecting horizontal poles in front and rear. The dandy was for 'lightweights', with the passenger sitting in a canoe-shaped contraption, carried by a complement of four coolies, alternating two by two. In 1884, a jampan with coolies cost three rupees or three rupees, eight annas for the steep climb from Rajpur to Mussoorie. A dandy cost about two rupees, all included.

33

During the latter half of the nineteenth century, the dak bungalow rest house in Rajpur was just one of several options for an overnight stay before proceeding up to Mussoorie. Julian Rust, who is credited with this view, was a well-known nineteenth-century photographer with a studio in Mussoorie.
(Kind courtesy of the late H. Michael Stokes, Kent, United Kingdom)

Outside of Rajpur, there was a one-pice toll bar for laden coolies, jampans paying eight annas; a dandy, four annas; a horse, four annas; and a pony for two annas.

This was the toll '…for the privilege of entering the gates of paradise as represented by a cool and bracing climate'.[13]

By the 1880s, one had two choices of road from the Rajpur toll gate. The first was the original, steep seven-mile (11.3 kms) Bridle Path route with many zigzags. The second more gradual ascent was by Mackinnon's Road, '…named after the designer and constructor, supported by a combination of capital contributed by those who had an interest in securing wheeled traffic to and from Mussoorie'.[14] In the 1880s, this road went only to Kulukhet.

If a traveller arrived in Rajpur in the evening, he would stay there for the night, since going up to Mussoorie was rather hazardous to a stranger on horseback and absolutely unadvised for the novice rider. Coolies would take the baggage

This early postcard shows a jampan, which resembled a chair, albeit covered by an oilcloth roof to protect the single passenger from rain and direct sunlight. Although not particularly well-paid (two or three annas for a one-way load), the local coolies were respected for their honesty and renowned for their ability to find virtually any house in Mussoorie or Landour for safe delivery of a traveller's chattel.
(Kind courtesy of the late H. Michael Stokes, Kent, United Kingdom)

ahead and were deemed very reliable, renowned for delivering the traveller's chattel safely to its destination. Women and children would generally travel by jampan.

At Jharipani, midway up the shorter seven-mile route and just before reaching the fourth milestone, was the famous halfway house which, in 1884 was '…in the last stage of decay'. Yet, at that time, the thirsty traveller was still able to refresh himself '…by a brandy or whiskey peg, a small bottle of claret, or a cup of tea, whichever might have been his "particular vanity"'[15] In fact, there were two halfway houses, one under European management that was licensed to sell liquor to soldiers and another under 'native management' that was not. Nearby to these houses was a 'very handsome' drinking trough for ponies and cattle, constructed by Maharani Krishna Kumari Devi, the wife of the deposed Maharaja Dev Shamsher Jang Bahadur Rana of Nepal who had put up at Fairlawn Palace (see Chapter 9).[16]

The first European grave in the area was located here (see Chapter 6).

This postcard photo shows the famous halfway house, located midpoint on the seven-mile
(11.3 km) Bridle Path between Rajpur and Mussoorie, where weary travellers could refresh themselves
'...by a brandy or whiskey peg, a small bottle of claret, or a cup of tea, whichever might have been
his "particular vanity"'. The earliest gravesite in the area (1828), seen above the upper house in the
photograph, is that of Captain Charles Farrington, an invalided soldier on his way to Landour,
'...whither he was repairing as a last hope...'
(Kind courtesy of the late H. Michael Stokes, Kent, United Kingdom)

Continuing from the halfway house on the short route, the traveller came to
Barlowganj, where there was a police post and another fork in the road. Those
who were headed anywhere east of Kulri, including Landour, took the 'upper road'
to the right, which was more popular. Those heading to Kulri itself, or westward
towards the library and beyond, could use either the upper road or the 'lower road'
that passed by the Crown Brewery and, in fact, was a continuation of the Mackinnon
Road to Rajpur.

In October and November, the order of traffic was reversed.

Then there is a general stampede from the hills, as though Mussoorie and
Landour were afflicted with the plague. Leaves are then expiring and visitors are
resuming their cold weather routine in the Plains, the ladies, especially, lingering
on long into November.[17]

Thus was travel to Mussoorie—and out—until 1899, when a railway line opened round the east end of the Siwaliks via Haridwar and through the eastern part of the Dun.[18] This greatly enhanced the popularity of the Station, as travellers from any part of India found it very convenient to travel to Laksar Junction (Laksar being in Haridwar district) and from there, to catch the Dehra Dun Railway to Dehra Dun itself. The Dehra Dun Railway was operated by the Oudh and Rohilkhand (O&R) State Railway. The O&R Line was often accused of running late, but it connected with every line in Upper India, '…and if it ran strictly to its time table there would probably be a great many more complaints from passengers who "got left" than there are.'[19]

For the jaunt between the Dehra Dun Railway Station and Rajpur, the dooly and gharry soon were replaced by a horse-drawn tonga or phaeton.

The Dehra Dun Railway Station. The railway first came to Dehra Dun in 1899, making travel to and from Mussoorie much easier than it had previously been.
(Photograph by Julian Rust from Bodycot, F. ['compiler'], Guide to Mussoorie with Notes on Adjacent Districts and Routes into the Interior, *Mussoorie: Mafasilite Printing Works, 1907, frontpiece)*

The 'Mackinnon Road' became known simply as the 'Cart Road' and was kept in fairly good order from Rajpur to within a short distance of Kulukhet (14 miles or 22.5 kms). In the early 1900s, it was tested for car travel. But it was in 1926 that the Honorable Nawab Mahommad Yusuf, the United Provinces' minister for local self-government, really opened the way for motor traffic to Mussoorie. In that year, he obtained for the Station a substantial loan from government for the construction of a pukkah motor road. Gradually, motor traffic nosed its way up to a terminus at Bhatta, then to Sunny View terminus in 1929-1930, then on to the Kincraig terminus. Rickshaws also carried downhill traffic. Initially, the road was not wide enough for two-way traffic, and there were 'gate timings' by which up and down traffic was regulated.

Before Independence and in Mussoorie itself, there were no cars, the road traffic consisting almost entirely of horses, rickshaws, dandies, doolies, kandies (woven baskets that were strapped to the back of coolies and used for carrying children or the sick) and—mostly—pedestrians.

> …anyone of any status had his own rickshaw pulled by four or five men known as jhampanies who dressed in the livery of their employer. It was a unique sight to see the number of liveried rickshaws on the Mall in those days.[20]

Of course, these well-fitted and manned rickshaws were for the very well-to-do; most houses settled for a dandy, although these still required at least four bearers. However, as wages increased and motorized vehicles became more common, these labour-intensive 'colonial' modes of transportation were less and less used. Rickshaws with two coolies pulling and two or three pushing were gradually replaced after Independence with three-wheeled cycle rickshaws. These cycle rickshaws still ply the Mall and beyond to the west. Dandies, doolies and kandies are now rarely seen, except perhaps for carrying village patients to hospital or at a village wedding to carry the bride. The only horses seen are those used for giving pleasure rides to tourists.

Those who studied in Mussoorie seem to have vivid memories of travelling to and from the Station. Bob Francis, a student at Woodlands School whose father was in charge of the Survey of India office in Dehra Dun (1922–1935), remembers it this way:

> Each summer the family would move to Mussoorie and stay there for the school year. My father would remain in Dehra Dun during the week, taking a tonga up to Rajpur (or walk up to Rajpur, if no transport was available) each Friday evening and then up to Mussoorie, returning each Sunday.
>
> In those days the journey for us to Mussoorie was like this: We would get

The Indian royals and well-to-do of Mussoorie kept rickshaws and liveried coolies for their exclusive use, although this was not the norm. More common was a modest dandy.
(Photo kind courtesy of John and Sonia née Payne Harriyott, England)

to Rajpur by tongas and hand over our luggage to an agency run by a European couple. They would arrange *phaltoos* [coolies] and transport; by dandy for the ladies and for the children by kandi. Ponies were also available.

We would then start the long hike through Rajpur Bazzar and then up the famous 'panch kainchi' [five scissor-like zig zags on the steep hillside] sharing

This photo from the 1950s shows three American missionary children in Landour—Karen Tamminen née Bowdish, Norman Van Rooy and Sue Steiner, being taken for an outing in a dandy. A dandy was a light canoe-shaped contraption of wooden frame covered with canvas and wax cloth, and usually borne by four bearers, alternating two by two. It was sometimes used for travel up to Mussoorie, especially by women and children. *(Photo kind courtesy of Steve Van Rooy, USA)*

the road with long lines of mules. At Oak Grove, we would rest at the Halfway House and have something to eat. Then it was on the road again past Fairlawn Palace, through Barlowgunj, past the red tank and on to Mussoorie.

These memories are very clear in my mind. The famous family story about me was as follows: I (age four) was in a *kandi* and some school boys started teasing me about riding my horse backwards. I got so annoyed I demanded to be set down and walked the rest of the way to Mussoorie.[21]

Marguerite Watkins, who grew up in the last two decades of British rule, remembers the excitement of going back up to Mussoorie in 1946 after the Second World War. For her, three days of travel started from Jabalpur on the Bombay Calcutta Mail—'always late'—on through Katni, Allahabad (with an eight-hour wait between trains), Kanpur, Lucknow, Faizabad, Shahjahanpur, Moradabad, Haridwar, and finally Dehra Dun. Writing nearly sixty years later, Watkins's excitement is still palpable:

As people jostled on and off the train, a monkey or two swung from the rafters eyeing our breakfasts. Crows called, hopping after crumbs, babies cried, steam hissed, bells clanged, and the cadence of Hindi, Urdu, English, homogenized into a background accompaniment to the calls of vendors and arguments between porters. Dust motes shone in sunlight; the sun had begun to warm the night air. A new day. A day closer to the mountains. Hissing and chuffing, the engine gathered speed, and last-minute boarders grabbed the outstretched hands of friends on the now-moving train as coolies hurled their baggage through windows. What a commotion; what bliss. Another day across the morning plains of India!

At Dehra Dun, there was the confusion of checking luggage and reuniting with school friends, as '…Chaperones heroically herded their charges into the correct bus, and porters heaved *bistars* [bedding] to its roof. In a gust of black petrol fumes and an ominous grinding of ancient gears, we were off.'[22]

Although it was the most direct route, coming up from Dehra Dun was not the only way of approaching Mussoorie. For those for whom trekking in the Himalayas had a strong appeal, there was the popular Shimla to Mussoorie trail, where '… the scenery throughout almost the whole route is delightful.' The distance was 142 miles (229 kms), divided into fourteen stages averaging about 10 miles (16 kms), with furnished bungalows available at each stage. In 1935 or thereabouts, when a guidebook for the trek was published, the trip was estimated to cost Rs 12 per day.[23]

Of course, travelling to Mussoorie was a quite different experience for India's royalty but still, it was a major undertaking, especially given extensive entourages and even greater heaps of baggage. The maharaja of Kapurthala, HH Brig. Sukhjit Singh, MVC,[24] recalled:

Virtually the seat of governance of the state [of Kapurthala] shifted, like the move of the government from Delhi to Simla, but in miniature. First of all the Comptroller of the Household would come up to make sure that everything was ready, because other houses would sometimes have to be rented to take the overflow from Chateau de Kapurthala. Then the Maharanis would move en bloc with a special train. The Senior Maharani would go in my grandfather's saloon and they would reserve two or three first class carriages for the others and their entourages. The baggage, the dogs and the horse would also go up and even some of my grandfather's more delicate birds who couldn't stand the heat of the plains, such as the Japanese pheasants and the monals. They went

Lakwar Village.

Lakwar (Lakhwar) Village, 1888. Lakwar, at an elevation of about 3,700 feet (1,128 metres), is located 15 miles (24 kms) to the west of Mussoorie, towards Chakrata. It was the last resting point but one on the foot trail from Shimla to Mussoorie. The District Board's bungalow at Lakwar was said to be a particularly good one. *(Photo by Mr and Mrs S.A. Hill from the Ballade of Photographs, 1888, captioned by Rudyard Kipling, Rare Book and Special Collections Division, Library of Congress)*

in their travelling-cages with their keeper and were housed for the summer in a specially constructed aviary.

Before we moved up, my sister and I would have to pay our respects to our various grandmothers, who always insisted that we couldn't leave until we had taken a little curd, a little sugar and a little money, which was auspicious for a journey. Then we would disembark from the train at Dehra Dun and go on horseback or in a *dandy* to Kincraig, where a rickshaw would take you on up to the house.[25]

In 1920, a Ford Model T was driven up from Rajpur via Jharipani to the Mall by Colonel E.W. Bell, a son-in-law of the Swetenham family of Cloud End Estate. Nonetheless, the lower down Kincraig remained the primary motor road terminus until well after the Second World War. From Kincraig onwards, the reliable coolies continued to shoulder the baggage. Returning students walked through the several miles to their schools. The smallest were certainly carried, and women were carried sometimes as well. Men and boys walked or rode horseback.

In those post-war days, Kincraig was described thus:

[It] was a treeless flat area on the hillside below the bazaar, the end of the motor road from the plains. A rock bluff rose above a dust-brown flat; neither grasses nor shrubs softened the perimeter. My friends and I had walked through a forest of oaks, ferns and flowering asters [from Woodstock School], and then a bustling bazaar to reach this barren place. But it seemed beautiful because we were going down, the first stage of the trip home.[26]

By 1954, owner-driven cars were routinely going up to Library Chowk, and special permit holders could go right up to Landour Bazaar.[27] And today, Kincraig's 'beauty' is still very much in the eye of the beholder. It has become a warren of auto repair shops and petrol pumps, certainly utilitarian, but hardly attractive as an entry point into the 'Queen of the Hills'.

In 1954, Mr Cornelius wrote in his guide to Mussoorie, '...we are quite sure that if this road building process continues, Mussoorie would appear like a glorious garden with beautiful cemented roads in and around it.'[28]

Little did he realize what impact traffic would have on the 'glorious garden'. Nonetheless, it is still true, as it was in 1860, that the trip to Mussoorie '...even to the most indifferent...cannot but be interesting.'

Notes

1. Kipling, Rudyard, *Writings in Prose and Verse, Early Verses, 1889-1896*, New York: Charles Scribner's Sons, 1920: 99.
2. Luard, John, *A Series of Views in India, Comprising Sketches of Scenery, Antiquities, and Native Character, Drawn from Nature and on Stone*, London: J. Dickinson, 1837.

3. Trower, Charles F. Trower, 33rd Bengal Native Infancy and 3rd Nizam's Cavalry, *Journal of a March from Midnapore to the Hills beyond Deyrah Doon, 1834-1835*, with sketches, unpublished.

4. Eden, Emily, *Up the Country, Letters Written to Her Sister from the Upper Provinces of India*, London: Richard Bentley, 1867: 114.

5. Parkes, Fanny, *Wanderings of a Pilgrim, in Search of the Picturesque, during Four-and-Twenty Years in the East; with Revelations of Life in the Zenana*, London: Pelham Richardson, 1850: 227 in vol. 2.

6. Eden, Ibid, p. 102-103.

7. 'Mountaineer' (pseudonym for W. Wilson), *A Summer Ramble in the Himalayas with Sporting Adventures in the Vale of Cashmere*, London: Hurst and Blackett, 1860: 1-3.

8. 'Mountaineer', Ibid, p. 6-80.

9. The SSLR was one of several small, narrow gauge (2' 6") concerns owned and worked by Martin's Light Railways, a management company based in Calcutta. The SSLR closed in 1970 but was taken over by the Indian Railways, the line converted to broad gauge and reopened to traffic. The SSLR was distinguished as being the first and only narrow gauge line ever to originate from Delhi.

10. Northam, John, *Guide to Masuri, Landaur, Dehra Dun and the Hills North of Dehra*, Calcutta: Thacker, Spink and Company, 1884: 6. Today, 125 years after original publication, this guidebook is again available, having been re-published in 2007 in the United Kingdom by Pagoda Tree Press, Bath. The author of this book—the earliest known guidebook to Mussoorie—was the proprietor of *The Himalaya Chronicle* which, in the 1880s, was published from Mussoorie twice weekly, usually only during 'the Season', although there was an attempt at year-round publishing.

11. The tunnel of the Mohan Pass, located between Landibara and Asaruri, was built in 1861 as a famine relief project.

12. Northam, Ibid, p. 14-16.

13. Northam, Ibid, p. 18-19.

14. Northam, Ibid, p. 19. Mr John Mackinnon was the Mussoorie Cart Road engineer who started the road project, having planned the whole thing on paper. He was instrumental in completing it from Rajpur to Kulukhet. Most of the European firms in Mussoorie, who obviously stood to gain by the construction of such a road, assisted Mr Mackinnon financially. This road would get their heavy stuff by wheeled carts to Kulukhet quicker and more cheaply. At first, much trouble was experienced during the rainy season on account of landslides and washouts, so it was neglected for some years. But Messrs Whymper and Company took the Crown Brewery on lease in 1876 and, along with Messrs Mackinnon and Company, they repaired the Cart Road and got it going again. 'Whympers Tank' on Brooklands Estate is still to be seen as a monument to the efforts of this great road-building venture, a hard task admirably taken up by these two companies (adapted from A. W. Cornelius' *Mussoorie Guide*, 1954; note that the Wympers tank are no longer visible, as they were in 1954).

15. Northam, Ibid, p. 22.

16. _____*Dehra Dun & Landour, Cantonments: Hand-book for the Use of Residents and Visitors*, Dehra Dun: Grand Himalayan Press, 1912: 9.

17. Northam, Ibid, p. 21.

18. For some years prior to this, there had been much discussion of running a line directly from Saharanpur through the Mohan Pass, a project that never was taken up and, so, today's Shatabdi services runs to Saharanpur and then back through Haridwar and along the eastern Dun route to Dehra Dun.

19. Bodycot, F. ('compiler'), *Guide to Mussoorie with Notes on Adjacent Districts and Routes into the Interior,* Mussoorie: Mafasilite Printing Works, 1907: 3-4. Travellers, except for those from the Punjab state, would come to Laksar Junction by the Oudh and Rohilkhand Railway, from Lucknow or Moradabad. Those from the Punjab would come to Laksar via Saharanpur. Interestingly, there are redundant sections of the Oudh and Rohilkhand Railway tracks holding up the roof of the south veranda at the historic Christ Church in Mussoorie (recycling at its best).

20. Allen, Charles and Sharada Dwivedi, *Lives of the Indian Princes*, London: Century Publishing Co. Ltd, 1984: 157.

21. Bob Francis reminiscing in a 2010 email exchange with the authors. When Bob's father, A.O. Francis, retired from the Survey of India in 1932, the family stayed permanently in Mussoorie until his death in 1961. Bob Francis now lives in Australia.

22. Watkins, Marguerite Thoburn, *Two Taproots: Growing up in the Forties in India and America,* USA: Xlibris Corporation, 2004: 96.

23. Davenport, Major C. *Simla to Mussoorie Over the Hills,* Calcutta: W. Newman & Co., circa 1935 (revised edition published in 2006 by Pagoda Tree Press, Bath): 1-15.

24. Allen, Ibid. MVC stands for Maha Vir Chakra, the second highest military decoration in India.

25. Allen, Ibid, p. 156–157.

26. The present Mussoorie Road was built up to Bhatta by 1930 and to Kincraig by 1936. After Independence in 1954 it reached the library and in 1957 it reached Picture Palace.

27. Cornelius, A.W., *Mussoorie Guide*, Dehra Dun: Vasant Press, 1954: paragraph 12.

28. Ibid.

A Thomas Alfred Rust photograph of the western end of the Mall, dated 1900. Maddock's School, including its chapel, can be seen where the Savoy Hotel was built only two years after this picture was taken. In 1900, the bandstand was still located immediately in front of the Library, rather than to the side as it is today. *(Courtesy of the National Army Museum, London)*

3

BUILDING THE BOLTHOLE

This was a town they had built altogether for their own indulgence, not for command, not for security, not even for profit, but simply for their own relaxation…
~ Jan Morris[1] ~

M ussoorie did indeed evolve over the years as a major resort—a place for relaxation—but in the period leading up to the establishment of Simla (now Shimla) as the summer capital, there was at least a suggestion in some circles that Mussoorie was in the running for this particular distinction. *The Hills*, the first newspaper to be published in Mussoorie, noted in its 12 December 1861 number:

> Now that there is a talk about removing the seat of Government to the Himalayas, a sanitarium like Mussoorie, offering as it does peculiar attractions on the score of climate, and centrically situated with respect to the Presidencies of Calcutta and Bombay, stands a fair chance of becoming, perhaps at a no distant date, the chosen residence of the Rulers of India.[2]

Mussoorie, of course, did not become the summer capital of British India. But like other sanitaria, it reached its apex as a British hill station during the reign of Queen Victoria (1837–1901), particularly in the period after the First War of Independence and with the advent of rail travel. Victoria's reign saw the high noon of Empire and, in the hills, the ambitious Victorians enthusiastically set about building the infrastructure within which their 'lives apart' could be lived.

Of course, this building could not be done without a phalanx of local workers. According to Dane Kennedy's estimate, which he based on census data, ten Indian workers were necessary to support each European.

> …the development of highland sanitaria generated enormous demands for native labor. Roads and bridges had to be constructed, land cleared and dwellings erected, provisions produced and marketed, visitors and their baggage brought up, fodder and fuel and water provided, and a myriad of domestic drudgeries carried out. These tasks the British relied upon Indians to do, and in large numbers…[3]

One may recognize 1823, when the two Fredericks—Young and Shore—built their shooting box, as the year Mussoorie was founded, although the 1908 *Imperial Gazetteer of India* noted that Mussoorie became a sanitarium in 1826...' Landour most certainly dates from 1827, when the East India Company gave approval to Colonel Young's proposal for the establishment there of '...a sanatorium for invalided British soldiers. But whatever the founding years, the Station—inclusive of Mussoorie and Landour— soon became a Victorian bolthole far away from the hustle and bustle, heat and dust, and illness and ennui of the plains. In fact, it was an 'out-of-India' place for the British, especially since it was never burdened with the bureaucracy attending a summer capital. It was a place for rest, recreation, recovery and severe aloofness, its 'official' role limited to providing a haven for sick soldiers and schooling for the sons and daughters of the Empire.

When Queen Victoria came to the British throne in 1837 at the age of eighteen, Mussoorie and Landour were just coming into their own. The Nepalese had been pushed back, Dehra Dun had become a bustling British cantonment and the abundant wildlife in the area made it a popular destination for those interested in shikar. Furthermore, the unknown reaches of the nearby Himalayas offered fabulous opportunities for adventurers and scientists. The hill station provided a restorative Elysium for soldiers of the East India Company, and many schools were being established to provide education and training to the next generation of rulers and administrators.

The confident Victorians were everywhere in the world, India was increasingly coming under their sway, and the cool breezes of Mussoorie had been discovered to waft eternal over the queen's representatives in India, that exceptional gem that soon became the brightest jewel in her crown.

But, of course, the British bubble burst. When Queen Victoria died in 1901 at the age of eighty-one, Indians were becoming ever more wary and weary of their foreign rulers. The First War of Independence had forever driven a wedge between rulers and ruled. Earlier confidences and close personal (and sometimes conjugal) relationships between the British and Indians had largely given way to the dictates of a rigid code of 'separateness' promoted, it is said, by the emergence in Britain of a robust evangelical Christianity and the arrival in India of British women in large numbers. Racism and severe class distinctions took deep root. Indians felt exploited economically. Twenty years into Victoria's reign and in an effort to assure more efficient rule, the British government took over full control of India from the East India Company, and soon (on 1 May 1876) the British queen was named empress of India. However, the demand for political voice, for freedom, grew louder as the decades passed. Ultimately, of course, the people had their say; India was freed from the bonds of colonial rule.

But that was nearly fifty years beyond the end of Victoria's reign and, in the meantime, there was much building to be done and pleasure to be had in Mussoorie.

It was during this Victorian Era—a period of industrial, political, scientific and military progress in Britain—that the Station saw its defining growth and development. Cottages and schools cropped up everywhere, shops well-stocked with Indian and foreign goods opened on the Mall and in Landour, smart hotels catered to the needs of demanding guests, roads were built within the Station, municipal regulations regarding sanitation, forestation and much more were put in place, and travelling up and down became easier (in any case, Mussoorie was always the most accessible of the major hill stations).

Of course, growth and development obviously have continued since the early 1900s, more recently at a breathless pace and perhaps not always for the better, but certainly Victorian Mussoorie came to epitomize a 'hill station ideal' and outlined for future generations the basic features of the town.

Mussoorie is said to have derived its name from the former abundance on its hills of the shrub *Coriaria Nepalensis Musari* (or Munsari). The common name—variously spelled as Musari, Munsari or Mansuri—eventually became 'Masuri'. The current spelling, Mussoorie, is credited to a local medium for advertisements:

> [*The Mussoorie Exchange Advertiser*] was…the semi-official murderer of the name 'Masuri' replacing the victim with 'Mussoorie'.[4]

The station is situated at latitude 30° 27' 30"; longitude 78° 6' 30", with Benog Hill to the west being the highest point on the Mussoorie side (6,901 feet or 2,104 metres above sea level) and Landour Hill being the highest point on the cantonment side (7,538 feet or 2,298 metres). The Mall is at 6,000 to 6,500 feet (1,828 to 1,981 metres), and parts of Landour are fully 1,000 feet (305 metres) higher than the Mall. The lofty and much admired range to the north extends from Nag Tibba in the west at 9,912 feet (3,022 metres) to Nandakot in the east at 22,504 feet (6,861 metres). To the south is the Dehra Dun Valley backed by the Siwalik Hills. The temperature generally falls in the range of 27° to 85° Fahrenheit (-2.8° to 29.4° Celsius). These are, of course, the technical parameters that make Mussoorie and Landour so favoured by nature and attractive to humankind.

An early postcard photo showing a splendid view of Benog Hill, located to the west of the Mall, with a water carrier in silhouette. Benog is the highest point on the Mussoorie side of the Station. Atop Benog is Jwalaji Temple. *(Kind courtesy of the late H. Michael Stokes, Kent, United Kingdom)*

In the very early days, Mussoorie and Landour were distinctly separate, with Mussoorie being the preferred location. It is said that in 1823, there was only one house in Mussoorie. Although, as Northam states in his 1884 guidebook:

> ...It is curious to think that the first construction was a small hut built as a shooting box, on the Camel's Back Hill, by Mr Shore and Captain Young in 1823. Being only a shooting box it can scarcely count as a house, but so it is.[6]

By 1828, there were sixteen houses in the Station (Mussoorie *and* Landour). About fifty-five years later, in 1884, the number had grown to almost 500 (340 European and 140 Indian houses), for once the attractions of the place had been discovered, the building of a few houses obviously led to the erection of many more. By the early 1900s, *The Gazetteer of Dehra Dun* reported there were 4,278 inhabited houses and a population of 14,689, of whom 3,418 were Europeans.[7] (Appendix B is a listing of the Station houses as recorded in 1929.)

The traditional houses in and around the Station were built strictly for hill conditions, put up on a rock base, with a skeletal wood frame of rectangles, diagonals, arches and triangles. The spaces in between were filled with mud, plaster, stones,

The snowy range beyond Mussoorie, photographed in 1900 by Julian Rust, who operated his photography shop out of Regent House in Kulri from 1893 to 1914. The Savoy Hotel was to be built later, below the newly built Chateau de Kapurthala, which is shown in this photograph with banners waving from the rooftop. *(Courtesy of the National Army Museum, London)*

'One might wander over a considerable portion of the globe, and penetrate into many remote corners in search of the picturesque, without finding an equal to the view, which, in clear weather, the residents may gaze on every morning of their lives.' 'The Mountaineer' (pseudonym of W. Wilson), 1860[5]

rubble and brickbats. The floors and ceiling were wooden, and the roofs either slate or shale or thatched with straw mixed with layers of earth, well beaten to hopefully make them impervious to rain and snow. The purported advantage of this type of construction was that it never collapsed en bloc—an important feature in an earthquake zone—and, whenever it did fall, it came down in bits and pieces, thereby reducing risk to life and property.[8]

However, the British settlers tended to build their houses as they did on the plains, with heavy thick walls and flat roofs, often with secondary pitched roofs of thatch or tin[9] to better protect them from the monsoons. This sort of construction came in for some criticism. ICS (Indian Civil Service) officer H.G. Walton, for example, was no fan of housing in the Station. He thought the architecture of private buildings—with the notable exception of Chateau de Kapurthala—to be at a very low level, most housing presenting '…the appearance of white and grey blotches on an otherwise pretty landscape…', and sadly built much like bungalows in the plains, quite unsuitable for the hills. He thought the interiors were not much better. And even at the time he was writing, in 1910–1911, he felt that houses were too closely situated in the central part of Mussoorie, particularly in the neighbourhood of the Himalaya Club and Kulri Bazaar, although noting that crowding would have been worse but for the introduction of a two-acre rule in 1894–1895.[10] Seeing Mussoorie today, that rule was obviously abandoned, and one wonders what Walton would think of today's congestion!

There were no land survey settlements of any kind in Mussoorie or Landour until the late 1820s, although revenue subdivisions had been established by Mr Thomas Palin Calvert as early as 1816 and, generally speaking, the boundary line between the East India Company-administered Dehra Dun district and the territories left to Sudershan Shah, the raja of Tehri who was reinstated after the British had driven out the Gurkhas, was the watershed line of the Mussoorie and Landour range. But, in reality, the European settlers took up what land they desired directly from the zamindars (landlords) of the villages on the slopes of the hills, despite the efforts of Frederick Shore to protect villagers' rights.[11]

The question of boundaries first cropped up when government established the convalescent depot at Landour in 1827.

> The fact that the land on the northern slopes of the hills was not in British territory being established from the records consulted, compensation was accordingly determined on, in the way of an annual quit-rent [to the Raja of Tehri], the Government paying Rs 70 per annum for the Landour Depôt, and the Civil Station, or Mussoorie proper, Rs 278 per annum. These rates have since been enhanced; but as the total area of Mussoorie and Landour (excluding Rajpur and Bhadraj, which were eventually excluded from the settlement, after it was first made) is nearly twenty square miles [32 square kms], about half of which, roughly speaking, was [Raja of] Tehri territory, a rent of say Rs 350 per annum was by no means excessive; about Rs 35 per square mile.[12]

In 1842, F.O. Wells, empowered by the company's Board of Revenue, made his famous settlement of lands in the Station. The next settlement was done in 1904 by Mr E.H. Ashworth. In the event, some properties such as Mullingar, Mullingar Cottage and part of Woodstock School straddled cantonment *and* municipal lands.

In 1862, Colonel Norman solved this vexing problem by simply excluding six properties (eleven houses) at the eastern end of Landour from taxes altogether. This happy arrangement for some was known as the 'Norman Guarantee'.

In 1903, municipal boundaries were revised, which resulted in a total area of 19 square miles (31 square kms), including the Landour Bazaar, which had been handed over to the municipality in 1897.[13]

Communication between Mussoorie and the rest of India, and, indeed, with the rest of the world, was greatly advanced by the Post Office Act XVII of 1837, the same year that Victoria ascended the British throne and during the time when Mussoorie and Landour were first being settled. This act gave the governor general the exclusive right of conveying letters by post for hire within the territories of the East India Company and, on this basis, the Indian Post Office was established on 1 October 1837. Thus, from its very earliest days, Mussoorie benefited from a postal service that had moved well beyond a relay of runners on foot. Mussoorie's General Post Office was first located at the entrance to Landour Bazaar but, in 1909, Rorleston House on the 'Grand Parade' was bought from Messrs Fitch & Co. and a new GPO building was constructed. This remains its present day location, although the Grand Parade portion of the Mall is no longer called that. Sub-post offices were set up in Landour, Library Chowk, near the Charleville Hotel, and in Barlowganj and Jharapani. Others, for example the Savoy branch, came much later. In 1865, a Head Telegraph Office was established in Kulri. And by 1910, Walton was able to boast that '…Mussoorie is well in advance of Nainital in the matter of telephones. Not only has it an exchange system of its own with some fifty subscribers, but it is also connected by a trunk line with Dehra…' which facilitated better business.[14]

Banking facilities were always available, although not always reliable. The North-West Bank opened in 1836, the first to be established in the Station. However, it failed in 1842. The Delhi and London Bank was opened in 1859, and in 1864 the Mussoorie Savings Bank was started (later, it was called simply the 'Mussoorie Bank'). In 1874, the Himalaya Bank was started by Mr F. Moss, but it too failed, and the building became the Himalaya Hotel. By 1900, the only one of the above banks that still existed was the Delhi and London Bank. Obviously, in the collapse of these banks, many residents of the Station suffered great financial loss. 'The Rambler' records a sad story:

It is possible that those 'in the know' were not aware of the new client [unnamed] they accepted at so precarious a time, but to the everlasting shame of one of these banks, on the eve of its collapse it accepted the life savings (Rs 64,000) of an old man and caused him to die of a broken heart.[15]

Over time, new banking firms came on to the scene. In 1892, the Alliance Bank of Simla Limited opened; in 1917 it became the Allahabad Bank. There was also the Bank of Upper India Limited, Messrs Bhugwan Dass & Company in Landour, and Mansa Ram & Sons Bankers. Mansa Ram & Sons Bankers was started in Landour in the 1920s (with branches in Dehra Dun, Saharanpur, Haridwar and Rishikesh) and was popular with the Landour-based missionaries because of its convenient location near Castle Hill gate. In 1955, Mansa Ram collapsed due to a liquidity crisis; however, creditors and depositors were eventually paid off by the court-appointed receiver after auctioning off the bank's extensive properties, including Mullingar (see Chapter 1). The Imperial Bank of India (IBI) was established in 1921 and soon had a branch in Mussoorie. A few years after Independence, in 1955, the IBI became the State Bank of India (SBI).

Although there are many latter-day banks in Mussoorie, the SBI is the oldest still in existence, operating on the Mall out of one of the Station's most historic buildings (originally the Himalaya Bank and later the Himalaya Hotel, not to be confused with the Himalaya Club). The cast-iron railings on the balcony of the SBI building still bear the VI (*Victoria Imperatrix,* Empress Victoria), a present-day reminder of a distant past.

It soon became necessary to attend to various civic amenities as well, and these were looked after by a municipal

In 1890, Mr Mansumrat Dass, son of the founder of Messrs Bhugwan Dass & Company, took over supervision of the bank branch in Landour. He was named to the Mussoorie Municipal Board in 1900, becoming the board's first Indian member.
(Courtesy of British Library)

committee (later to become a 'board'), Mussoorie being one of the first hill stations to enjoy local self-government.[16] Already established by 1842, the committee was made up of twelve members, some of them elected to three-year terms (open to re-election) and some ex officio such as the district superintendent of police and the civil surgeon. The functions of the committee were to look after sanitation in the Station (the Bhilaru sewerage shoot, built at a cost of Rs 70,000, was a major undertaking in later years), to regulate and control the building of houses and to see to '...all matters that may conduce to the convenience and welfare of the residents'. Importantly, the committee had power to levy certain taxes, both against proprietors and tenants, and to disperse funds and generally to regulate and control the finances of the municipal system.[17] Mr Mansumrat Dass of the banking establishment of Messrs Bhugwan Dass & Company in Landour was the first Indian to sit on the municipal board, having initially been named a member in 1900.[18]

In 1871, the Bellevue Estate on the slope of Vincent Hill was purchased by the committee from Mr G. Hunter and adapted to the purposes of a town hall, including an auditorium for public performances and meetings, a band gallery and of course, offices. Until the Rink was built in 1890, all major public events were held in the town hall. In 1877, the municipal office was moved to the Kutchery on the Mall and, subsequently, a two-storied building was erected close by in Kulri as the municipal office with a boardroom and offices for staff.[19] Shortly after the municipal office vacated Bellevue, it became home to the exiled Afghan Amir Mohammad Yaqub Khan (see Chapter 9). Today, Bellevue is called Radha Bhawan; it is under dispute and, sadly, is in an extremely dilapidated condition.

The historical railing at the State Bank of India still bears the VI (*Victoria Imperatrix*, Empress Victoria) that tells of its colonial past. One of the most historic of all the existing structures in Mussoorie, the SBI building originally housed the Himalaya Bank. Later, it became the Himalaya Hotel and then the Imperial Bank of India. After Independence, the Imperial Bank became the State Bank of India.

(Courtesy of Mela Ram & Sons, Mussoorie)

BHUGWAN DASS & Co.

Tea planters, Timber Merchants Commission Agents and House Proprietors. The Premier Bankers of Dehra Dun.

ESTABLISHED 1856.

BRANCHES AT:— MUSSOORIE & SAHARANPORE

Fixed Deposits with Rs. 100 minimum for 3, 6, 8 and 12 month —Terms on application.

Current Accounts with Rs. 100 minimum. Interest half-yearly on maximum monthly balances not below Rs. 1000, at 2% per annum.

Loans and Advances on approved security *Bills* on London bought and sold. *Drafts and Hundis* issued and cashed on the principal towns in India. Moderate commission.

Banking Business of every description transacted at reasonable Exchange, Interest and Discount.

Life and Fire Insurance effected through leading Insurance Companies. Terms on application.

Estates, land and house property bought, sold and hired. Moderate Commission

Bhugwan Dass & Co. was one of the leading banks in the Station during the early 1900s. Its hillside branch was located in Landour. *(From Bodycot, F. ['compiler'], Guide to Mussoorie with Notes on Adjacent Districts and Routes into the Interior, Mussoorie: Mafasilite Printing Works, 1907)*

The construction of roads within the Station was high on the agenda of the municipal committee. One can most easily understand this priority after reading an early account from Emily Eden. Emily was the sister of Governor General Lord Auckland and in 1838 was visiting Mussoorie and Landour with her brother (see Chapter 10) when she described their progression through Landour:

In the afternoon we took a beautiful ride up to Landour, but the paths are much narrower on that side, and our courage somehow oozed out; and first we came to a place where they said, 'This was where poor Major [William] Blundell and his pony fell over[20], and they were both dashed to atoms—and then there was a board stuck in a tree, 'From this spot a private in the Cameronians fell and was killed.' Just as if there were any use in adding that he was killed, if he fell—anybody might have guessed that. Then _____, who lived up here for three years, said he would take us home by a better path, and unluckily it was a worse one, and we had to get off our ponies and lead them, and altogether I felt giddy and thought much of poor Major Blundell![21]

A view of the Station's Municipal Hall (far right) and Club (left). Originally, the municipal offices
were on the Bellevue Estate on the slope of Vincent Hill. These offices were moved in
1877 to the Kutchery on the Mall. Later, this two-storied Municipal Hall
building was erected close by in Kulri.
(Photo by C. Nickels. Kind courtesy of the late H. Michael Stokes, Kent, United Kingdom)

But, gradually, significant progress was made on roads in the Station and, in 1884,
Northam was able to report that '…there are abundant opportunities, especially for
the pedestrian, to seek and find peripatetic pastures new'.[22] Indeed, for the horseman
or the pedestrian, Mussoorie furnished all that could be desired. By this time, the
Mall was well laid out from the post office in the east to the library in the west.
This was, of course, the primary promenade, although 'furious riding' was strictly
prohibited by the authorities.

The notion that Indians were not allowed on the Mall in Mussoorie is belied
by photographic evidence, and nowhere in the Station's earliest by-laws is reference
to such an onerous and racist restriction to be found. This may have been due to
Mussoorie not being a summer capital, for certainly the British in Mussoorie well
understood the symbolic significance of commanding and holding 'their' ground,
and such restrictions apparently did exist at official hill stations.[23]

As the Mussoorie landscape was characterized by steep ups and downs, the level
gradient of a well-maintained Camel's Back Road running from the Mall near the

library and rejoining it near the Rink was particularly popular for morning and evening constitutionals or physical exercise, and it still is. Camel's Back takes its name from a rock outcropping that resembles a seated camel. Along Camel's Back Road is Scandal Point, presumably so named because it was a favourite meeting place for young amoureux.

A Fitch & Co. postcard. Scandal Point on Camel's Back Road was so named as it was a favourite meeting place for young lovers. Obviously others too, including children, enjoyed the splendid views. The level, well-maintained roadway made it an easy path for guardians and their charges. The message on the back of this card reads, 'Margaret and I often walk westward along this road from 5-7 p.m. We usually sit for a time in this little pavilion. From it one gets a glorious view of the sunset. There are always many nurses or ayahs along the road with their little English charges and…one often sees Indian men with them, helping to tend the babies. The building [of the road] was a tremendous feat of engineering.' *(Kind courtesy of the late H. Michael Stokes, Kent, United Kingdom)*

Then there was the road from the library to the Charleville Hotel (now the Lal Bahadur Shastri National Academy of Administration). From the gates of the Charleville, Dick Road led to the Botanical Gardens, also sometimes known as the Municipal Gardens or Company Bagh, and another road dipped down to Happy Valley. The Tullahmore Road led to the Convent of Jesus and Mary (Waverley), and for those wanting to stroll further afield, the Everest Road led off to George Everest's Park Estate and Cloud End. Or one could walk down to Barlowganj and return by way of the path in front of the Antlers, a quintessential hill station cottage. In Landour, there was the road around Castle Hill (now closed to the public). And, of course, by this time (1880s) the road through the Landour Bazaar was well laid out. Hence, Emily Eden may have felt no trepidation in progressing from Kulri to St Paul's without a thought of Major Blundell.

An early twentieth-century postcard showing young mothers with their children at the Municipal Gardens, well-attended by bearers. *(Kind courtesy of the late H. Michael Stokes, Kent, United Kingdom)*

A 1906 postcard showing rickshaw drivers near Christ Church gate, towards the western end of the Mall. Road maintenance was a major and successful undertaking by the progressive Mussoorie Municipal Board. *(Kind courtesy of the late H. Michael Stokes, Kent, United Kingdom)*

As the civilian population continued to grow, the need for a hospital became increasingly obvious. Invalided soldiers had their medical facilities in the cantonment, but what about the general public? Despite the obvious need, this was a priority that was only later attended to on a modest scale through a combination of public and private resources for, in 1907, Bodycot's *Guide* recorded:

> A few years ago there were no such institutions [hospitals] in Mussoorie, sadly needed as they were in a station to which so many [civilian] invalids come to recover their health. Invalids who were ordered into a hill hospital or who required special treatment had to be sent to Naini Tal or Simla, to receive the attention their cases required.[24]

However, by the end of the Victorian era and thanks to Major W.G. Alpin, IMS (Indian Medical Service), who was civil surgeon in the years around 1900, St Mary's Cottage Hospital was established in a house called 'Landour View' on Wynberg Road (now Civil Hospital Road) with funds raised by subscription and donations (not until 1909 did the government sanction an annual grant). St Mary's Cottage Hospital still operates—now called 'Civil Hospital'—in a building constructed in 1916. There was also a hospital opened in 1903 near the main post office, strictly for Europeans and Eurasians '...who were unable to afford the cost of medical treatment, medicines and nursing in their own homes'.[25] This facility was supported by donations and by collections from patients who were able to pay. Yet, these two modest facilities were considered inadequate, even at the time, for so large and important a hill station. Finally, in 1931, several Christian missions joined together to open the Landour Community Hospital on the Tehri Road for the civilian and local village population. Today, this recently renovated hospital is operated by an Indian organization, the Emmanuel Hospital Association, although more complicated medical cases are generally sent to Dehra Dun or beyond.

Nursing homes for elderly Europeans were a regular feature of pre-Independence Mussoorie, available for those who required fairly constant care and could pay the relatively steep rates. By the early 1900s, there were three such facilities. One of these was Evelyn Hall, inclusive of adjacent cottages, at the top of Evelyn Hall Road above Christ Church. Excellently situated with an expansive view of the snows, Evelyn Hall previously had been the headquarters of the Great Trigonometrical Survey and home of the 'Great Theodolite' (see Chapter 10). The Evelyn Hall Nursing Home closed in 1934; however, the privately owned hall itself still occupies its commanding position. The other two nursing homes in the Station were at Grey Castle, located near Evelyn Hall and at the Monastery in Happy Valley. Inmates at these facilities would often spend the cold weather season in Dehra Dun or elsewhere on the plains. There was also a maternity home at Rock Cliff on Camel's Back Road.

Even before electricity came to Mussoorie there were street lights that extended as far down as Barlowganj. The first street lights—installed about 1875—were set on so-called 'Rurki' lamp posts that, for beauty at least, were not universally appreciated. But apparently they were improved upon and in 1907 Bodycot wrote, with considerable civic pride:

> The lighting of Mussoorie Roads…by clean and handsome-looking [carbide or acetylene gas] lanterns with decent looking lamps inside them…is a bright and shining example, and the Lucknow Municipality, while waiting for the promised electric luxuries in store for them in the sweet bye-and-bye, might meanwhile send a deputation up to Mussoorie to study the question of street lighting.[26]

This postcard photo from the very early part of the twentieth century shows the Library Chowk portion of the Mall. Note the 'Rurki' carbide lamp in the foreground.
(Kind courtesy of the late H. Michael Stokes, Kent, United Kingdom)

Two years later, on 24 May 1909—celebrated at the time as Empire Day—the electric lights of Mussoorie were switched on, no doubt to the great envy of Lucknow. For it was the progressive Mussoorie Municipal Board that, as sole proprietor, had taken up a state-of-the-art hydroelectric scheme to address the need for both water and electricity. From 1893 to 1909, Mussoorie's water supply was provided by steam pumping or gravitation from the Chalmer Khud, Khattapani and Brooklands springs, and also from the Mackinnon spring below the library.[27] This having become inadequate, the Station's sanitary engineer put forth a scheme to produce both electric power and more water, with Kempty Falls as the source. But Kempty Falls was in the territory of the raja of Tehri; negotiations failed, and an alternative plan at Bhatta Falls in British territory was implemented, although at considerable cost overrun. At the time this project was completed, the lift of water—1,700 feet (518 metres)—was the highest in Asia and one of the highest in the world. By today's standards, the project was miniscule but to the credit of its engineers and builders, it is still providing electricity to the Barlowganj and Jharapani sections of Mussoorie. While electricity reached the Mall in 1909, it was not until some years later that power was extended to the further reaches of the Station. So, for example, Wynberg Allen School did not get electricity until 1913.[28] (see Appendix C for ICS officer I.C. Walton's 1911-detailed description of this project.)

The enthusiasm of the Mussoorie Municipal Board in providing lighting in the Station extended to many other civic areas, and their aggressive approach to developing and maintaining the Station can best be seen in their regulations and by-laws. The very long list of possible offences (liable to a fine) included:

- Letting out, throwing or allowing to flow on any road, street, or bye-way, or waste land, foul water, filth, urine or refuse of any other description...
- Burial, cremation or other disposal of dead bodies in any place not sanctioned by the Board...
- Keeping an open smith's forge, or tannery, or a piggery, within 100 yards of public roads...
- Cutting or injuring trees or fences on any public road or place...
- Sounding drums or other musical instruments so as to cause annoyance to the public, in disregard of the prohibition of the Board...
- Dogs on the road from the General Post Office to the entrance of the Happy Valley between the hours of 4 p.m. and 8 p.m...

- Posting bills, advertisements or notices of any kind in public places, or on any public building, contrary to the order of the Board...
- Neglect on the part of the keeper of any house or place of public entertainment or resort, to prevent drunkenness, gambling or disorderly behaviour...
- The frequenting by prostitutes, eunuchs or bad characters of any kind, of any public place, road or thoroughfare, or any doorway, house, roof or open place abutting on any such public place, road or thoroughfare, so as to cause annoyance to the occupants of houses or property in the vicinity, or to passersby...[29]

And the rules and regulations went on and on. The Victorians were relentless in their attempts to 'maintain order' but, fortunately, their rule-making didn't seem to interfere with Mussoorie, which came to be known as a carefree station away from officialdom. Station leaders had put in place the necessary physical infrastructure and, side by side, Victorian entrepreneurs, soldiers, priests and arbiters of entertainment and fashion had created the social infrastructure that, together, achieved the goal of a place simply for relaxation.

Notes

1. Morris, Jan, *Stones of Empire, The Buildings of the Raj*, Oxford: Oxford University Press, 1983: 198. Morris is speaking here of Darjeeling but the sentiment applies even more so to Mussoorie; Darjeeling became the summer capital of Bengal, while Mussoorie never gained 'summer capital' status.
2. *The Hills*, 12 December 1861: 170.
3. Kennedy, Dane, *The Magic Mountains, Hill Stations and the British Raj*, Delhi: Oxford University Press, 1996: 175.
4. Williams, C. ('The Rambler'), *A Mussoorie Miscellany*, Mussoorie: Mafasilite Press, 1936: 30.
5. 'Mountaineer' (pseudonym for W. Wilson), *A Summer Ramble in the Himalayas with Sporting Adventures in the Vale of Cashmere*, London: Hurst and Blackett, 1860: 10.
6. Northam, John, *Guide to Masuri, Landaur, Dehra Dun and the Hills North of Dehra*, Calcutta: Thacker, Spink and Company, 1884: 25.
7. Walton, H.G. *The Gazetteer of Dehra Dun*, Reprint, Dehra Dun: Natraj Publishers, 2007: 243 (first published in 1911).
8. This type of construction is called dhajji, which literally means a patchwork quilt. Thus a dhajji house is a patchwork of timber and stone. It is no longer so common but can be seen.
9. The process of hot-dip galvanizing, which increased the durability of corrugated metal sheets,

was patented by Henry William Craufurd in 1837. The credit for the first manufacture of galvanized corrugated iron sheets, in 1843, goes to John Porte in Southwark, Scotland. A year later, the Phoenix Iron Works in Glasgow went into mass production. Corrugated iron sheets became popular and most of the production was earmarked for the colonies. By 1891, British production of corrugated iron exceeded 200,000 tons, with 75 per cent of the production being exported to India and other colonies.

Although very noisy during heavy monsoon rains and under the feet of native monkeys, the sheets were easy to transport, quick and simple to install and highly durable. In very short order, galvanized iron sheets became the de facto roofing standard throughout the hill resorts. They did not contribute to a picture-perfect image of a Victorian village, but in the colonies, alas, finer details had to give way to pragmatism (from Bhatt, Vikram, *Resorts of the Raj, Hill Stations of India*, Ahmedabad: Mapin, 1998: 67-68).

10. Walton, Ibid, p. 244-245.
11. 'The Rambler' records, 'Sometimes the sale was transacted directly between the zamindar [landlord] and the prospective settler and was generally a fair and amicable transaction, but often a settler's servants were left to do the bargaining and to avoid the sahib's displeasure in case of failure, all sorts of threats and stratagems were employed to make the zamindars relinquish their holdings, often at ridiculously low terms, the compensation for which 'bargain' was invariably an extra large tip for the servant. Thus did Mr. Shore take up the cause of the zamindars, but was robbed of success by the zamindars themselves who could never be persuaded to appear at the Kutchery (court), either as complainants or to give evidence' (from Williams, C. ['The Rambler'], *A Mussoorie Miscellany*, Mussoorie: The Mafasilite Press, 1936: 22).
12. Bodycot, F. ('compiler'), *Guide to Mussoorie with Notes on Adjacent Districts and Routes into the Interior, Mussoorie*: Mafasilite Printing Works, 1907: 31.
13. Walton, Ibid, p. 256.
14. Walton, Ibid, p. 248.
15. Williams, Ibid, p. 19.
16. Walton, Ibid, p. 251.
17. Northam, Ibid, p. 40.
18. *Cyclopedia of India,* Calcutta: The Cyclopedia Publishing Company, 1908: 293 in vol. 2.
19. Bodycot, Ibid, p. 143.
20. Major William Blundell died on 2 Nov 1831 and was buried in Landour cemetery, according to burial records at St Paul's Church, Landour.
21. Eden, Emily, *Up the Country*, London: Richard Bentley, 1867: 115-116.
22. Northam, Ibid, p. 34.
23. There are numerous references in today's literature (and on the Internet) mentioning that major parts of hill stations were actually closed to Indians, e.g., the offensive signage 'Indians and Dogs Not Allowed.' However, the authors have found no Mussoorie or Landour pictures of such signs, while numerous historic pictures do show Indians strolling on the Mall. And

unlike in Shimla and Darjeeling where Indians were relegated to living at symbolically important lower elevations, the Indian population of the Station occupied higher ground, since most of them lived in the Landour bazaar area. Regardless, racism certainly was widespread in the nineteenth century, among the British and also among Indians.

24. Bodycot, Ibid, p. 144.
25. Ibid.
26. Bodycot, Ibid, p. 9.
27. Chalmer Khad spring is located below Bellevue/Radha Bhawan and Guru Nanak School. Khattapani spring is towards the northwest of Landour, from where water is still being pumped up to Mussoorie. There were also lime kilns at Khattapani, used for mortar in building Station houses. Brooklands spring is near Wynberg Allen School.
28. Ruskin Bond, quoting the principal at the time: 'On the 14th of April [1913] the work of Electric Installation began; on Empire Day [24 May] we used our electric lights for the first time; they are a great comfort' (Bond, Ruskin, *The Story of Wynberg Allen, Mussoorie*, Landour: Wynberg Allen School, published on the occasion of the centenary, June 1988, p. 11).
29. Excerpts from 'Municipal Board Regulations, Bye-laws, &c' as contained in Hawthorne, Robert, Ed., *The Beacon's Guide to Mussoorie*, Mussoorie: The Beacon Press, 1890.

An 1871 view of the
Landour bazaar. From its
earliest days, this bazaar was,
and still is, the great purveyor
of goods for local residents.
(Courtesy of British Library)

4

AN ELYSIUM FOR TOMMY ATKINS

Nothing can be imagined more delicious to an invalid, half dying
under the burning sun of India, than the being removed into the fine,
bracing, and cool atmosphere of this station…
~ Anonymous (from a miscellaneous paper) ~

Frederick Young felt much the same way about the attractions of the hills above Dehra Dun, and it was he who first pushed Calcutta for the establishment of Landour[1] as a high–altitude sanatorium for the British Tommies[2]…an antidote to the sickness and death, ennui and boredom that plagued soldiers on the plains. It would be an Elysium far away from the heat, dust and pestilence of the plains.

And certainly high and cool it was, and is, for parts of Landour are fully 1,000 feet (305 metres) 'closer to heaven' than the Mall in Mussoorie. The highest point in the cantonment, and in the entire Station, is Landour Hill, at 7,538 feet above sea level (2,298 metres), located just above St Peter's Church. The second highest point is Lal Tiba at 7,464 feet (2,275 metres). Both of these peaks tower hundreds of feet over the highest points in Mussoorie. Lal Tiba, earlier called Depot Hill in reference to the convalescent facility, offers a splendid view of the Dun as well as the snowy peaks, but today, access is limited as it has been taken over by Doordarshan and All India Radio as a transmitter site. A 'new' Lal Tiba nearby must now suffice for tourists who make it this far from busy Mussoorie Bazaar.[3]

In 1827, Young gleefully wrote home, '…It is certainly the most charming climate in the world and its merits have at last been acknowledged by Government!' Calcutta had accepted his proposal to erect in Landour both barracks for convalescent European soldiers and bungalows for sick and convalescent officers, sanctioning a regular establishment of a commandant and staff. 'This will make our situation more lively and gay, which was all it wanted to render it most enviable.'[4]

However, the government's own rationale was not about liveliness and gaiety. It was about convenience and saving money:

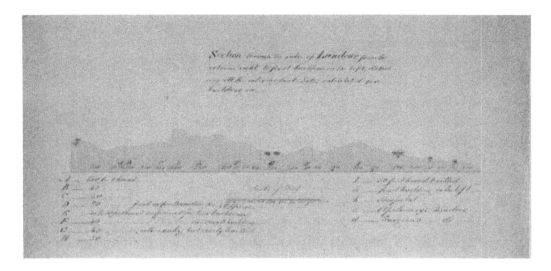

This is the earliest known schematic drawing for the establishment of Landour, described as a 'Sketch of Proposed Convalescent Station', dated 1827. At this early time, Landour was better known than Mussoorie. *(Courtesy of British Library)*

> The establishment of this station [Cantonment], so convenient for the invalids of Meerut, and other great northern cantonments, will be a great saving to Government, who were obliged, before its creation, to send their sick servants to the Cape of Good Hope, or at least to sea.[5]

The government paid a quit rent of Rs 70 per annum to the raja of Tehri and the mahant (priest) of Dehra, who in return absolutely ceded the cantonment land.[6] In December 1827, a detachment of Pioneers[7] under Captain Robert McMullin came up from Meerut and started building the British Station Hospital and Landour Depot and, for the convenience of the Pioneers and invalids, merchants were encouraged to set up shop.

By 1828, Major Nicholas Brutton of the 11th Light Dragoons was commanding the depot, supervising eighty officers and men (including some invalids) who were living in tents, '…and many of the sick are already, from the effects of the delightful climate, recovering'.[8]

But the living situation for the invalids was basic indeed in 1828. Captain Thomas Skinner of the 31st Regiment visited Landour in that year and reported on the conditions:

There were no houses completed yet on the ridge; and the officers and soldiers, with all those who had arrived for their health, were still in tents. Everything was very wild about them; and a little specimen of the domestic arrangement of one, with whom I went to breakfast this morning [15 April 1828], will show that their ménage was not quite in high order. On preparing to sit down, we found that the goats that were to give us milk had run away to the highest crags, and were browzing [sic] upon almost inaccessible places. We decided upon a chase, and scrambled in pursuit of them. My host, I found, was well accustomed to the sport, for it had been his daily exercise since his arrival. In an hour we succeeded in driving them down, and had the mortification, on our return, to see a greyhound scampering away with the only provision from the larder...I must certainly commend my friend for his hospitality, although I confess his intentions were not so well fulfilled as a hungry traveller could desire.[9]

But better accommodations were soon built and, from April 1829, regular batches of sick Tommies were being sent to Landour, and the cantonment soon had its own cluster of officers-in-charge. Overall in-charge was the commandant who was assisted by the station staff officer (SSO), medical officer, chaplain, staff sergeant-major, quartermaster sergeant and orderly room sergeant.

But not everyone was satisfied with the arrangements. When annotating his sketches in 1837, Captain Luard made this comment about the lack of consistent and good management at the depot:

...Houses for officers, barracks for the men, and hospitals were constructed at considerable expense and with great credit to Capt McMullin, who had the superintendence and planning of the whole. [But] the full benefit of such an establishment has been in some measure frustrated by a spirit of false economy.

No part of our military establishment requires more rigid discipline than the hospital; and the constant attention, not only of the medical men, but of officers appointed to superintend every branch of such an establishment, is absolutely necessary; [but] to avoid expense, an invalid commandant, invalid officers, and an invalid surgeon, have been appointed to do these duties! Many of them so absorbed in their own complaints, as to be totally unequal to attend to the wants of others; and these officers are ordered of course to rejoin their regiment when recovered, and fresh invalids permitted to replace them.[10]

Whether Luard's complaint was justified or not, the depot continued to grow, so that by the turn of the century there was an average of 350 troops posted to Landour during the Season (April–October), including soldiers on sick leave. In these early years, the depot closed in late October and did not open again until April. During winter, only a few officers were left in charge. In July, there was what was called 'half-time relief'; men who had had three months or more in the hills were sent down, giving place to others desiring and getting approval for a change for the latter half of the hot weather and rains.

Junior non-commissioned officers (NCOs) at Landour in 1900. The highest NCO rank was sergeant, usually called daffadar in the East India Company (EIC) Army and later in the British Indian Army. The life of NCOs was often dangerous and, when in camp on the plains, boring and hot. A stay in the Landour Depot was, of course, an immense relief to these soldiers.

(Courtesy of the National Army Museum, London)

Later, facilities included a more complete Military Hospital, located above Kellogg Church near the top of Depot Hill, with many nearby bungalows used as barracks. The hospital was said to have had a 'tropical diseases specialization', although it probably took not only malaria and other such cases common in the plains but also those suffering from the venereal diseases that plagued British soldiers. Numerous other private houses in other parts of Landour were also rented by the military to accommodate officer patients.

In 1906, Frederick Young's house, Mullingar, was taken on by the military as a Furlough Home for Soldiers on leave from the plains; it had 300 beds and, unlike facilities in the earlier period, was kept open throughout the year. Later, there was a Furlough Home in Kirklands and Westonel, near what is still the (Masonic) Lodge Dalhousie.

A much-expanded Mullingar, seen in this postcard photo (far lower left), was a Furlough Home for Soldiers from 1906–1914. It housed 300 soldiers and was kept open throughout the year. This photo was probably taken before 1905, since it shows the original and larger St Emilian's Church (far upper left), which was destroyed in the 1905 earthquake and rebuilt in 1908 on a smaller scale.
(Kind courtesy of the late H. Michael Stokes, Kent, United Kingdom)

In the years just before and after 1900, there was no Officers' Mess in the cantonment, only a so-called 'Sergeants' Mess'. However, there were amusements and recreation for the soldiers such as a reading room, library, billiard room, the Landour Theatre near Sisters' Bazaar for amateur theatricals and other entertainments—sometimes in historical records erroneously referred to as the 'Shakespearean Theatre'—a coffee shop and the RATA (Royal Army Temperance Association) room. It is unclear how many soldiers frequented this latter establishment! By 1936, there was a Landour Military Families' Club. And there were various alternatives for Christian worship for the British soldiers in the cantonment. In 1907, Bodycot noted in his guidebook that,

> ...The Reverend Mr. Kitching is the Church of England Chaplain, St. Paul's Church; Father Jerome has the care of the Roman Catholics and St. Peter's Roman Catholic Chapel; while the Reverend Mr. Woodside looks after the Wesleyans, &c.[11]

Despite their hard life relative to more senior officers, the NCOs in Mussoorie clearly added to the amusements in the cantonment.
(Courtesy of the National Army Museum, London)

During the early years, Landour with its depot was better known than Mussoorie, which consisted of only a few houses and had no official establishment like the military presence in Landour.[12] And the two were quite separate and apart, as it was only later that Landour establishments—primarily shops—came further down the hill, and Mussoorie itself moved eastward. The bazaar that gradually grew up along the narrow neck of land that connects what was known as Club Hill with the Castle Hill and again with the western slopes of Landour, eventually joined the two hill stations. Club Hill is no longer called that, but it is still the site of the Himalaya Club Hotel. Castle Hill is the estate of the Survey of India, but the castle is no longer recognizable.

This 1865 photo of the Castle and Castle Hill Estate was taken by the famous nineteenth-century photographer, Samuel Bourne, who was a partner with Charles Shepherd in the well-known firm that bore their names. The firm had studios in Bombay, Calcutta and Simla. The castle was home to Maharaja Duleep Singh during the seasons of 1852 and 1853. *(Courtesy of British Library)*

CASTLE HILL ESTATE

Castle Hill Estate was originally developed by Mr George Bladen Taylor on 182 acres in Landour.* A so-called 'ground rent paying' property, the houses there were originally known as Woodcroft and Greenmount. A playing field '…where Mussoorie's big hockey and football tournaments have been played for years…' was part of the estate, and is still known as Taylor's Flat. Taylor also built All Saints' Church on the property for the convenience of the residents, but this was demolished in 1948 (see Chapter 6 for a picture of the former All Saints' Church).

In time, '…Mr [probably, Frederick 'Pahari'] Wilson bought the estate and, then, when one of Mussoorie's fluttering banks crashed and lengthy litigation followed, Mr Wilson engaged Mr [Henry] Vansittart to watch his interest and we are told the estate eventually passed into Mr Vansittart's hands for comparatively, "a mere song".**

Vansittart was superintendent of Dehra Dun in the 1840s.

In the early 1850s, the government purchased the estate, renovated the buildings and made it over as a summer residence for Maharaja Duleep Singh, who lived there during the Season in 1852 and 1853. The estate then passed back into private ownership until 1908 when the Survey of India acquired it, along with its now eight houses, for offices and residences. The eight houses on the property were Dunedin, Dunedin Cottage, Fowl House, St Rogue, Hazeldene, Craignish, Abbotsford and Melrose (the latter two houses both paid tribute to the popularity of Sir Walter Scott: Abbotsford was the name of Scott's home located in Melrose, in the Scottish Borders to the southeast of nearby Edinburgh). The District Gazetteer of 1934 noted that 'the Castle Hill Estate of the Survey of India was vacated in 1932' but this was obviously only temporary, as the survey continues to this day to occupy the site.***

---

*There was a George Bladen Taylor described as 'an Indian master mariner' who was definitely in India during the 1830s (Kolsky, Elizabeth, *Codification and the Rule of Colonial Difference*, USA: Urbana-Champaign, University of Illinois, 2005: 101). While the unusual name suggests this may be the same Taylor who first developed what was later named Castle Hill Estate, this has not been confirmed.

**Williams, C. ('The Rambler'), *A Mussoorie Miscellany*, Mussoorie: Mafasilite Press, 1936: 36.

***Superintendent, Printing and Stationery. *District Gazetteers of the United Provinces of Agra and Oudh, Supplementary Notes and Statistics up to 1931-2 to Volume I (D), Dehra Dun District*, Allahabad: United Provinces, 1934: 4.

The estate affords lovely walks, but the Survey of India has kept it closed to the general public for many years. There is a circular road level with the gate and, previously, there was also a lower circular road. The hill to the north, still within the estate, is tunnelled. The tunnel is not natural; it was bored by a Pioneer detachment to carry water from Kattapani to the Kulri area.

The Taylor's Flat playing field, which was also sometimes called simply 'The Flats', was a part of the original Castle Hill Estate, developed by George Bladen Taylor.
(Kind courtesy of the late H. Michael Stokes, Kent, United Kingdom)

In the early 1900s, Landour Cantonment was a block of about a square mile and a half towards the east end of the Mussoorie settlement. Mussoorie surrounded Landour on all sides. In 1912, it is recorded that there were eighty private houses in Landour, the majority of them held by their owners in 'fee simple', the grant having originally been made under the Wells' Settlement of 1842.[13] Locations that are familiar even today, such as the Childers group of houses to the north—Childers Castle, Childers Lodge and Childers Cottage[14]—and Elcot House, Oakville, most of the Woodstock School property and certainly South Hill to the east, were always outside the cantonment proper. Still, the Landour Cantonment consisted of 1,070 acres when the bazaar was included.

For seventy years, from the establishment of the cantonment in 1827 until 1897, the Landour shops along the southward spur were under the control of the commandant. However, in 1897, the military authorities turned over the bazaar area to the Mussoorie municipality. Upon this change in jurisdiction, the cantonment henceforth commenced where the road runs east towards what is now the Landour Community Hospital and onwards to Woodstock School. The Char Dukan (four shops) area was and still is a central location in the cantonment. There are a few additional shops further to east from Char Dukan at Sisters' Bazaar, so named after what was a sisters', in other words, nurses' dormitory at the location.[15]

At this time, Landour Bazaar consisted of some 300 shops. There are probably no more than this today. In the early 1900s, it was said that:

> In this Landour Bazaar are...shops of all kinds, petty dealers in fruit and vegetables, grain merchants, banias [traders and merchants] of all sorts and sizes, cloth merchants, mahajans [usually, moneylenders] and native bankers. It is one of the best supplied bazaars in India; the majority of the larger dealers are direct importers from the European manufacturer in their particular lines, and one can get here almost anything one requires.[16]

By 1900, Rokeby (once owned by Frederick 'Pahari' Wilson), Theodore Lodge and Ivy Bank were boarding houses. These are names and places that are still familiar today. Rokeby is now Rokeby Manor, a boutique hotel.

Neither Landour nor Mussoorie has a wealth of grand buildings, primarily because neither ever served as a summer capital like Shimla did for the central government or Darjeeling for the Bengal government. Still, there are several historically important buildings in the Station. In Landour, like in Mussoorie, several of these have weathered the ravages of time and an often aggressive climate. Recently, the buildings of both St Paul's Church and St Peter's Church have regained new life (see Chapter 6). The nearby Woodstock School buildings, notably Midlands, previously known as 'The College', for it once housed a teachers' training facility, have undergone much renovation in recent years. And the cantonment area is kept pristine by regulation and the keen eyes of its military guardians, as is the Survey of India's Castle Hill Estate, although the eponymous castle building itself is no longer recognizable. The Landour Bazaar has fared less well in terms of maintenance and appearance, but nonetheless

Gulam Mahomed was a Landour merchant dealing in goods imported from England, and with '…every requisite for Gentlemen and *Shikaris* proceeding into the interior'.
(Photo kind courtesy of Hugh Rayner, United Kingdom, and quote from advertisement in Northam, John, Guide to Masuri, Landaur, Dehra Dun and the Hills North of Dehra, Calcutta: Thacker, Spink and Company, 1884)

is still the best shopping area in the Station, as far as local residents are concerned.

Formerly the most visible landmark in the bazaar area, the municipality-owned Clock Tower, was built in 1938–1939 by Ugrasen Verma, a local contractor, for a sum of Rs 14,000.[17] It was in a rundown state for many years, with the clock stuck at 2.45! The tower has now been razed to the ground and discussion is underway on how to restore it. The Clock Tower location informally marks the boundary between Mussoorie and Landour.[18]

While there are not many other major buildings in Landour, it is peppered with bungalows. In contrast to the strict grid pattern of the cantonments on the plains, these cottages within and outside of the cantonment proper were arranged to take advantage of the irregular contours of the hillsides and the excellent prospects. Sites that offered a view of both the snowy ranges and the Dun were, and certainly still are, at a premium. The less sunny northern slopes were less desirable…at least for the living. The Protestant and Catholic cemeteries were placed here, and are still in use, although today there is a less rigid separation of the two branches of Christianity, this happy reconciliation apparently having been brought about by overcrowding in the upper Protestant section! (See Chapter 6 for a discussion of cemeteries in the Station.)

While Landour expanded over the years, it has never seen the growth that Mussoorie has experienced. According to the 2001 Indian Census, Landour had a population of only 3,500, which is not a great deal more than the 2,500 'native population' recorded in 1884, almost 120 years earlier (neither of these figures would have included military personnel, students and other part-time residents). This contrast in growth with Mussoorie is probably due to the Cantonments Act of 1924, which virtually banned any new construction and the felling of trees, combined with limited non-cantonment land in Landour suitable for building purposes. And even if there had been land available for building in the non-cantonment areas of Landour, any new construction was more recently further limited in this ecologically fragile area by a judicial constraint. In recent years, the entire area has benefited tremendously from the reforestation efforts of the Indian military's Eco-Task Force.

The building prominently shown in this postcard photo is still standing in Landour but alas, the twin turrets are gone.
(Kind courtesy of the late H. Michael Stokes, Kent, United Kingdom)

The earliest and quite transient population of Landour was British, primarily military, for of course the cantonment had been established for the benefit of British soldiers and officers.

However, as we have seen, from the earliest days shopkeepers were encouraged to take up residence there. These small-scale businessmen came from as far away as Gujarat, Bombay and Lahore to serve the growing town. In 1947, the ethnic mix of Landour changed dramatically, with the departure of most of the Britons as well as many Muslim shopkeepers (see Chapter 11 [postscript]).

Christian missionaries were present in large numbers in Landour for over one hundred years, until the 1970s. Most of them had children in Woodstock School. In many cases, mothers would spend the hot weather in Landour with the children, taking them out of boarding for the duration of their stay, while fathers would continue to work at their mission stations on the plains, coming to Mussoorie only for holidays. Many mission organizations owned bungalows in Landour for the use of their members, but these were largely sold off to Indian buyers in the 1970s. There is still a considerable expatriate presence in Landour, now made up of (non-missionary) Woodstock teachers and students, as well as students at the Landour Language School (where most study Hindi, although some other Indian languages are also taught).

The Guard Room from Theatre Road in upper Landour across from Kellogg Church. The soldiers on duty here were responsible for maintaining security and orderliness in the cantonment. Theatre Road was named in reference to a hall for amateur theatricals and other entertainments (not to be confused with Picture Palace in Kulri). *(Kind courtesy of the late H. Michael Stokes, Kent, United Kingdom)*

Today, the cantonment is visually dominated by the government-owned Doordarshan and All India Radio transmission towers atop Lal Tiba. Hopefully, a Municipal Clock Tower will once again loom over the lower bazaar area, as it did for so many years. Closer to the ground, the cantonment area is largely controlled by the Ministry of Defence Research and Development Organization's Institute of Technology Management (ITM). This is quite unlike Mussoorie, which is defined largely by shops and hotels catering to tourists. For Landour, this circumstance has served exceptionally well, as traditional military discipline has assured the upkeep of the area and maintenance of the forests.

As a result, Landour is still very much the Elysium that Frederick Young sought out nearly 200 years ago, although Tommy Atkins is, of course, long gone.

Notes

1. The name 'Landour' may have been given by the British officers who founded the cantonment, probably drawn from Llanddowror, a village in Carmarthenshire in southwest Wales. If indeed named by British officers, this would track with the Scottish place name 'Kincraig' and the Irish name 'Mullingar'. However, Ganesh Saili, a local historian, suggests that the name may well have been given by traders setting up shop in Landour and may derive from '...the princely state of Landaura, near Roorkee' (Saili, Ganesh, *Mussoorie Medley, Tales of Yesteryear*, New Delhi: Niyogi Books, 2010: 21).
2. 'Tommies', a general and informal term to describe all British soldiers, came from Tommy Atkins, the nickname for a private soldier derived from the specimen entry on an army form on which soldiers were required to enter their personal particulars. It is said that the first duke of Wellington, Arthur Wellesley, who successfully led the army of the East India Company against Tipu Sultan at the Battle of Seringapatam in 1799, chose the name.
3. 'Tiba' is a local word for hill or peak. The highest peak in the region, but not within the cantonment or station, is Nag Tiba (Serpent's Peak) at 9,912 feet (3,022 metres).
4. Jenkins, Louisa Hadow, *General Frederick Young, First Commandant of Sirmur Battalion (Second Gurkha Rifles)*, London: George Routledge & Sons, Ltd, 1923: 74.
5. Bodycot, F. ('compiler'), *Guide to Mussoorie with Notes on Adjacent Districts and Routes into the Interior*, Mussoorie: Mafasilite Printing Works, 1907: 69.
6. _____*Dehra Dun & Landour, Cantonments: Hand-book for the Use of Residents and Visitors*, Dehra Dun: Grand Himalayan Press, 1912: 7.
7. The origin of the Pioneer Corps dates back to 1758 in Madras (now Chennai, Tamil Nadu state), where the first Pioneer companies were formed. Pioneer units were, and still are, intended to provide disciplined and well-trained manpower, where civilian labour is either not available (as in Landour in 1827) or its employment is not desirable for reasons

of security or ability. By the time of the First World War, there were as many as twelve Pioneer regiments in the British Indian Army. Today, there are Pioneer units in both the Indian and British armies.

8. Bodycot, Ibid.

9. Skinner, Thomas, *Excursions in India; Including a Walk over the Himalaya Mountains, to the Sources of the Jumna and the Ganges* (2 vols), 2nd edition, vol 1, London: Richard Bentley, 1833: 210-211.

10. Luard, John, *A Series of Views in India, comprising sketches of Scenery, antiquities, and native character, drawn from nature and on stone*, by Captain John Luard, London: J. Dickinson, 1837.

11. Bodycot, Ibid, p. 65.

12. _____*Dehra Dun & Landour*, Ibid, p. 7.

13. _____*Dehra Dun & Landour*, Ibid, p. 8.

14. The Childers group of houses was probably established by Col Michael Childers of the 11th Light Dragoons. Since 1990, Childers has been known as the Nahata Estate. Today, the structure at its gate is famous as 'Binocular Point', for on a clear day and with powerful binoculars one can see the Himalayan peaks, Bandarpunch and Srikantha.

15. The greater part of this information on the early days of the Landour Cantonment was taken from Bodycot, Ibid, p. 64-69.

16. Bodycot, Ibid, p. 64-65.

17. The Clock Tower contractor, Ugrasen Verma, also built the Kateswar Temple to the west of the Mall.

18. Some say the lower boundary between Mussoorie and Landour is the Picture Palace in Kulri Bazaar, which is along what was once called the 'Grand Parade'. Even in 1884, 'Grand Parade' was considered a 'most inappropriate' appellation (Northam, Ibid, p. 48).

The Mussoorie Seminary, later called the Maddock's School, was privately established in 1834 and taken over by the Church of England in 1865. It survived for only sixty-six years (until 1900). It was said to have failed because the young British graduates could not find work in India appropriate to their training. Yet, other such schools like Bishop Cotton in Shimla and St Paul's in Darjeeling did survive, and records suggest that bad financial management may have been the main reason for closure. The site of Maddock's School is today occupied by the Savoy Hotel, just above Library Chowk.

(Courtesy of Alkazi Collection of Photography, New Delhi)

5

EDINBURGH-IN-THE-HILLS

When Memory, midst scenes of strife or care,
Will fondly turn to years and comrades here,
It well may be, Young Student, you will say,
"God Bless the School! Our happiest days were there".
~ *From S.J. Darcy's poem, 'Stet Fortuna Domus' (Let the Fortune of the House Stand)*[1] ~

Like all the great hill stations that were established in India in the first half of the nineteenth century, Mussoorie also soon became home to numerous schools, planted in the Himalayan foothills away from the heat of the plains and originally catering mainly to British and Anglo-Indian children whose parents had not the means or desire to send their offspring 'home' for education. Many of these schools exist—indeed, thrive—to this day, testimony to their ability to adapt, to modern times, their offerings of '…scholastic excellence, development of character, sportsmanship, punctuality and discipline.'[2]

John Northam's 1884 guidebook gives Mussoorie's many schools the shortest possible treatment:

> Their name is legion, but as…comparison would be odious, the details of each must be left to its own announcements. It may be remarked, however, that Masuri [Mussoorie] is fast becoming one vast seminary, and may be termed the Edinburgh of India.[3]

An Edinburgh-in-the-Hills or not, Mussoorie certainly was able to boast several outstanding boarding schools even from its earliest days, and today arguably stands foremost among hill stations for its educational institutions. Fortunately, later writers were not so sparing as Northam with information on the Station's schools, nor were the institutions themselves reluctant to aggressively advertise their advantages, so today there is excellent archival information available about the early growth of this 'industry' in Mussoorie and Landour.

The very first school to be established in Mussoorie and, indeed, the very first

European school of any standing to be established anywhere in the Himalayas, was the Mussoorie Seminary. It came into being in 1834 when John Mackinnon, a retired army schoolmaster, brought his private school from Meerut in the plains to Mussoorie. Originally located on the site of the Old Brewery to the west at the foot of Benog Hill[4], the seminary catered to young British and Anglo-Indian boys. Mauger Monk, a teacher at the school, wrote home in 1840 that Mackinnon was '…making money fast…'[5]. Nonetheless, Mackinnon later retired from education, opting for brewing beer as a livelihood (see Chapter 7 for a discussion of Mackinnon's career in the brewing industry), while the school itself continued to be run for some time by Mr Henry Ramsey, who lived at Wycliffe across the road from the Chateau de Kapurthala. However, Ramsey apparently did not succeed at the job, and the school temporarily closed in 1850. Shortly thereafter, the chaplain of Christ Church, Reverend William Maddock, invited his brother, Reverend Robert North Maddock, to come to India to re-establish the seminary at a new location immediately above the Municipal Library. Known informally from this time as 'Maddock's School', it was considered a very pukkah establishment and the fees were high. Nonetheless, Reverend R.N. Maddock beggared himself by pouring his own savings into the venture and, apparently with no other viable option, he offered the school for sale.[6]

In 1865, the school was purchased for £12,000 sterling by the Church of England's Diocesan Board of Education. This purchase was inspired and strongly supported by Bishop George Edward Lynch Cotton, the Church of England's second metropolitan of India, whose grand vision was a string of public schools in the hills.

In late 1866, the new owners put the school under the charge of Reverend A.O. Hardy, who had been the domestic chaplain to Bishop Cotton. (It is said that Thomas Hughes, in his book *Tom Brown's School Days*, based the famed Hardy of Eton on A.O. Hardy.) Hardy served for three years and was succeeded by Reverend Arthur Stokes, who headed the school for thirty years from 1869–1899.[7] Under Stokes's leadership the school—by now sometimes called Stokes School—was said to '…improve in every way…' and enrollment peaked only to drop off later in the century. Stokes oversaw the building of an Anglican chapel that his predecessors had envisaged (the chapel no longer exists).[8]

The school motto was 'Promite Vires', which the boys translated as 'Promote your Men'.[9] These young men were sons of public works department officers, police officers, assistant commissioners, employees of the survey department, apothecaries, planters, merchants, hotel proprietors, surgeons, veterinarians, bank managers, college

An 1877 photo of students in front of the Maddock's School chapel, which was built during Reverend Arthur Stokes' thirty-year tenure as principal (1869–1899). Like the school, the chapel too no longer exists (see Chapter 3 for a view of the chapel in its original setting). 'On the dismantling of the school chapel after 1899, the stained glass windows were re-erected in All Saints' Church, Mussoorie, and probably the brass memorial plates also.'

(Photo and quotation from the Register of Stokes' School, Mussoorie, 1867–1900, in the collection of the Society of Genealogists, London) officials and 'persons of private means'.[10] It is recorded that boys leaving Maddock's went regularly to the Thomason College of Civil Engineering in Roorkee.[11] Some obtained places at Calcutta University, and many resumed successful scholastic careers at schools back in England. Notable graduates include William Willcocks (later, Sir William) who oversaw construction of the first Aswan Dam during 1889–1902. Another graduate, Mr C.M. Gregory, not only built the Hotel Cecil (now Mussoorie's Prince Hotel) but also many of India's earliest and largest railway bridges. Students also included boys from the Skinner and Corbett families, two names still widely recognized in modern India.[12]

In 1867, there were 904 pupils in the school. But by 1899 there were only twenty-eight senior boys and forty-one junior boarders and two junior day boys. Perhaps self-servingly, Stokes attributed the falling enrollment to the lack of good government positions open to graduates, which therefore discouraged parents from spending more on their sons' education than they could help. There was worse to come on the financial front.

> In that year [1899], the Calcutta newspapers were flooded with letters from
> parents worried by rumours of the school's closure, which led the Government to
> initiate an enquiry. Several alarming facts came to light: the school's endowment
> had been diverted from the legitimate purpose of paying the Headmaster's salary
> in order to meet an overdraft with the Mussoorie Bank, and the school was
> heavily in debt. To make matters worse, school premises were in a very bad
> state of repair. The writing was on the wall.'[13]

In August 1899, a commission including the archdeacons of Calcutta and Lucknow decided to close the senior department and carry on only a preparatory school at the Abbey and to sell the school estate. (The Abbey was a junior school to the west, near Park Estate, that had been opened in 1896 by a former Maddock's pupil, Mr W.C. Hörst.) 'In September, notice was sent to parents informing them of the change contemplated. This led to many protests on the part of the parents, but without avail.'[14]

The Mussoorie Seminary/Maddock's School closed in 1900. It had lasted just sixty-six years.

In 1901, the property was sold and the Savoy Hotel was opened on the site (see Chapter 7).[15]

Bishop Cotton's grand vision for exemplary public schools in the Himalayan foothills had resulted in three leading hill schools being established during his bishopric, all at one time or another supported by the Bishop Cotton Memorial Endowment Fund. The Bishop Cotton School in Shimla (est. 1859) and St Paul's in Darjeeling (est. 1864) are thriving to this day and are amongst India's oldest and most prestigious boarding schools. But the bishop's vision failed to take permanent root in Mussoorie.

The second oldest European-style hill school in the Himalayas, Waverley[16] Convent School, was also founded in Mussoorie, lending some validity to the Edinburgh-in-the-Hills appellation. Founded in 1845 by the Religious of Jesus and Mary, Waverley, unlike Maddock's School, continues to this day as a premier educational institution and, as such, is the oldest continuing school in the Himalayas.[17] The school was built on the Waverley Estate that was sold to the Catholics by an Italian, Paolo Solaroli (b.1796–d.1878), probably near the time of his return to Italy. Solaroli had become exceedingly wealthy as a mercenary soldier and financial advisor in the employ of Begum Sumru of Sardhana (near Meerut in Uttar Pradesh state)[18]. He was married to the begum's adopted daughter Georgiana, the natural sister of the begum's adopted son and heir, David Ochterlony Dyce Somber (b.1808–d.1851). Back in Italy, Solaroli eventually became the marquis of Briona in recognition of his military and diplomatic service. The Waverley Estate is located far above the Mussoorie Library at nearly 7,000 feet (2,134 metres) above sea level and with an excellent view of the snows, enjoyed even by Princess Mary during her 1906 visit to Mussoorie.[19]

Paolo Solaroli (1796–1878), the soldier of fortune who sold his Mussoorie estate to the Catholic Church for the establishment of Waverley Convent School. Later styled the marquis of Briona (Italy), Solaroli's origins were humble but he amassed a vast fortune in India while working for the Begum Sumru of Sardhana. *(Courtesy of St George's School, Mussoorie)*

It is quite possible but not certain that Waverley Estate was named after a Sir Walter Scott novel that was popular at the time (The novel *Waverley* was written in 1814 and often is regarded as the first historical novel). Originally, there were two schools, Waverley and Belmont, the former for children paying full fees, and the latter for those admitted at lower rates or as charity cases.[20]

'This well known and deservedly popular institution…' is said to have sheltered many 'refugees' from the plains during the First War of Independence in 1857. On 4 April 1905, its buildings were severely damaged by the earthquake that shook the entire Station; however, it was soon rebuilt on new and improved plans. Given government recognition only in 1895, fifty years after opening, Waverley is today affiliated to the Indian Certificate of Secondary Education (ICSE), offering education and training up to class ten to girls from across India and of all religious backgrounds (boys were admitted up to class four until 1966). Belmont was amalgamated into Waverley in the 1940s. Today, next door to Waverley is the convent-run co-educational Hindi-medium St Lawrence School for local children, established in 1962. The Jesus and Mary nuns maintain a beautiful and historic chapel on the estate that dates back to the school's earliest days.

BEYOND AGRA:
NOTES ON THE FOUNDING OF WAVERLEY CONVENT SCHOOL*

Bishop [Joseph Anthony] Borghi, on his return from France, said that as soon as possible, he would send the Sisters to Mussoorie to establish a new Convent there. It would also serve as a summer resort for the Sisters of Agra.

The Profession Ceremony of M. [Mother] St [Saint] Thais, M.St Fabian and M. St Borromeo took place on 24th March 1845 in Agra and on 25th March the pioneers left for Mussoorie.

1845, Waverley Mussoorie Community: The pioneers of the new house in Mussoorie were M. St Gonzaga, M. St Leo, M. St Joachim, M. St Basil, M. St Cecilia, M. St Athanasius, M. St Thais (English) and M. St Fabian. [In these earlier days, nuns were given the names of saints. The founding sisters at Mussoorie were almost all from France.]

*Excerpts from Mitra, Alica, *A History of the Congregation, the Religious of Jesus and Mary in India, 1842-1993*, New Delhi: Delhi Province of the Religious of Jesus and Mary, circa 1999: 16-18.

25th March 1845 was Easter Monday. Mother Therese with the 8 religious set out to make a foundation at Mussoorie in the Himalayas, where Bishop Borghi had purchased for them a very attractive property, 6.400 feet [1,951 meters] above sea level and 4 kms [2.5 miles] from Landour. The Landour property was found unsuitable for a school, besides it was located too far out. Bishop Borghi bought the Waverley Estate from Signor P. Solaroli who had been the Begum of Sardhana's Bank Manager.

The Bishop made sure that the journey to Mussoorie would be comfortable. Three carriages drawn by oxen would take about 20 days to reach Dehra Dun. Fr Michael Angelo, Chaplain of Sardhana, would accompany them; he had been sent for this purpose. From Dehra Dun at the foot of the mountain, the Sisters sat in sedan chairs carried by 4 men, who lifted the chairs on their shoulders and climbed up the winding paths of the bare mountain to arrive at Mussoorie.

There were 3 houses on the 9-acre property: Waverley', the largest, became the residence of the sisters and of the First Class Boarders. 'Belmont' housed the Chapel, the Parlour and the Second Class Boarders. The smallest house was the residence of the Chaplain, Fr. De Brione. The Schools were called 'Waverley' and 'Belmont'.

May, 1845-Waverley Boarding School: Waverley Boarding School was opened on 1st May 1845. By June there were 7 boarders and some day pupils, who came for Drawing and Music lessons. Music was the rage; Mother Therese asked Mother General to send someone trained in Music. The Sisters hoped that the Boarding School would expand in the New Year.

November, 1845-Waverley Orphanage: That November an Orphanage was started. The 5 girls for this Institution were lodged in 'Belmont'. They were to help in the housework and learn 'flower-making'.

There is no mention of the early suffering and privations endured by the valiant Sisters.

There were times when they did not have sufficient to eat. The best went to the children always, as was the teaching of our Foundress. For two or three years they slept on carpets, left by the previous owner. Any income was spent on the children's comfort, not on themselves. All these hardships went to make this establishment a beautiful one.

An early view of Waverley House. This building is the original Waverley House, the largest of three homes on the Waverley Estate, which were purchased by the Catholics from Paolo Solaroli, who was in the employ of Begum Sumru of Sardhana. *(Kind courtesy of the Congregation of the Religious of Jesus and Mary, Rome)*

A 1920s view of the main entrance area of Waverley Convent School, looking similar to how it appears today. *(Kind courtesy of the Congregation of the Religious of Jesus and Mary, Rome)*

A classroom at Waverley Convent School, circa 1922. The oldest still-operating school in the Himalayas, Waverley opened its doors on 1 May 1845 with seven boarders and a few day students. Today, it has hundreds of students, both in Waverley and in the affiliated St Lawrence School for local children. *(Kind courtesy of the Congregation of the Religious of Jesus and Mary, Rome)*

The elegant 'children's dining room' at Waverley Convent School, circa 1922. *(Kind courtesy of the Congregation of the Religious of Jesus and Mary, Rome)*

A circa 1922 view of one of the girls' dormitories at Waverley Convent School. *(Kind courtesy of the Congregation of the Religious of Jesus and Mary, Rome)*

Belmont House at Waverley Convent School, one of the three original houses on the Waverley Estate. Opened in November 1845, Belmont housed the second-class boarders, children who were orphans or whose parents could not pay full or even any school fees. The nineteenth-century distinction between fee-paying and non-paying students gradually ended, and in the 1940s Belmont was amalgamated into Waverley. *(Kind courtesy of the Congregation of the Religious of Jesus and Mary, Rome)*

Vue de la maison Belmont, Mussoori.

In its early days, Waverley offered '…a sound Catholic and general English education…' And even though the convent was quick to point out in its advertisements that '…the religion of Protestant children is not interfered with…', it is hardly surprising that in those conservative times, non-Catholic Christians residing in India were desirous of a similar but staunchly Protestant school for their daughters who were not destined to return to Britain for their education.

Thus came about Woodstock School. From the outset, Woodstock was an undertaking that included not just the British in India but the Americans as well. And it was the Americans who eventually took the lead role in running the school.

In 1852, British officers and two American missionaries formed a company that in 1854 opened the Protestant Girls' School in Caineville House, Mussoorie. Given that it was a 'company' that formed the school, it is probably for this reason that Woodstock School was—and sometimes still is—referred to as the 'Company School'. Contrary to popular assumption, there is no historical evidence of any formal connection between Woodstock School and the East India Company.

The British officers who were involved in setting up the school were Colonel Boswell, Colonel Brooke Boyd and Captain William Alexander. The two Americans were from the American Presbyterian Mission in Dehra Dun, Reverend David Herron and Reverend J.S. Woodside. The chaplain of Landour, Reverend William Jay, also played a role.

These men asked the London-based Society for Promoting Female Education in the East to send out some lady teachers, and in late 1853 four teachers arrived in Calcutta.[21] Of these, one actually never made it to Mussoorie, having accepted a proposal of marriage before ship's docking. According to the records of the Church Missionary Society, the remaining three teachers—Mrs Bignell and her assistants, Miss Ayton and Miss Birch—reached Mussoorie on 18 February 1854. On 6 March the school was opened with seventeen pupils.[22]

Mrs Bignell (principal) and Miss Ayton returned to England within two years. Miss Birch married and opened a private school in Shimla. But the Protestant Girls' School survived.

In 1856, the school moved to Woodstock House in Landour, which it rented from the estate of Lieutenant Colonel Bradshaw Yorke Reilly of the Royal Engineers (Reilly died on 5 November 1853 and is buried in the Landour Cemetery). Reilly also owned the neighboring houses called Upper Woodstock and Woodstock Cottage, later renamed 'Tafton', and these too became part of the Woodstock campus. In circumstances similar to Waverley Convent School, Woodstock School took its name from Colonel Reilly's estate, the estate itself probably having been named after the then-popular Sir Walter Scott novel *Woodstock or The Cavalier* (published 1826).

In both 1861 and 1862, there were name changes; first, from the Protestant Girls' School to 'The Woodstock Establishment' and in 1862 to 'Woodstock School', the name the school still retains. In 1867, the '…Trustees on behalf of the Society' purchased Woodstock House and Woodstock Garden (where the recently renovated Boys' Hostel is now located) from Lieutenant Colonel Reilly's widow, Emily Reilly. The three trustees were George Bladen Taylor, who developed what came to be known as Castle Hill Estate; Captain Adrian Deneys Vanrenen, the owner of Edgehill; and Reverend John S. Woodside, a well-known Presbyterian missionary at the time in Dehra Dun.[23]

(L) Captain Adrian Deneys Vanrenen, the early owner of the Edgehill Estate in Landour, and (R) Reverend John S. Woodside, a Presbyterian missionary in Dehra Dun, were two of the trustees who saw to the purchase of Woodstock House and Woodstock Garden in 1867 for Woodstock School. The third trustee involved in the purchase was George Bladen Taylor of Castle Hill Estate. *(Courtesy of British Library)*

It was at about this time that the school ran into difficulties. When the school was founded, the Church Missionary Society (of the Church of England) and the allied Society for Promoting Female Education in the East had rather rosy expectations of the support they thought would come from within India.

> The Christian Community in India, parents especially, warmly welcomed the proposal of the Committee, and came forward liberally with promises of help during the first years of the Institution, until it shall become self-supporting: there is therefore no reason to expect further demand on the Society's income. The necessarily large expense incurred in sending out the Agents and School Apparatus has not yet been covered by special contributions.[24]

Founded in 1854, Woodstock was in its early years a school for Protestant girls. It later became fully co-educational and non-denominational, as it is today. Although much changed, this 'Quad' area of the school is still recognizable. *(Kind courtesy of the late H. Michael Stokes, Kent, United Kingdom)*

A late nineteenth-century view of Woodstock School, taken by a photographer from the famous G.W. Lawrie studio in Lucknow. Woodstock, first known as the Protestant Girls' School, opened in 1854 at Caineville House in Mussoorie but two years later shifted to its present location in Landour. *(Courtesy of the Mount Holyoke College Archives and Special Collections, South Hadley, Massachusetts, USA)*

But these expectations of local support were not fully realized, and it was only in 1870 that the Society for Promoting Female Education in the East ended its connection with the school:

HIMALAYAS.—Landour.—Various circumstances connected with this Station, necessitating a serious outlay in carrying on the Woodstock School, the Committee have decided upon dissolving their connexion [sic] with it; and the completion of Miss Freer's engagement for five years' service afforded a suitable opportunity for so doing. The Committee regret that justice to the other Agents, for whose support they are responsible, and the heavy liability that would have been incurred by further perseverance in carrying on the School, render this step inevitable.[25]

Poor administration, the inability to secure teaching staff and the withdrawal of support from the society caused Woodstock to shut its doors in 1871. The London Society put the property up for sale.

But help was on the way. Two local Presbyterian missionaries—Reverend J.S. Woodside again, as well as Dr. Samuel H. Kellogg, after whom a Landour church is named (see Chapter 6)—put out a plea for assistance to reopen the institution, as a school for missionary children. In response to their appeal, there arrived on 30 June 1872 the famous 'Buy Woodstock' cable from the Presbyterian Ladies' Society of Philadelphia (USA), and the school reopened on 1 March 1874.[26]

In March 1877, Mrs Eliza Jane (née Foster) Scott of the North India Mission of the Presbyterian Church, USA, who was appointed by the Presbyterian Ladies' Society of Philadelphia, assumed charge of Woodstock. Perhaps not coincidentally, given Mrs Scott's nationality and connections, it is from about this time that the school saw an increase in the number of American children. In the earlier years, most students were British and Anglo-Indian.

Mrs Scott was a graduate of Mount Holyoke Seminary (now Mount Holyoke College, one of the 'Seven Sisters' colleges in the USA). By 1890, Woodstock School had five teachers who were alumnae of Mount Holyoke Seminary. As one of these colleagues remembers:

Mrs. Scott raised the school from insignificant conditions to be a worthy class of Mount Holyoke. It scored in the first rank among the schools of India under her… [and] the names of Miss Lyon [founder of Mount Holyoke] and Mount

Holyoke were often on our lips. In 1890, there was quite a Mount Holyoke circle at Woodstock. Mrs. Scott, class of 1852; Miss Hettie Scott [the daughter of Mrs. Scott],1879; Miss C.C. Giddings and Miss Mary Bailey, both of 1884. Also Miss Clara G Williamson, 1872.[27]

Another account notes that Mrs Scott, as principal of Woodstock School, 'was one of the early disciples of Mary Lyon and a pioneer in women's education in India'. Mrs Scott served as principal until her death in 1892, when another Mount Holyoke Seminary graduate, Effie Victorine (née Hallock) Braddock took charge (1892–1895). After 1895, Miss Clara Chandler Giddings, who had been a teacher at Woodstock for five years, took over as principal. In total, Woodstock was under the leadership of Mount Holyoke Seminary graduates for over twenty-one years (1877–1898).

(L) Mrs Eliza Jane Foster Scott, principal of Woodstock School, 1877–1892. Mrs Scott was the first of three Mount Holyoke Seminary (USA) graduates who served successively as principals of Woodstock School during the years 1877–1898. *(Photo from Jones, Edith, Caroline Wilkie and Mary I. McGee, Woodstock School, the First Century, Landour, Woodstock School, second printing, 1999 [first printing, 1954])*

(R) Miss Clara Chandler Giddings was the last Mount Holyoke Seminary principal of Woodstock School. She worked at Woodstock for eight years, serving as principal during 1896–1898. *(Courtesy of the Mount Holyoke College Archives and Special Collections, South Hadley, Massachusetts, USA)*

The staff of Woodstock School in 1885. At that time, three staff members were from the Mount Holyoke Seminary (USA). In this photo are Miss Clara Williamson (seated first row, second from left; Mount Holyoke Seminary 1872), Mrs Eliza Foster Scott (seated second row, second from left; Mount Holyoke Seminary 1852) and Miss Hettie Scott (third row, centre; Mount Holyoke Seminary 1879). The seminary had a very close association with Woodstock School, providing teachers and three principals to Woodstock School during the late nineteenth century.[28] *(Courtesy of the Mount Holyoke College Archives and Special Collections, South Hadley, Massachusetts, USA)*

In 1896, Reverend and Mrs H.M. Andrews, also of the North India Mission, were appointed joint principals. Between 1913 and 1922, several missionaries from the Punjab were in charge of the school in turn, with the North India Mission generally in control, sometimes along with the so-called 'Mission and Church of the Punjab'. From 1923, a much broader union of missionaries became involved with the management of the school.

Under this Protestant missionary leadership, the school catered primarily to girls whose parents were missionaries, although boys up to the age of twelve also attended. In a 1907 advertisement, the school boasted that '...The moral, religious and refining influences surrounding the students are of the highest order, and the student spirit is excellent'. In particular, religious training was given a prominent place ('...fortunately we are not troubled with "Education Bills" in India...'). It also was said that stress was laid on dormitory accommodations, '...little "cubicles" being provided for pupils, affording privacy, as a contrast to the publicity of the general huge bedrooms, and a prize is given for the neatest and most tastefully arranged cubicle.'[29]

Through the years, Woodstock School (motto, 'Palme Non Sine Pulvere'—not the palm of victory without the dust of struggle) saw many changes in its physical facilities as well as its curriculum. Early on, additional classrooms, teachers' quarters, dining and assembly halls, an infirmary, an art studio, and music rooms were added (Woodstock was and still is known for its strong music programme). At the beginning of the twentieth century, the school was elevated to a college, in affiliation with Allahabad University, and a teachers' training programme was added.

The principal—or, rather, joint principals—who perhaps had the most far-reaching impact on Woodstock's future, were Reverend Allen E. Parker and his wife, Irene. Arriving at Woodstock in 1922, they were co-principals during the inter-war years, overseeing numerous changes. The college courses were dropped, and the school was made into a fully co-educational, inter-denominational and multinational boarding and day school, offering a programme of study starting from kindergarten and concluding with either Senior Cambridge credentials or the equivalent of an American high school diploma. Taking advantage of the Himalayan location, outdoor education and exploration were emphasized, a practice that continues till today. Workaday skills were not neglected, although they remained reflective of the gendered disparities between women and men which was common at the time; a 1936 advertisement promoted '...manual training for boys' and '...cooking and sewing for girls' (This so-called 'Industrial Arts Department' no longer exists).[30] Physical facilities were expanded, including a new playing field and a new hostel to accommodate the inclusion of boys into the student body.

While many American students of missionary parents were evacuated to the United States during the Second World War[31], the school at the same time experienced an influx of students from other parts of the British Empire, particularly Burma and Malaya and from as far away as China, with parents viewing Woodstock as a safe haven during troubled times. Thus, at the end of the war, returning Americans found a much more diverse student body than it had been before.[32]

The co-principals, Mr and Mrs Allen (Irene, née Glasgow) Parker headed Woodstock school during the inter-war period (1922–1939), changing the school from a girls' seminary to a fully co-educational institution that was multinational, with American children in the majority. *(Photos from Jones, Edith, Caroline Wilkie and Mary I. McGee,* Woodstock School, the First Century, *Landour: Woodstock School, second printing, 1999 [first printing, 1954])*

Mrs Irene Mott Bose, an American married to an Indian who was a High Court judge in Nagpur, had brought their two children up to Mussoorie in 1942. She wrote about Woodstock:

> The children are happy and like it and the staff seem competent. On the debit side they have...picked up the most appalling language since coming; doesn't speak well for a Mission School! It is probably due to a lot of evacuee children they have taken in.[33]

Apparently, Mrs Bose didn't put herself and her children in the 'evacuee' class.

The post-war Indian Independence period saw high staff turnover and weak finances. Nonetheless, in 1959, Woodstock became the third high school outside North America and the first school in Asia to receive accreditation from the Middle States Association of Colleges and Secondary Schools (USA). Further strengthening of the curriculum came with the introduction of cross-cultural courses in social studies, literature, art and religion. Indian universities became more accepting of the American Woodstock diploma, allowing for easier placement of graduates in Indian colleges and universities.

Up to this point in Woodstock's history, most—although certainly not all—students were children of missionary parents. But with the departure of many missionaries from India in the 1970s, Woodstock faced the option of again closing or redefining its mission. Its leader at the time, Reverend Robert ('Bob') Alter, chose the latter route. The school deliberately shifted from being a 'missionary school' to a school with a more international student body, staff and curriculum, with an ever-stronger Indian cultural component. ESL (English as a Second Language) courses were added to meet the needs of non-English speaking students and, later, innovative computer technology courses were introduced, along with more contemporary classes, such as environmental sciences. The religious life of the school became decidedly more inclusive. The transition was a success. In December 2002, India's *Outlook* magazine ranked Woodstock as the Number 2 residential school in the country.[34]

Today, the school caters to about 500 students from over twenty countries, Indian students of course being the largest single national group. Armed with an American high school diploma, many graduates go to the United States or other countries for higher education, although an increasing number remain in India for further studies. Among Woodstock's distinguished graduates is Brigadier Hukam (Kim) Singh

In 2004, Woodstock School celebrated its 150th year anniversary, at which time the Government of India issued this commemorative first day cover stamp.
(From the authors' collection)

Yadav of the Indian Army who fought on the Burma front during the Second World War, served as aide-de-camp (ADC) to the last British viceroy of India, Lord Mountbatten, and later taught at India's Defense Services Staff College. Woodstock graduate Gerry Williams was named Artist Laureate of the state of New Hampshire, USA, in 1998.[35]

While Woodstock was serving primarily the educational needs of the children of foreign Christian missionaries, it was Wynberg Allen School[36], initially called the Christian Training School and Orphanage, which took up in 1888 the task of educating the children '...of the large European and Eurasian (Anglo-Indian) community in the Northwest Provinces and Oudh, now the United Provinces'. The school's founders, Mr Alfred Powell, Mr and Mrs Arthur Foy of Germany and Brigade Surgeon J.H. Condon, were so-called Non-Conformists

Christians[37] from Kanpur. However, from the first, no child of any denomination was refused admission if space and funds allowed. Destitute orphans were admitted free of charge. Arthur Foy became known as the 'foster father of the Wynberg Home for the poor', a tribute to his many years of involvement with the school.

Classes first began in 1890 at Rockville bungalow in Landour (now often called the 'Haunted House'), located beyond what was a toll bar at Jabarkhet along the Tehri Road. While at this location, the school enrolled up to twenty children, although it began with far fewer.

The founders of Wynberg-Allen: (L–R) Alfred Powell, member of the Board, 1887–1911; Brigade Surgeon J.H. Condon, MD, member of the Board, 1893–1901; Mrs Arthur Foy, member of the Board 1887–1898; Arthur Foy, chairman of the Board, 1887–1897.
(Courtesy of Wynberg Allen School and Mela Ram & Sons, Mussoorie)

The school was started (by Mrs E.C. Barton-West[38]) with two pupils, Peter and Mary Cables[39]. Under the building was a charcoal bhatta (kiln) and when this burst, the school was 'burnt out' but without injury to anyone. The institution was moved to Abbotsford and Dunedin (bungalows) on the Castle Hill Estate, and was eventually opened on its present site in March 1894.[40]

The move to the Wynberg Estate in 1894 was made possible by H.G. Meakin of Poona (now, Pune, Maharashtra state), who donated the Rs 20,000 needed by the school to acquire their own building. Meakin was a brewer and the founder of what today has become Mohan Meakin Ltd, the maker of famous Indian brands such as Old Monk rum, and Golden Eagle and Lion beers. Over the years, other important donors have included the Maharaja Holkar of Indore, the maharaja of Vizianagram (now part of Madhya Pradesh state) who contributed significantly after the 1905 earthquake, and David Sasson & Company (shipbuilders in Bombay, Calcutta and Karachi).

The girls' section, Wynberg Homes as it came to be called, also accepted boys up to twelve years of age. The nearby 'Bala Hissar' was the older boys' school. It was so named because the building was where the ex-amir of Afghanistan, Dost Mohammad Khan, had been kept under house arrest by the British during 1839–1842 (see Chapter 9). The original Bala Hissar building no longer exists, having been replaced in 1975 by the Lehmann Building, named after Dr Geoffrey Lehmann, who was a doctor at the Herbertpur [Uttarakhand] Christian Hospital, and for thirty-seven years, chairman of the Wynberg board of directors. The science block within the building is named after Major Harsh Bahuguna, who did his schooling at Wynberg Allen and was a member of the successful Indian Everest Expedition in 1965.[41] Other famous graduates include several Second World War heroes such as Charles Dyson (Distinguished Flying Cross), Minoo Dinshaw (Navy) and Dinshaw Eduljee (Air Force Cross).

In 1916, a governing body, the Wynberg Homes Society, was formally established for Wynberg, with the explicit purpose of '...providing for and giving to children, wholly or partly of European descent, an education based on Protestant Christian principles; to maintain such children and to give them an academic and practical training conducive to economic welfare and happiness.'

Henry D. Allen, vice-chairman of the board of directors, proposed a separate school for older boys and, in 1926, the senior boys were transferred from the Wynberg Estate to the new Henry Allen Memorial High School on an adjacent hill. In 1963, Wynberg Homes—by this time called the Wynberg Girls' High School—and Henry Allen Memorial School were merged into a fully co-educational institution, Wynberg Allen School (motto, 'Excelsior'—ever upward). With this merger, the expanded Wynberg Homes facility became the Junior School and the Henry Allen campus became the Senior School. Today, the school has about 700 students; very few of them are either Christian or of European descent, although the school respects and maintains its Christian ethos. Under the control of the Wynberg Homes Society, a board of management oversees the day-to-day affairs of this ICSE (Indian Certificate of Secondary Education)-affiliated institution.[42]

In lasting memory of its founders, Wynberg Allen School has three houses, appropriately named Powell, Foy and Condon. There is also a house named after Henry D. Allen.

Perched on a hilltop overlooking Barlowganj[43] in lower Mussoorie, St George's College is the second oldest (after Waverley) of the early Mussoorie schools that still exist. Founded in 1853 in a cottage called 'Manor House' that was first built by a Mr Hutton, the property was purchased in January 1853 for the school by a Mr Carli. Later that year, the school admitted its first students. To this day, its graduates are called 'Manorites' and, indeed, the school itself is often referred to as Manor House. The founding of St George's (motto, 'Virtuset Labor'—[success...] by virtue and exertion) was inspired by the archbishop of Patna with the object of educating Roman Catholic boys. Capuchin Fathers ran the school until 1894 but, in that year, agreed to turn over St George's to the Patrician Brothers. The Capuchins indicated that their reason for leaving the school was a desire to return to religious and missionary activities, which had become increasingly difficult due to a shortage of Capuchin priests. Upon their departure, Reverend Brother Stapleton of the Brothers of St Patrick was appointed principal.[44]

St. George's College, Mussoorie.

An early view of St George's College in Barlowganj. St George's was founded in 1853 and is the second oldest of the early Mussoorie schools that still exist (Waverley Convent School is the oldest). *(Photo compliments of the Delany Archives, Carlow College, Ireland)*

Since that time and to this day, the Patricians have run St George's. In 1894, the Patricians also took over the St Fidelis' School and Military Orphanage that had been moved by the Fathers of the Agra Mission from Shimla to Mussoorie in 1866. 'St Fids', as it was affectionately called, was for children of the domiciled Catholic community, although non-Catholic children were always admitted. St George's and St Fidelis' were amalgamated in 1948, when Brother Bernard Byrne was the St George's principal. Subsequently, St George's established a school—Nirmala Inter-College[45]—for local and workers' children on nearby Fox Hill. Today, St George's has an enrollment of about 700 residential and non-residential boys (now, mostly non-Catholic boys), from all over India as well as from neighboring countries. Nirmala is co-educational with about 500 day scholars. St George's early graduates took a course of study designed to prepare them—like Maddock's students—for the Thomason College of Civil Engineering in Roorkee, the survey department and the military.[46] Today, St George's is affiliated to the ICSE (Indian Certificate of Secondary Education) Board and Nirmala students take the State Board examinations.[47]

The Patrician Brothers of St George's and St Fidelis' Schools, circa 1920. The Brothers of St Patrick took over running the school in 1894 and have been doing so ever since.
(Photo compliments of the Delany Archives, Carlow College, Ireland)

From the beginning, St George's had military connections, in that it admitted orphans from the military and received for many years a military subsidy. Over the years, this traditional connection and a continuing emphasis on not only academics but also sports has enabled many former students to distinguish themselves in related fields. Besides producing several Olympic gold medalists[48], well-known graduates include General Shankar Roy Chowdhury, former chief of army and former Rajya Sabha (Upper House of the Indian Parliament) member; Air Chief Marshal D. La Fontaine; Lieutenant General Stanley Menezes, former vice-chief of army and recipient of the Param Vishisht Seva Medal and the Shaurya Chakra (both Indian military decorations); Harsh K. Gupta, leader of the Indian expedition to the Antarctic; and Major Haripal Singh Ahluwalia, the first Indian on Mount Everest (29 May 1965). Other famous graduates include the actor Saeed Jaffrey (*The Man Who Would Be King, Gandhi,*

Passage to India) and Dr M.S. Gill, Rajya Sabha member and senior Government of India official who over the years has held many key positions, including that of election commissioner.

Hampton Court, located on the grounds of what was once the Calcutta Hotel[49], is the only school in Mussoorie with a royal monicker, as it almost certainly takes its name from Hampton Court Palace, which is located along the Thames River in East Molesey, Surrey, near London (like Mussoorie, it too is a major tourist destination).[50] Started in 1876 by Reverend Henry Sells as a strictly non-denominational institution, Hampton Court was purchased in 1895 by Miss Florence Holland and then became known informally as 'Miss Holland's School'. (Miss Holland herself was the first Latin MA of the Bengal University and winner of a Roychand Premchand Grant.) Earlier, Miss Holland had started a school at Arundel Cottage near Wynberg Allen but, upon purchase of Hampton Court, moved her school there. Hampton Court School continued to be run by Miss Holland until 1921, when she put the entire facility up for sale.

Miss Florence Holland was one of several young women who started schools in Mussoorie. These were well-educated young ladies who were able to apply their skills in education, one of the few vocations that was acceptable for a nineteenth-century woman. Note in this 1907 Hampton Court School advertisement the presence of 'home cows' on the campus.
(Advertisement from Bodycot, F. ['compiler'], Guide to Mussoorie with Notes on Adjacent Districts and Routes into the Interior, *Mussoorie: Mafasilite Printing Works, 1907: facing p. 36)*

The attractively situated Hampton Court property was taken on by the Religious of Jesus and Mary, after a visit by Reverend Mother Clare, the superior general of the congregation, to the Indian subcontinent. In response to requests from Waverley and other parents for a school focused on the needs of their young sons, the sisters opened Hampton Court Preparatory Boys' School in 1922 for boys from Class I–IV. The early years of the school saw a shortage of teaching personnel, as the only nuns available for the school came from the New Delhi Day School, itself newly founded, and secular teachers were brought on board. Seventy-six years later, in 1998, the boarding section was closed and classes up to the tenth standard were added, this change coinciding with a growing desire to more broadly serve the local population. The school is open to all local children '…without distinction of caste or creed.' Today, the school is co-educational with approximately 600 day students and is affiliated to the ICSE (motto, Loyalty…to God, Self, Family, Fellowmen, School and Nation).[51] Ruskin Bond, well-known author and resident of Landour, studied at Hampton Court, as did Hugh Gantzer, retired Indian naval officer and well-known and active resident of Mussoorie.

A postcard photo of Miss Florence Holland's School, which she ran from 1895–1921. Subsequently, the facility was used briefly by the Seventh Day Adventists (1921–1922). Since 1922, the Sisters of Jesus and Mary have been in charge of Hampton Court School at this ideal location on the southern flank of the Mall. *(From the private collection of the late H. Michael Stokes, United Kingdom)*

From what has been seen so far, it would appear that only the Christian-inspired population was involved in establishing educational institutions in the Station. In the earliest years, this was indeed the case in this very British hill town. However, by the 1930s, there were a number of schools specifically for Indian students, such as the Ghananand High School and Intermediate College below Kincraig, the Islamia School, the Arya Kanya Pasthshala and the Sanatan Dharm Kayna Pathshala. Now there are many new schools, primarily secular but some inspired by Hinduism and other religions.

The railway companies of India were another important element in putting Mussoorie on the map as the 'Edinburgh of India'. These companies established Oak Grove School, '...the coming together of three of the greatest gifts of the 19th Century: railways, hill stations and public school culture.'

It was in 1887 that an offshoot of the Lahore Railway School, known as the 'Sind-Punjab Railway School' was started on the property that was later developed by Maharaja Dev Shamsher Jang Bahadur Rana as the Fairlawn Palace, four miles below the Mall on the Bridle Path down to Rajpur (see Chapter 9). Subsequently, the authorities of the East Indian Railway became involved with the venture and, in 1888, the Oak Grove Estate in Jharipani (near Fairlawn) was bought and the first building, designed by Mr R. Roskell Bayne, chief architect of the East Indian Railway (EIR), was constructed. This was the boys' section which opened in June 1888 under the headmastership of Mr A.C. Chapman. A girls' department opened the following November. Numbers increased rapidly, all children of railway workers and mostly Anglo-Indian. In 1894, the Sind-Punjab Railway School, run by this time by the North Western Railway of which the Sind-Punjab Railway had become a part, was permanently closed and the students came over to the EIR's Oak Grove facility. In time, more land was purchased for Oak Grove, facilities expanded, and a junior department was added in 1912. By 1936, Oak Grove (mottos from the famous *Mundokoupanishad* shloka [poetic verse]—'Take us, O' Lord, from Darkness to Enlightenment' and 'Studiis et Rebus Honestis'—for study and other honest pursuits) had an estate of over 250 acres, including playing fields and even a miniature rifle range. It was said to be '...undoubtedly one of the best, if not the best, school property in these hills'.[52]

One of the Oak Grove teachers in the 1950s was Miss Doris Garlah of the Woodlands Estate family (see below). Miss Doris, 'very good at maths and generally very accomplished', must have been quite popular, for the school records still note that it was she who in 1957 announced the first ever mid-term break at the school and, topping even that, she gave the girls '...the treat of treats' in 1960, allowing them to listen in by radio to Princess Margaret say 'I do' in her wedding to Antony Armstrong-Jones (earl of Snowdon)![53]

Today, Oak Grove serves approximately 600 children of the Indian Railways, overseen by a board of directors whose members are railway officials. Successful students are awarded the CBSE (Central Board of Secondary Education) diploma.

Although a railway school, Oak Grove—like St George's—had its own cadet corps that taught young boys basic military skills. Even though many of the students were not destined to enter active military service, it was thought that such training served as an excellent means of instilling discipline.
(Kind courtesy of Paul Rowland and Steve Leake, United Kingdom)

Besides several schools for local children and Mussoorie's oldest school, Mussoorie Seminary, there were a number of other educational institutions that did not survive the winds of change that continued to sweep over Mussoorie. Of the very oldest schools, there are several that now only exist in distant memory.

Caineville House School, called the Caineville Diocesan Girls' High School, is one such.[54] Its establishment in 1864 was also inspired by Bishop Cotton and, in this case, promoted by the Anglican Archdeacon of Calcutta, John Henry Pratt[55], who was particularly interested in the education of Anglican girls in India. Miss Scanlon opened the school with only four students (Miss Scanlon also taught music at Woodstock School). Two years later, it had fifty-six pupils on the books. '…Special attention [was] paid to French, drawing, music, dancing, and physical drill'.[56] Miss Frances Adams later took over the school and served as principal for forty-seven years (1894-1940). A memorial plaque to Miss Adams can be seen in Christ Church.[57] Caineville House School received Board of Education approval '…for the purpose of the registration of teachers…' in November 1905[58] but closed in 1948. The small number of British girls who remained were transferred to All Saints' School in Nainital (All Saints' continues today as a major hill school for girls). In the bazaar, the school was sometimes called Miss Cundle's (or Miss Candle's) School,[59] no doubt harking back to Miss Scanlon's days. In 1950, two years after Caineville closed, Shishu Niketan, an English medium school, moved into the property but shifted to Clement Town in the Dun Valley in the late 1960s and is now called Raja Ram Mohan Roy Academy. Today, the 60-acre Caineville Estate below Library Bazaar is the administrative wing of the Indo-Tibetan Border Police (ITBP) Academy. The ITBP camp as a whole is still one of the most beautifully wooded parts of modern Mussoorie.

Postcard photo of Caineville House School, which closed in 1947. The school in the bazaar, sometimes called 'Miss Candle's School', was established in 1864 by the Church of England for the education of Anglican girls not destined to return home to England for their studies. Today, the property is part of the Indo-Tibetan Border Police camp, and the old school assembly hall is the mess. *(Kind courtesy of the late H. Michael Stokes, Kent, United Kingdom)*

Caineville was for Protestant girls whose parents could pay. Another school, Dumbarnie, was a partner institution for the poor...and the girls from each sat on opposite sides of the aisle every Sunday at Christ Church.[60]

In fact, Dumbarnie was an amalgamation of two separate smaller institutions.

In 1896, an appeal for funds was taken up and by 1898 the Church of England Orphanage was started with sixteen children in Rockcliff bungalow to the north below Gun Hill. In 1899, the school moved to Chapelton to the west of the Convent of Jesus and Mary. The Dumbarnie Estate on the Vincent Hill Upper Road where Sir Proby Thomas Cautley had lived was purchased in 1907, and the school moved there. A year earlier, in 1906, Reverend Maurice Wilfred Ragg, the station chaplain, had established a small facility to address the needs of poor children under five years of age; in 1914, this became the Lady Hardinge Nursery. Finally, in 1923, the Hardinge Nursery and the Church of England Orphanage merged and became known as the 'Dumbarnie Homes and Orphanage'. The children were not all actually orphans; the school provided a home and education for children of domiciled British parents who could not afford to bear the normal expenses of educating their children. Dumbarnie closed in 1947, and the estate is now part of the residential and day school Manava Bharati School (CBSE).[61]

(L–R) Cecil, Doris and Edith were the children of Thomas Hector Garlah and Alice Maude Garlah, who started the Woodlands School in Landour. It operated from 1888–1960s; in its later years, it was run by Cecil and Edith. Edith died in 2006, at the age of ninety-nine years, the last of the Garlah family that had been in Mussoorie since the nineteenth century. *(Kind courtesy of Arthur and Dagma Houghton, Landour)*

In 1888, Mr Thomas Hector Garlah and his wife, Alice Maude, started a school in Willow Lodge, which they moved in 1898 to the Dingle (both in Landour). In 1905, they purchased the Woodlands Estate, which became both residence and school. Woodlands School '...made a speciality of giving the very young an excellent grounding in school life while living in a real home' (the pupils were children of residents and visitors to the station).[62] Mr T.H. Garlah was said to have had quite a reputation as a disciplinarian, carrying a cane of which he made good use! His wife was the de facto housemother, looking after the general welfare of the children. After the death of the parents, the Garlahs' son Cecil and daughter Edith ran the school until Cecil's death in the 1960s, when the school permanently closed. Upon closure, Miss Edith Garlah went to work at Wynberg Allen. Miss Edith died in 2006, just five months short of one hundred years old, the last of a family that had been in Mussoorie since the nineteenth century. All of the Garlah family are buried in Camel's Back Cemetery. Woodlands Estate itself remains home to several Anglo-Indian families.

In about 1884, Frederick Young's Mullingar House became the property of the Philander Smith Institute for Boys, founded by the Methodist Episcopal Church (USA) with funding from Adeline Smith, the widow of Philander Smith. Smith had been a successful Chicago businessman and liberal donor to Christian missions in Asia. The institute moved to Nainital in 1905…but not before the Philander boys had been caught developing their 'philandering' skills! In her 1997 book, Ruth Unrau humouringly relates their attempts at flirting with the Woodstock girls:

> Church-going and religious education have always been a part of the Woodstock program. In those early days when Woodstock was a school for girls, a procession of dandies carrying the staff and the less able-bodied snaked through the bazaar, followed by a crocodile of little girls going two by two. The destination was Union Church in the bazaar. The boys from Philander Smith Institute on Mullingar Hill systematically timed their migration so that they could pass the long line of Woodstock girls.[63]

In Nainital, the Philander Smith Institute was amalgamated with the Oak Opening Boy's High School to become the Philander Smith College. Jim Corbett was a student at this institution. During the Second World War, Philander's Nainital became the Hallett War School and, from 1947 onwards to today, the Birla Vidya Mandir School for Boys.[64]

There were numerous small, private schools that came and went rather quickly over the years.

In 1896, the Modern School was established at Bassett Hall by Mr Frederic Maurice Smith, to prepare boys for the English public schools '…at the age of fifteen or sixteen, so as to avoid the failures so often incurred as the result of sending boys home at too early an age…Those who are not destined to go home are carefully prepared for Indian careers...'[65] The school had an impressive curriculum that extended from English, Latin, divinity and arithmetic to trigonometry, physics, political economy, Indian history and bookkeeping (Smith himself was a mathematics honours graduate from Cambridge). Nonetheless, in 1906, the Modern School was denied recognition by the Board of Education in London, even though the application was endorsed by the Mussoorie civil surgeon (regarding health standards) and by the inspector of European Schools for the United Provinces. Denial was on the grounds '...that the number of pupils in the higher divisions is too small for the School to afford experience of the character contemplated for the Regulations in question.'[66] The Modern School closed shortly after this lethal blow. A similar fate awaited the Junior Mussoorie School at the Abbey for boys under fourteen years, which had been taken on by the Lucknow Diocesan (Anglican) Board of Education upon the demise of Maddock's School.

The Landour Academy, also at Mullingar House and run by Mauger Monk and his brother-in-law, Rev. Isaac Lewin, did not long outlive Monk's death in 1849 (see Chapter 10 for more on Monk's life). The Landour Boarding and Day School also did not survive for long, despite initial success and laudable ambitions. It was established in 1906 by Mr George Moore—formerly of the Philander Smith Institute, Landour and Nainital—paying great attention '...to the development of good manners, of truthfulness, and a high sense of honour, and it is the aim of all concerned to develop these noble and manly qualities more by personal persuasion than by punishment.'[67]

At one time, there was also a rather unique Summer Home for Soldiers' Children, established in 1870 with funds raised by General John Biddulph, the first British agent in Gilgit (1878–1881). The Summer Home was initially run by Reverend J.A. and Mrs (Charlotte) Stamper in Bassett Hall (now, the Kasmanda Palace Hotel), located just above Christ Church. But after one year, Glenburnie, located near the Municipal Gardens to the west, was purchased for the home from the estate of General Sir Charles Reid.[68] Strictly for British children, the Summer Home was described as '...the only institution of its kind in India.'[69]

The necessity for this Home is perhaps not so urgent now as it was in the old days when it was started, when not a single depot had any 'family quarters'; but there are still very many soldiers' wives, who for want of available quarters cannot get to the hills, or who object to leaving their husbands, but are anxious about their children in the heat and surroundings of their plains-station, and who are more than thankful to have such a place as the Glenburnie Summer Home to send them to. The help of visitors to Mussoorie for this institution, which is not so well known as it deserves to be, is solicited.[70]

The summer home closed in the late 1930s.

SUMMER HOME

FOR SOLDIERS' CHILDREN
AT MUSSOORIE. HIMALAYAS.

ESTABLISHED 1876.

MANY friends have asked me for a short account of this Institution. I have now much pleasure in writing it.

In the Spring of 1876 there was much writing in the Indian newspapers, on the subject of the misery and suffering of European children in India, especially the Soldiers' children; and any one [sic] who is acquainted with the army, will know that these pictures were not overdrawn. English people have not, and never can have any idea of the Indian climate, or what it is to have hot weather for seven months of the year, and even though many people find their health none the worse for it, and some Officers' and Civilians' children can stand it pretty well, still this is not the case with Soldiers' children.

In order to have a chance of standing the climate, every comfort must surround the child; nurses must be ready to take charge of it if the mother is ill; constant care must be exercised, and every luxury must be procurable in case of sickness. This can never be the case with Soldiers' children where the mother is very often extremely sickly herself, and has no means or knowledge to provide what is necessary. Even if the health of the child is not actually bad, still the hot weather brings misery and confinement such as English children have no experience of.

After this correspondence, it was determined to do something, and General Biddulph opened a subscription with a view to help in some way. Mr. Stamper and I took the greatest interest in the subject, and had long had a plan in view, viz. : to take the children who required change up to the Hills for the hot weather, returning them to their parents when the heat was over; and as I was going to the Hills that year with my own little girl, Mr. Stamper allowed me to write a few regiments, saying that I would take a few children, say ten or twelve, up with me, and keep them as members of my family until my return. The answers to these letters were so overwhelming that I had 45 children on my list before I could refuse one, and it required some sternness to stop there. Such a charge made us very anxious, but all went well. A large house was secured at Mussoorie at a moderate rent for the season. A hard-working and clever Soldier's wife promised to come with me as Matron, to which establishment the Commanding Officer at Landour enabled us to add a Serjeant as Schoolmaster.

On the hottest night I ever remember we began our journey, meeting the different parties of children at the railway stations as we went along; Mr. Stamper and I and our little girl travelling with them, and after two nights of train and omnibus, we reached Mussoorie all well. The Doctor who attended us shook his head at my party and said they would never all survive to return, as they were too sickly to live; but thank God they all got on well and went down at the end of five and half months so rosy and fat that their own parents hardly knew them.

In 1877 I went up again with a party of 50, who all did well. A home was also opened at Murree for the Punjab children, but is closed this year as the fund was not able to pay for two houses.

About money matters: General Biddulph gave me Rs.500* to start with, and afterwards undertook to raise all the money we required; and so far the subscriptions have covered all expenses. But we found that it was very difficult and uncertain a matter to get a large house at a low rent, that we were obliged to purchase one for the purpose; and accordingly bought General Reid's House, "Glenburnie," for Rs.13,000. This sum is partly paid, but there is a debt of Rs.3,000 on the house, which makes us all very anxious. During my management there were only the children's expenses to think of, as mine, including house-rent, were paid by Mr Stamper; but last year as I could not continue the management, we were obliged to engage a paid Superintendent, and her salary is a serious though necessary item. The parents pay for their children as far as their means allow, viz.: Serjeants 5 or 6 Rs [sic]. And Privates 3 Rs.[sic] a month. This, however, hardy covers the cost of food only. Government has helped us by giving the children free railway passes up and down; still part of the travelling expenses fall on the fund. With all economy, each child costs the fund quite Rs. 50 for the season beyond what parents pay.

Our great wish is to make the Institution a permanent one. It has been successfully started, and everything is in perfect working order. It only now requires that the house should be fully paid for, and to have a sufficient sum in hand for working expenses. The Afghan war took away many regiments who helped us; and so many officers have had expenses connected with this war that our funds suffer; so we have to try and make a little interest in England. Could our English friends see the happy rosy faces, hear the merry voices, and witness the excellent appetites of our Glenburnie children, they would wish us well, especially if they saw the contrast of the pale, languid brothers and sisters in the plains and saw them in the hospital, suffering from ophthalmia, diarrhea and fever, covered with mosquito bites and prickly heat, for which change of climate is the only cure. Sixty children are going up this year, to be increased to eighty if funds allow.

Subscriptions will be very acceptable, and may be paid "To the account of Rev. J.A. Stamper," (Chaplain of Umritsur) City Bank, Threadneedle Street, E.C., from whence they will be forwarded to General Biddulph's Fund.

CHARLOTTE STAMPER.

June 6ᵗʰ, 1879.   *Hon. Sec. Summer Home.*

˙Note—Ten rupees may be calculated at £1.

A funds appeal for the Summer Home for Soldiers' Children, which operated out of Bassett Hall above Christ Church for a short time and, later, from Glenburnie near the Municipal Gardens. The home closed permanently in the 1930s.
(Transcribed from a printed leaflet in the Mrs S. Laughton papers at the Centre of South Asian Studies Library, University of Cambridge, UK, kind courtesy of Ms Rachel M. Rowe, librarian)

Of all the old 'no more' Mussoorie schools, Vincent Hill School is remembered as the most unusual. The school—known variously during its early years as Annfield School, Mussoorie Primary and Intermediate School, and Mussoorie Primary and Middle English School—was first opened in 1911 by the Seventh-day Adventist (SDA) Mission[71] on the twenty-three acre Annfield Estate in Landour. Mrs Edith Bruce was its first principal.[72] In 1919, the school purchased the forty-nine acre

Vincent Hill property and, during the transition from Annfield, moved temporarily into Hampton Court (1921–1922). On 15 March 1922, the school, now named Vincent Hill, opened at its recently acquired property southwest of Library Bazaar, and the Annfield Estate was sold.

The location itself, Vincent Hill, is named after Lieutenant General William Vincent (b.1781–d.1859), who served variously in Java, Singapore, Burma and at several locations in India. He died in Mussoorie on 28 August 1859 at the age of seventy-five and is buried in the Camel's Back Cemetery. Eventually, the property

The original entrance to the Vincent Hill School, circa 1925. *(Kind courtesy of Peter Haynal, USA)*

The purpose-built main building of Vincent Hill School, as it appeared in 1922. This building provided classrooms, a chapel, cafeteria and administrative offices. An addition was later added to the middle section. *(Kind courtesy of Peter Haynal, USA)*

(L) Mrs Edith Bruce was the first principal of Vincent Hill School (1911–1913). At the time, the school was called Annfield and was located in lower Landour. (R) A.J. Olson was the school's principal when it moved in 1922 to its Vincent Hill location. Olson served as principal from 1922–1927. *(Kind courtesy of Peter Haynal, USA)*

came into the possession of Mr John Dyer. Dyer's widow and inheritor remarried and, as Mrs Ellie Keelan, she sold the estate to the Seventh-day Adventists. The Keelan family remained associated with Vincent Hill School through to its closure.

(Top) Vincent Hill girls at their cooking lesson. The school was known for giving pupils extensive training in manual and household duties. (Bottom) Vincent Hill School students exercising during the 1920s. *(Kind courtesy of Peter Haynal, USA; photo of girls cooking lesson is from the collection of Gerald Christo, Hosur, India)*

From 1922 until 1955, the Vincent Hill School offered a twelve-year curriculum that, at the high school level, prepared students for the Senior Cambridge Certificate. But in that year, an American curriculum was introduced in order to better serve the missionary children. From this point onwards, the school mainly served the Seventh-day Adventist overseas missionary community, whereas heretofore it had also attracted students from among domiciled Europeans and Anglo-Indians of the SDA church community. It was also reported that '...many of the students are trained for Holy Orders, or for colportage [the distribution of religious publications, books and tracts by carriers called "colporteurs"].' The school was said to differ also in that it relied as little as possible on hired labour, pupils being given extensive training in manual and household duties. '...The excellent products from the school bakery, hawked around the Station, is testimony of what the students are capable of in the culinary department.'[73]

In the mid 1920s, the school became a junior college and became known as Vincent Hill School and Junior College. In 1951, the junior college work was discontinued, thus ending high hopes of joining a worldwide circle of SDA colleges that was being established during this period.

At the end of 1969, the school was also closed because, according to the SDA Encyclopedia, the Indian government policy on granting visas restricted entry of qualified personnel into the country who might serve as teachers of the American curriculum. Also, for the same reason, the missionary clientele gradually diminished, making it impossible to have a well-balanced educational programme. And, having switched to an American curriculum, the school was really no longer attractive to those SDA Anglo-Indians who stayed in India after independence. In short, no 'business plan' was put forward to address the realities of vastly changed circumstances. With the closure of the Vincent Hill School, which never had an enrolment of more than just over one hundred, remaining SDA students of mainly United States, Canadian and Australian missionary families were sent to the SDA's Far Eastern Academy in Singapore.[74] Vincent Hill School had operated for only fifty-eight years. The Vincent Hill Estate was sold to the Sikh community for its new school.

In 1969, the very year that the SDA's Vincent Hill School closed, the Guru Nanak Fifth Centenary School opened on the same site. Named in memory of Sri Guru Nanak Devji on the occasion of his 500th birth anniversary, the Guru Nanak School (motto: Come to Learn, Go to Serve) is managed today by the Fifth Centenary School Society. The old Vincent Hill facility is used by the Guru Nanak boys; girls and junior boys are housed on the nearby Shangri-la Estate, which was purchased by the society in 1977. Of all the newer schools in the Station, this Sikh school is considered by many to be one of the most successful.

The late twentieth century saw the arrival of many new schools in the station, a circumstance that will undoubtedly assure Mussoorie's place in the field of education for years and years to come. These schools are indeed 'legion': the Central School for Tibetans, Mussoorie Modern School (not to be confused with the earlier 'Modern School'), Mussoorie Public School, Pine Wood School, Mussoorie International School, St Clare's Convent School[75] and many more.

So, while there were numerous schools that did not survive, the late twentieth century saw many new ones arise. It is likely the trend will continue, if the infrastructure of this fragile hill station can bear an ever-greater 'load'.

It is a tribute to the leadership of some of the oldest schools that they still exist today, given the radical changes that took place in the late nineteenth and twentieth centuries, namely, increasingly easier travel between India and Europe, less assurance of good postings for the English in what became increasingly 'Indianized' services and, later, Independence itself, along with the departure of most Europeans.

However, any such tribute to leadership cannot be extended to the schools with an Anglican provenance. Of all the 'old' schools that did not survive, those with a Church of England (Anglican) provenance were the hardest hit. In 1924, the Church of England's bishop of Nagpur, Eyre Chatterton, wrote:

> Up to the present time the Roman Church has had a great advantage over our Church, in that it is able to secure the services of well-qualified teachers at no great cost. We look forward to the time when our Church of England will provide teaching brotherhoods for the benefit of European schools in India.[76]

In fact, that time never came, at least not in Mussoorie. All of the Church of England (Anglican) schools established in the Station—Mussoorie Seminary/Maddock's, Caineville House, Dumbarnie and the Junior Mussoorie School—ultimately failed. But it wasn't only for lack of teachers 'at no great cost'. These schools had been set up only for British and sometimes Anglo-Indian children. When most of the children left with their families in the 1940s, that was a death knell, since the schools had largely lost their clientele and there was no shift to an Indian student body. As we have seen, a similar fate awaited the Seventh-day Adventist Vincent Hill School.

However, clearly the administrators and faculties of Waverley (established 1845), St George's (1853), Woodstock (1854), Hampton Court (1876), Oak Grove (1887), and Wynberg Allen (1888) did adapt successfully. If they had not, these schools too would not exist today. In each case, school leadership significantly altered the visions and objectives of their institutions to address the educational needs, no longer primarily of the British in India but of Indians themselves, while steadfastly maintaining a dedication to '…scholastic excellence, development of character, sportsmanship, punctuality and discipline.'

This response assured their very survival and has carried them successfully into the twenty-first century.

WHAT'S IN A NAME?

In its short life of sixty-six years, the Mussoorie Seminary had two other names, Maddock's School and Stokes' School, after two of its headmasters. Waverley was sometimes called the Convent School or the Kala (black) School, in reference to the nuns' dress, and there was a Belmont School on the same premises. Today, there is a St Lawrence School on the campus. Caineville was called Miss Cundle's, the Miss Candle School, or Miss Candle's School, probably bazaar versions of the headmistress's name, Scanlon. Woodstock School was first called the Protestant Girls' School, then the Woodstock Establishment and finally Woodstock School. However, the folks in the bazaar called it the Company School. Some still do, and the fact that Woodstock never had any formal or direct connection with the East India Company apparently doesn't matter. Wynberg Allen was variously called the Christian Training School and Orphanage, the Wynberg Orphanage for Poor and Destitute Anglo-Indian Children, Wynberg Homes (girls), Bala Hisar (boys), Wynberg Girls' High School, Henry Allen Memorial Boys' School and—the most wonderful—Bobby Sahib's School. Bobby Hesseltine had run the Mussoorie Hotel in the main Wynberg building and Bobby Sahib's Hotel became, of course, Bobby' Sahib's School. The Sind-Punjab Railway School became Oak Grove School or, if you asked in the bazaar, it was simply Fairlawn, after the estate that was the school's first home. During its life of only fifty-eight years, Vincent Hill School had five other names: Annfield School, Mussoorie Primary and Intermediate School, Mussoorie Primary and Middle School, Vincent Hill School and Junior College, and Vincent Hill College. Apparently, this was all too much for 'The Rambler' who wrote in his 1936 guidebook, 'Hampton Court was once the Calcutta Hotel and the illiterate therefore called the school the "Calcuttiya School".' But who was The Rambler to complain? His real name was Charles Williams.

Notes

1. S.J. Darcy, a Patrician Brother, was a greatly respected and loved instructor (and poet) who taught at St George's College, Barlowganj for almost thirty years (1920–1949). 'Stet Fortuna Domus' is also one of the mottos of the Harrow School, London.

2. Williams, C. ('The Rambler'), *A Mussoorie Miscellany*, Mussoorie, The Mafasilite Press, 1936, from an advertisement contained therein for Col Brown's Cambridge School, Dehra Dun.

3. Northam, John, *Guide to Masuri, Landaur, Dehra Dun and the Hills North of Dehra*, Calcutta: Thacker, Spink and Company, 1884: 48.

4. The so-called 'Old Brewery' opened in 1830 but closed in 1832 (only to reopen later as the 'Mackinnon Brewery'). Benog Hill is at a height of 6,901 feet (2,104 metres), atop of which is now the Jwalaji Temple.

5. Morgan, Andrew, ed., *Mussoorie Merchant, the Indian Letters of Mauger Fitzhugh Monk, 1828-1849*, Bath: Pagoda Tree Press, 2006: 27.

6. Upon sale of the school, Reverend Robert North Maddock (MA, Oxford University) retired to the plains but returned to Mussoorie in 1867 to initiate a new headmaster. Whilst there, he died of smallpox in March 1867 at St Helena's, the headmaster's house that was adjoining the school. The house, St Helena's or St Helen's, still stands and is now part of the Kapurthala Estate. There is a beautiful memorial plaque in Christ Church, remembering Maddock 'who was called to a heavenly home on the eve of departure to an earthly, after 17 years of faithful work as headmaster of Mussoorie School....multis ille bonis flebilis occidit (bemoaned by many good men)'.

7. There is a memorial inscription in Christ Church in honour of Lt Col John Wilfred Stokes, Reverend Arthur Stokes' eldest son.

8. In an appendix to Bishop Cotton's memoirs, published in 1871, it is stated: 'The school at Mussoorie still remains a higher class school [compared to the Bishop Cotton School in Shimla] of nearly 100 boys. The fees are higher than at Simla, and a liberal rather than a commercial education is given, the standard of instruction being more advanced both in classics and mathematics. Boys have passed from it in quite recent years with credit through the entrance examinations of the Calcutta University and of the Roorkee College. There are two very good exhibitions, founded by the original proprietor, the late Rev R Maddock, who liberally remitted for this object £1,000 of the money he received on the sale of the institution. The school prospered much for three years under the Rev A O Hardy, domestic chaplain to Bishop Cotton, who undertook the charge of it at the close of 1866, when efforts to procure a headmaster had been beset with the difficulties which too often impede their selection in India. An University man succeeded Mr. Hardy when, at the end of three years, he resumed his work as a Government chaplain' (from an appendix [p. 574] contained in the *Memoir of George Edward Lynch Cotton, D.D., Bishop of Calcutta and Metropolitan, with Selections from his Journals and Correspondence*, edited by Mrs Sophia Anne Cotton [wife of Bishop Cotton], London: Longman, Green and Co., 1871).

9. *Promite Vires* more correctly translates as 'put forth thy strength'.

10. Craig, Hazel Innes, *Under the Old School Topee*, Putney: British Association for Cemeteries in South Asia (BACSA), 1990: 32.

11. The Roorkee College, established in 1847, was the first engineering college in the British Empire. It was renamed the Thomason College of Civil Engineering in 1854, after Sir James Thomason, chief engineer-in-charge of the Ganga (Ganges) Canal. In 1949, it became the first engineering university of independent India and, in 2001, it was again renamed the Indian Institute of Technology Roorkee. Under whatever name, this university, which was 150 years old in 1997, has remained one of India's premier institutions of higher learning.

12. Three sons of Alexander Skinner—Albert Edward Skinner, Robert Hercules Skinner and Stanley Edgar Skinner—attended Maddock's School. Sons of Christopher Corbett at Maddock's were Christopher Edward Corbett, John Corbett, Maurice Corbett and Archibald D'arcy Corbett.

13. Craig, Ibid, p. 33.

14. *Register of Stokes' School,* Mussoorie, 1867-1900, p. 169 (in the collection of the Society of Genealogists, London).

15. Williams, Ibid, p. 58-60.

16. The Survey of India's 1929 map of Mussoorie uses the spelling 'Waverly', as do some other early publications. However, today the Convent of Jesus & Mary calls its estate 'Waverley', so that is the spelling used here.

17. The Religious of Jesus and Mary (Religieuses de Jésus-Marie) is a Roman Catholic order for education, founded in October 1818 at Lyon, France by Claudine Thévenet (later, Mary of St Ignatius, canonized in 1993). In 1842, Lyon sent nuns to India, where several houses were set up, the first or 'foundation' house being in Agra. To the present time, the Convent of Jesus and Mary oversees a network of girls' schools in India and Pakistan. In India, the Jesus and Mary schools boast many notable graduates, among them Sheila Dikshit, former chief minister of Delhi; Aung San Suu Kyi, Burmese democracy activist; Priyanka Gandhi Vadra, daughter of Indian politician Sonia Gandhi; Sujata Madhok, journalist and social activist; the late Jessica Lal, ex-model, brutally murdered in 1999; and Preity Zinta, Bollywood actress.

    Fanny Parkes noted during her 1838 travels that 'There is also a girls' school at Mussoori (sic)', but it is unclear what school this might have been, since Waverley didn't open until 1845. Perhaps it was a small institution run out of a bungalow, but this is only speculation. Parkes also mentions that on 17 April 1838, 'A long ride round Waverly (sic) was the evening's amusement'; at the time, this would have been Paolo Solaroli's estate and not yet Waverley School (from Parkes, Fanny, *Wanderings of a Pilgrim, in Search of the Picturesque, during Four-and-Twenty Years in the East; with Revelations of Life in the Zenana*, London: Pelham Richardson, 1850: 230-231 in vol. 2).

18. Begum Yohanna Sumru, daughter of a Muslim nobleman, converted to Catholicism and, through her marriage to the mercenary Walter Reinhardt, came into control of a jagir (grant of lands) in the Doab region between the Ganges and Yamuna rivers. She built what is now

the Basilica of Our Lady of Graces in Sardhana, near Meerut (Uttar Pradesh state). Begum Sumru died on 27 January 1836, 'fortified by the last rites of the church'. Her state, but not her personal property, was taken over by the British Indian government.

19. 'Earlier, on 2 March 1906 Waverley was honoured by a Royal Visitor, the Princess of Wales, the future Queen Mary. She enjoyed the matchless panorama of the snowy Himalayan Range clearly visible from the Waverley verandah' (from Mitra, Alica, *A History of the Congregation, the Religious of Jesus and Mary in India, 1842-1993*, New Delhi: Delhi Province of the Religious of Jesus and Mary, circa 1999: 62).

20. In the nineteenth century, it was common for a school to, in effect, have two parts, as a means of preserving the social distinctions of the day. One was usually a boarding school for children whose parents could afford to pay for their education; the other was for orphans and children whose parents could not pay school fees. The former subsidized the latter.

21. The Society for Promoting Female Education in the East closed down in 1899, however, the Church Missionary Society took over some of its activities.

22. Church Missionary Society's *Missionary Register*, Vol. 43.

23. Information taken from Unrau, Ruth, *Hill Station Teacher*, North Newton, Kansas: Kidron Creek Publishers, 1997: 15; and from Jones, Edith, Caroline Wilkie and Mary I. McGee, *Woodstock School, the First Century*, Landour: Woodstock School, second edition, 1999: 1-3.

24. Church Missionary Society's *Missionary Register*, Vol. 43.

25. _____*The Thirty-Eighth Annual Report of the Society for Promoting Female Education in the East*, Cheapside, London: Suter and Co., 1872: 27. It is interesting to note that in the same number it is written, 'The Caineville [House] School fully retains its reputation under the superintendence of Miss Scanlon, who derives much help from the teachers sent out by the Society.' Yet, as it turned out, it was Woodstock School that survived and prospered while the Caineville House School closed in the period leading up to Independence.

26. Presbyterianism is a family of Protestant Christian denominations. Historically, its adherents follow the Christian precepts of the sixteenth century reformer, John Calvin, although today there is said to be great diversity among the various denominations. Presbyterianism originally evolved primarily in Scotland. Its governance is typified by the rule of assemblies of 'presbyters' or elders, and thus the name.

    When the Presbyterian Church in India was merged into the present-day Church of North India (CNI), part of Woodstock's Landour property conveyed to the CNI.

27. Mary Lyon was the founder of Mount Holyoke Seminary, now Mount Holyoke College, located in South Hadley, Massachusetts, USA. She was a powerful advocate for the development of women's education in the United States, having studied under Reverend Joseph Emerson in Byfield, Massachusetts, in the early nineteenth century. One of Mary Lyon's former pupils wrote that Emerson's '...schools in Byfield I may safely call the prototype, not only of Mount Holyoke, but of all modern institutions for the higher education of girls. We know not what India owes to Mary Lyon and Reverend Joseph Emerson' (details from unpublished correspondence, courtesy of the Mount Holyoke College Archives, USA). It is interesting to

note that David Ochterlony, hero of the Anglo–Nepalese War of 1815–1816, also studied as a young boy in Byfield, Massachusetts.

28. Staff of Woodstock School in 1885: First row (L–R): Miss Wilson, Miss Clara Williamson (Mount Holyoke Seminary, class of 1872), and Miss Griffith. Second row (L–R): Miss Anderson, Mrs Eliza Jane (née Foster) Scott (class of 1852 and principal of school), Miss Anna Scott. Third row (L to R): Miss McNair, Miss Hettie Scott (1879), Miss Mary Fullerton.

29. Bodycot, F. ('compiler'), *Guide to Mussoorie with Notes on Adjacent Districts and Routes into the Interior,* Mussoorie: Mafasilite Printing Works, 1907: 153.

30. From an advertisement contained in Williams, Ibid.

31. Marguerite Thoburn Watkins, writing in 2004, poignantly describes her evacuation from Woodstock and India in 1942, when she was eleven years old: 'I think of the start of our trip as a spring evening in Mussoorie when the grownups shut the door to a Fir Clump living room with the children left outside to play unsupervised on the graveled flat. It was long past time for home and homework. Closeted inside were all the adults from both Fir Clump and South Hill, their hushed voices indistinguishable from the sounds of evening— crickets, leaves in the wind, crack of twig, the hills settling down. The mixed-age group of youngsters did not divide as usual by year and interest, but hung together, realizing that something important was happening behind those doors.

'In India we seemed always to have been at war, yet it had not directly affected Americans. Now here we were, amusing ourselves outdoors as the shadows lengthened and our mothers whispered about things unfit for the ears of children—Japanese prison camps with their privations and atrocities. Three months later we were on the deck of the troop ship S.S. Brazil'. (From Watkins, Marguerite Thoburn, *Two Taproots: Growing up in the Forties in India and America*, USA: Xlibris Corporation, 2004: 17).

32. Watkins, Ibid, p. 104.

33. Owens, Patricia, ed., *An American Memsahib in India, the Letters and Diaries of Irene Mott Bose, 1920-1951*, London: The British Association for Cemeteries in South Asia, 2006: 177.

34. The Doon School for boys in Dehra Dun was ranked #1 residential school by *Outlook* magazine.

35. Information on today's Woodstock School adapted from various school sources.

36. The name Wynberg may have its origins in South Africa. De Oude Wjinbergh (Old Wine Mountain, anglicized to Wynberg) was originally a Dutch farming neighbourhood located in what today is a picturesque and historical suburb of Cape Town. This neighbourhood became the site of a garrison town after the British takeover of the Cape Settlement in 1795. As Cape Town was a major stop for ships en route to India, many troops spent considerable time here, and it is not inconceivable that an army officer may have found his way to Mussoorie and named his property 'Wynberg'. However, no definite proof of this connection or any other connection to the name Wynberg has been found. The name 'Allen' has a much clearer provenance, of course, being the surname of Henry D. Allen who inspired the establishing of a separate senior school for boys.

37. 'Non-Conformists' or 'Dissenters' were Protestant Christians who did not conform to or follow the governance and usages of the Church of England. The movement started in Great Britain in the seventeenth century. In recent years, these distinctions have become quite blurred, especially among the minority Christian population in India where many Protestant church factions have merged.

38. Mrs Barton-West served Wynberg Allen School from 1890 until 1895. A plaque in honour of her service, donated by her son, John O.N. West, and daughter Annie S. James, still hangs in the Wynberg (Junior School) dining hall.

39. Mary Cables later became a helper in the 'baby home' or nursery which had been set up as a 'blessing' to poor European and Anglo-Indian widows who were now able to go out to work and make a living for themselves and their children.

40. Bodycot, Ibid, p. 154.

41. According to Ruskin Bond's account, the Bala Hisar had an unlucky reputation. In 1925 the Boys' School had a new master, Mr McIntosh, who had come over from the Philander Smith College, Nainital. He had not been long in Bala Hisar when he had a providential escape from sudden death, having reluctantly gone to a cinema show, only to find upon his return that his rooms were on fire. '...the "Bala Hisar"... appeared to have been jinxed. Some years earlier, Captain Charles Henry Deane Spread, of the Invalid Establishment, Landour, was struck by lighting and killed at Bala Hisar. He was preparing to develop some photographic plates and in a heavy shower was collecting rain water for the process from the guttering when he was struck dead.' A similar fate befell a Mr Fitzpatrick, but we do not have the details.' (Bond, Ruskin, *The Story of Wynberg Allen Mussoorie*, Landour: Wynberg Allen School, published on the occasion of the centenary, 1988: 16-17).

42. Information on Wynberg Allen was obtained from various school sources, and from Ruskin Bond's *The Story of Wynberg Allen Mussoorie*, Landour: Wynberg Allen School, 1988.

43. Barlowganj is named after Colonel Charles Grant Barlow, whose residence was 'Barlow Castle'. Barlow Castle, which reportedly was not much of a castle, had both an earlier and later names. Originally, it was simply a thatched bungalow known as 'Ravens Wood'. Much later, Barlow Castle became Whytbank Castle, owned by Major General Edmund Wintle of the Bengal Staff Corps. This was sold in 1928 to the Johnstone family of the Alliance Bank (from Williams, C. ['The Rambler'], *A Mussoorie Miscellany*, Mussoorie: Mafasilite Press, 1936: 40). In 1938, Whytbank Castle came to be owned by St George's College, and was used to house wealthy St George's students who resided there as so-called 'parlour boarders'. In the 1990s, St George's sold the Whytbank property. The Jaypee Residency Manor Hotel now occupies the site.

44. The Catholic Capuchin order arose in Italy in the early sixteenth century. Its members are committed to a life of austerity, simplicity, poverty and preaching, according to the principals of St Francis of Assisi. The name comes from the Italian word 'capuccio' which means 'hood'; the usually coffee-coloured hood formed a part of the monks' religious dress. Cappuccino coffee has its roots in the same word!

The Patrician Brotherhood (Brothers of St Patrick) was founded in Ireland in 1808 by Bishop Daniel Delany, '…guided by the spirit of St Patrick…', the patron saint of Ireland. At the time that he founded the order, Delany was the bishop of Kildare and Leighlin. The Patricians first came to India (to Madras, now Chennai) in 1875. Today, the brotherhood runs twenty-four schools across India, including St George's.

45. 'Nirmala' is a common Hindi name meaning 'pure' and, in this context, refers to Our Lady of Immaculate Conception.

46. Bodycot, Ibid, p. 37.

47. Information taken from interviews. In Christian hagiography, St George (b. circa 275–281– d.23 April 303) was a soldier in the Guard of the Roman Emperor Diocletian. St George, the patron saint of England, is venerated as a martyr and immortalized in the tale of George and the Dragon. There is a wonderful statue on the Mussoorie campus of St George slaying the dragon.

48. Ten former pupils of St George's and Oak Grove School represented India in Olympic hockey between 1928 and 1936. They won a total of fifteen gold medals. St George's students included George Marthins (1928), Maurice A Gateley (1928), William Goodsir-Cullen (1928), Carlyle Carroll Tapsell (1932 and 1936), Earnest Goodsir-Cullen (1936), and Lionel Emmett (1936). Eric Pinniger (1928 and 1932), Leslie Charles Hammond (1928 and 1932), Richard James Allen (1928, 1932 and 1936) and Richard Carr (1932) were past pupils of Oak Grove School. Also, Neil Nugent from St George's won a bronze medal for Great Britain in the 1952 Helsinki Games.

49. Williams, Ibid, p. 61.

50. It is not entirely clear why this name may have been chosen for the school. Its selection may be related to the historic link between Hampton Court in England and the Senior Battalion of the Gurkhas, which was sometimes temporarily stationed at Hampton Court up to the early 1900s. The Battalion's permanent headquarters were in Dehra Dun, and an officer from there may have had some influence in naming the estate.

51. Information on Hampton Court from Williams, Ibid, p. 61, as well as from interviews taken at the school, and promotional materials obtained from the headmistress in August 2009.

52. Williams, Ibid, p. 62.

53. Oak Grove information, including quotes, was taken from the school's promotional material and from on-site interviews.

54. Caineville was originally a private home ('Caineville' is a Scottish/English family name), to which wings containing classrooms and dormitories and enclosing a large quadrangle were added. A dining hall, drill hall and lavatories were added later. There were three large playgrounds on the sixty-acre estate of well-wooded land. (British Library)

55. Archdeacon Pratt was a true 'Renaissance man'. Even though he was a churchman, his literary output during his Indian career was chiefly of a scientific character. Valuable papers appeared from time to time between the years 1853 and 1862, in the journals and *Philosophical Transactions* of the Royal Society, and in the publications of the Asiatic Society of Bengal.

These included, 'The Effect of the Local Attraction on the Plumb-line Caused by the Himalaya and other Mountain Ranges of India,' 'The Influence of the Sea on the Plumb-line of India', 'The Great Indian Arc of the Meridian', 'The Probable Date of the Vedas', and 'The Constitution of the Solid Crust of the Earth'.

Occasional papers of a similar but lighter character were also contributed to the *Calcutta Review* and other Indian publications. In 1856, Pratt edited 'The Notes of the Eclectic Society'. Just before his death in 1871, he issued the sixth edition of his best-known work, *'Scripture and Science Not at Variance,'* wherein he embraced modern scientific discoveries and the theories of Lyell and Darwin, but refuted that these conflicted with the Biblical Book of Revelations, saying that true science 'can do nothing against the truth'. Pratt died at Ghazipur in the United Provinces (Uttar Pradesh state) on 30 December 1871 while on what he described as 'my last winter tour' (adapted from *The Venerable Archdeacon Pratt, Archdeacon of Calcutta: A Sketch*, by I. Cave Brown, Bengal Chaplain, contained in *Mission Life*, Volume III, Part 1 [New Series], 1872: 163-69).

56. Bodycot, Ibid, p. 153.
57. There is also a memorial plaque in Christ Church remembering Margaret Elizabeth Clarke, who had been headmistress of the Caineville House School as well as Montrose House School. Presumably, the latter school was in Montrose House on Camel's Back Road, which at one time also housed trigonometrical facilities (Survey of India).
58. This approval was contained in a letter dated 10 November 1905 from the Board of Education, Whitehall, London. The letter noted that 'I am to add that the Board have had some hesitation in according recognition in view of the small number of pupils in the Upper Forms of the School.' (British Library)
59. Williams, Ibid, p. 66.
60. Dumbarnie is a Scottish place name. The girls' attendance and seating at Christ Church is recalled by Mrs Dagma Houghton of Woodlands Estate, Landour (2009).
61. A plaque, installed in 1917 as 'a memorial to Revd Maurice Wilfred Ragg, Chaplain of [Christ Church] Mussoorie 1910—1915, to whose efforts the founding of the Lady Hardinge Nursery was largely due' can still be seen at the Manava Bharati School.
62. Williams, Ibid, pp. 62-63.
63. Unrau, Ruth, *Hill Station Teacher*, North Newton, Kansas: Kidron Creek Publishers, 1997: 59.
64. Information on Philander Smith was provided by the staff at a small liberal arts 'Historically Black College' in Little Rock, Arkansas, USA called Philander Smith College, this college being another example of Smith's largesse.
65. Bodycot, Ibid, p. 154.
66. Letter S. 9620/05 from the Board of Education, Whitehall, London to the Under Secretary of State for India, dated 5 January 1906. (British Library)
67. Bodycot, Ibid, p. 156.
68. Reid was commandant of the Sirmur Battalion of Gurkhas [2nd Gurkha Rifles]. He died of cholera at the siege of Delhi on 6 October 1857. Sirmur is a district in the state of

Himachal Pradesh; Nahan is its main city.

69. Northam's 1884 guidebook states, 'Any soldiers [sic] child, with the following exceptions, can be admitted; those ineligible are:- children of mixed parentage; children suffering from contagious disorders; children under three years, unless accompanied by an elder sister; boys over 12 year [sic] of age' (Northam, Ibid, p. 45).

70. Bodycot, Ibid, pp. 157-8.

71. The Seventh-day Adventist (SDA) Church is a Protestant Christian denomination distinguished mainly by its observance of Saturday, the original seventh day of the Judeo-Christian week, as the 'Sabbath' or their particular day of worship. The Adventists first came to India as missionaries in 1893.

72. Even though the school was opened only in 1911, the SDA first purchased property in Mussoorie in 1907 for a sanitarium and a place where the SDA workers '...could go for a rest from the hot and humid climate of coastal cities and the torrid heat of the interior. Late in 1907 the work of the Calcutta Sanitarium was transferred there.' (Neufeld, Don F., ed., *Seventh-day Adventist Encyclopedia*, Second Revised Edition, Vol I, Hagerstown, Maryland [USA]: Review and Herald Publishing Association, 1966: 750).

Vincent Hill principals were Mrs Edith Bruce, 1911-1913; G.F. Furnival, 1914-1919; T.D. Rowe, 1920-1921; A.J. Olson, 1922-1927; I.F. Blue, 1927-1930; D.W. McKinley (acting), 1931; I.F. Blue, 1932-1939; R.A. Garner, 1939-1942; C.A. Schutt, 1943-1945; H.T. Terry, 1946-1947; R.E. Rice (acting), 1948; W.C. Mackett, 1948-1952; M.O. Manley, 1952-1955; H.H. Mattison (acting), 1956; M.O. Manley, 1957-1962; W.G. Jensen, 1962-1964; A.W. Matheson, 1964-1967; I.D. Higgins, 1967-1969.

73. Williams, Ibid, p. 63-64.

74. Neufeld, Don F., ed., *Seventh-day Adventist Encyclopedia*, Second Revised Edition, Vol II, Hagerstown, Maryland (USA): Review and Herald Publishing Association, 1966: 839-840. Information also provided in private correspondence with Peter Haynal, USA, a former VHS student.

75. St Clare's School property includes what was once the Hindustan Hotel in lower Landour.

76. Chatterton, Eyre, *A History of the Church of England in India*, London: SPCK, 1924, Chapter XXII.

An 1860s photograph showing Christ Church much as it looks today. Christ Church dates back to 1836, and is the oldest Protestant church in the Himalayas. The church celebrated its 175th anniversary in May 2011. *(Photo kind courtesy of Peter Tiller and Marilyn Metz, London)*

6

EYES TO THE HILLS

I will lift up mine eyes to the hills, from whence cometh my help.
~ Psalm 121.1 (Holy Bible) ~

An 1884 guidebook to Mussoorie recorded that '…In 1835, the European population felt strong enough to build a church…'[1] And then some! For by 1907, there were no less than eight churches in Mussoorie and Landour, and a second St Emilian's on Club Hill was under construction (the first was destroyed in the 1905 earthquake).

Of these earliest churches, all but two continue to this day, and many more houses of worship of all faiths have been added to the ecclesiastical landscape.

Given the British provenance of the town, it is hardly surprising that some of the most prominent—and certainly among the oldest, if not the oldest—houses of worship in Mussoorie are Christian ones. The earliest of these churches were built for the European residents. During the early years of British India 'official Christianity' was not of the proselytizing kind, even though '...it was always assertive and assured, knowing itself to stand somewhere near the centre of imperial power, and it provided an inescapable reference point among the stones of empire.'[2]

Just as at the centre of English villages stood an Anglican church, so too in the hill stations of India. Later, other churches were built by missionary groups, primarily to serve local Indian Christians[3], but it was invariably an Anglican church that took centre stage.

Mussoorie was no exception.

The oldest Protestant church in Mussoorie—and, indeed, the oldest such church in the entire Himalayan region—is Christ Church, the foundation stone of which was laid on 16 May 1836 by the bishop of Calcutta and metropolitan of the (Anglican) Church of England in India, Reverend Daniel Wilson. On that day, Reverend Wilson wrote in his diary:

Dorothy 'Dollie' Hickie was for forty years the organist at Christ Church. The youngest daughter of Michael Corbett Hickie, who was a tax collector in Delhi, Dollie lived most of her life at Henry Villa, to the west of Library Bazaar. She died in 1917 and was buried in Camel's Back Cemetery. There is a memorial plaque in Christ Church fondly remembering her years of service to the church, and there are plans afoot to renovate the historic organ that Dollie played.

(Kind courtesy of Richard Hickie, United Kingdom)

On Saturday [16 May 1836] we laid the foundation stone of Christ Church, Mussoorie. The whole Christian population poured out; I suppose four or five hundred persons. The scene on the gently sloping side of the hill was exquisite and the entire ground around the circuit of the foundations was crowded. The Himalayan Mountains never witnessed such a sight. I began with some prayers from the service for consecrating churches, slightly varied. Then my chaplain read Psalm lxxxvii. Mr Proby read Haggai 1st; and the whole assembly sung the hundredth psalm. I made a short address. The senior civilian, Mr. Hutchinson, next read the deed of gift. Colonel Young, Political Agent (the King, in fact, of the Dhoon) read a copy of the inscription. All was now ready, and I descended into the deep cavity in the mountain and laid the stone in the name of the Father, the Son, and the Holy Ghost. The Lord's Prayer and Benediction closed the service. As we were departing, the band of the Ghoorka regiment struck up the National Anthem, which echoing and re-echoing amongst the mountains, was the finest thing I ever heard. Afterwards I entertained the Committee at dinner. We sat down, twenty-one, in camp fashion – each one sending his own chair, knives, forks, plates, and spoons. God be magnified! The whole celebration was unique. It will be the first church raised amidst the eternal snows of Upper India, and all planned, executed, and money raised in a single month. Nine months will finish it.[4]

Wilson came back to Mussoorie and consecrated the church in April 1839.

But before this stone-laying occasion, there had been some controversy within the young congregation regarding an ideal location for the church, although from the beginning there was probably little doubt that this church, which would serve the British civil establishment, would corner an excellent spot somewhere along the Mussoorie ridge. Initially, a site was selected near Zephyr Hall in the Kulri section of the Station, but this was opposed by Mr John Mackinnon, founder of the Mussoorie Seminary and '…one of the leading men in Mussoorie owing to his energy and public spirit', on account of the distance from his school. At this time, his seminary was located far to the west at the foot of Benog Hill, beyond what is today the Lal Bahadur Shastri National Academy of Administration. A happy compromise was much facilitated when Mr J.C. Proby of Meerut donated a plot '…out of his own garden'[5] near the Mussoorie Library, just above where the Camel's Back and Mall roads meet.

Who was this generous donor, now rarely remembered? Schooled at Rugby and Cambridge, John Carysfort Proby (b.1798–d.1868) was an East India Company chaplain in the Bengal Presidency from 1824–1843, serving in Calcutta, Allahabad and Meerut. Proby was the son of a minister, and he married a minister's daughter, Lydia Martin Brown, in Calcutta in 1826. While posted to Meerut, three of their young children died within a four-month period in early 1836, the same year that he donated a portion of his Mussoorie land for the establishment of Christ Church. It was a poignant tribute to a man's faith, no doubt sorely tried by the sudden loss of his little children. In 1846, ten years after Christ Church had been established, the surviving Proby family returned to Cheesehill, Winchester, where Reverend Proby had served before leaving for India.[6]

Bishop Wilson had no misgivings about the kind of building that should be constructed for this early church in the Himalayas. '…This will be the first church built in India after the pattern of an English parish church…' Wilson recorded in his diary. And indeed, the church is a classic of Cotswold-style ecclesiastical architecture. Built with private donations, the tower and nave (main section) of the church were erected under the leadership of Captain Rennie Tailyour of the Bengal Engineers. When the chancel (altar and choir area) and side transepts were added in 1853, the church presented—as it still does—a classic cruciform shape, in that the layout of the building is in the shape of a cross. In 1870, Mr Lionel Douglas Hearsey, member of the locally well-known Hearsey family and grandson of Hyder Young Hearsey, donated the bell chimes that are in the tower, today only sparingly used. The first Christ Church chaplain was Reverend Henry Smith.

As the premier church in the Station, Christ Church attracted in its early days a large Sunday crowd during the Season. Mrs Robert Moss King, wife of the collector of Meerut, records the scene outside Christ Church on Sunday, 16 October 1878:

> It is a funny sight to a newcomer on going to church to see the crowds of dandies ranged outside, looking like miniature canoes that have been beached. If the congregation consist of 200 woman and 100 men, that means 200 dandies, which, with an average of three coolies to each, gives 600 attendant coolies, besides 100 ponies and 100 syces. So you can fancy the crowd outside the church. An Indian crowd, however, is never noisy or rough, and somehow or other everyone finds his pony or dandy without any trouble.[7]

There is a deodar tree (*Cedrus deodara*) in the Christ Church gardens that, as noted on a plaque, was planted after morning worship on 4 March 1906 by Mary of Teck,

HRH the Princess of Wales, who later became Queen Mary. She and the Prince of Wales (later, King George V) were on a tour of India at the time, and the princess had come up to the hills for a visit, planned at the last minute (see Chapter 9). The tree still stands, and there is a recently restored railing and a second, new plaque to commemorate the 1999–2000 repair work.

In the 1930s, there occurred an incident at Christ Church that showed a rather less-than-sympathetic government attitude, even towards frailty and illness among her 'subjects'. The incident and government reaction to it is amusingly recorded by 'The Rambler' in his 1936 guidebook:

(L) Christ Church was constructed in 1836 under the leadership of Captain Rennie Tailyour, Bengal Engineers, with additions undertaken in 1853. The above inscription, which can still be seen in the church, reads: Christ Church, Mussoorie, Nave and Tower erected, by private subscription, A.D. 1836. Transepts, Chancel and Gothic Roof added, by private subscription, A.D. 1853. Architect:- Captain Thomas Renny Tailyour, Bengal Engineers. Chaplain:- The Reverend Henry Smith, M. A.'
(Kind courtesy of Marty de Montereau, France)
(R) The historic William Hill pipe organ in Christ Church. It has not functioned since the 1960s, but efforts are underway to restore it. *(Kind courtesy of Marty de Montereau, France)*
In 1888, Mussoorie's Beacon Press released *Mussoorie Portraits in Rhyme, Taken during the Season by 'May'*. Christ Church was home to the Mussoorie Choral Society, and one of the verses rhymed praises for fundraising through music:

At Christ Church, all the season through
Sweet melody's been made,
And all the proceeds have been given
The Summer Home to aid. (British Library)

Pandit Motilal Nehru [the father of Jawaharlal Nehru, who had a seasonal residence in Mussoorie] was very ill in 1933 and the Reverend T.W. Chisholm, chaplain at that period, in his usual Sunday service prayers for the sick sought God's help for the Pandit. There was an immediate storm in the Government teacups and the reverend intercessory was reprimanded, so that in these years of our Lord, Holy Orders can be interpreted to mean wholly Government orders.[8]

Reverend Erik Templeton, Christ Church priest, standing between Skinner's Horse (1st Horse) honour guards at the October 2005 dedication of a memorial plaque to Brigadier Michael Alexander Robert Skinner, commander of the Indian army's Skinner's Horse (1960–1963) and a leading member of Christ Church. Michael Skinner's great-great-grandfather, James Hercules Skinner, raised Skinner's Horse in 1803. There are numerous other memorial plaques in Christ Church, dating to as early as 1851.
(From the authors' private collection)

Over the years, Christ Church has most certainly had its ups and downs. As it had been a house of worship almost exclusively for the British, their departure in the 1940s and 1950s left the church facing hard times. Its membership plummeted and the building fell into near ruin. Even as recently as 1997, Ruth Unrau wrote, '…There is no money now to restore this once vital church, to replace broken window panes, to paint walls, or to fix the roof. It is sad to see a church die.'[9]

Happily, Unrau's gloom and doom prognosis didn't materialize. Christ Church was saved from the wrecking ball largely through the efforts of the redoubtable Maisie Gantzer, secretary of the Save Mussoorie Society (see Chapter 10). And particularly in the last ten years, Christ Church has come back to a more active life, with the restoration of its beautiful and historic stained-glass windows[10] and numerous other improvements that have been funded by both grant-making foundations and individual donors of many faiths, who have been keenly interested in the preservation of this valuable historic site.

The interior walls of the church are covered with memorial plaques, evocative reminders of its colonial *and* more recent past. The newest inscription honours the memory of the late Brigadier Michael ('Mike') Alexander Robert Skinner (b.1920–d.1999). Brigadier Skinner served as commander of his ancestor's Skinner's Horse (1st Horse) from 1960–1963. He was a native of Mussoorie and an active member of Christ Church (see Chapter 10).

Today, Christ Church is one of three parishes in Mussoorie that are part of the Church of North India (CNI) that was formed in 1970 from the merger of several strands of Protestantism.[11] Its architectural features and, in particular, its coloured windows and evocative memorial inscriptions make it a popular tourist attraction.

Christ Church was an Anglican (Church of England) establishment, and so was St Paul's in Landour, the garrison church which was consecrated on 1 May 1840, again by Bishop Wilson. (Apparently, the good bishop enjoyed coming up to Mussoorie, which was not an easy trip from Calcutta in the mid 1800s.) Thus, both churches are of the same vintage and, in fact, present a similar exterior appearance, although St Paul's is somewhat the smaller of the two. Whereas Christ Church mainly served English civilians—many of whom were the 'leading citizens' of their day—St Paul's was primarily used by British (Protestant) officers and soldiers stationed, recuperating or on leave in the cantonment. Recognizing St Paul's close association with the military establishment, it was amusingly referred to in 1884 by Mrs Robert Moss as 'the church militant'.[12] Jim Corbett's parents were married in St Paul's in 1859.[13] Carol Evans and Tom Alter, the Bollywood star and 2008 recipient of the Government of India's Padma Shri Award, were married there in 1978.

With its military connections severed after 1947, St Paul's managed to 'hang on' in the cantonment with support from a core group of foreign and Indian staff from Woodstock School. But even so, St Paul's was closed over the years on an off-again-on-again basis. Today, its band of worshippers still includes school and local residents; and recently the building itself has been completely renovated through the generosity of Mr Sanjay Narang, a well-to-do Woodstock graduate, who fondly remembers from his student days this centerpiece in the Char Dukan (four shops) area of the cantonment.

From 1840 until 1848, Christ Church and St Paul's were served by the same chaplain (priest). However, by 1848, both congregations had grown sufficiently to each have their own priest. Today, two ministers serve these parishes, together with the Hindustani Church on the campus of Woodstock School.

St Paul's Church in Landour was established in 1840 for use primarily by British officers and
soldiers in the cantonment. The building was renovated in 2008 and now serves a
civilian congregation, made up largely of Woodstock School staff and students.
(Courtesy of the National Army Museum, London)

The third of the earliest Anglican (Church of England) houses of worship in the
Station was All Saints' Church on the grounds of the Castle Hill Estate. This church
was built for the convenience of residents by Mr George Bladen Taylor who owned
the estate before it was taken over by the government and became Castle Hill.
It is said that Reverend Robert North Maddock laid the foundation stone and
the boys of his school sang in the choir.[14] By 1948, All Saints' was no longer in
use and, with permission from the Anglican bishop of Lucknow, the building was
dismantled. The material and fittings, such as the pulpit, moved to the Hindustani
Church building.[15]

A rare photo of All Saints' Church (far left), on the grounds of the Castle Hill Estate, circa 1880s. The church building no longer exists. *(Courtesy of British Library)*

Later, two other Anglican churches came up in the Station. These were Hooper Memorial Church, near the Charleville Hotel or what today is the Lal Bahadur Shastri National Academy of Administration, and the Church of the Redemption near the Ralston Estate in Barlowganj. The Hooper Church was named after Reverend William Hooper (b.1837–d.1922, in Mussoorie). In the early 1900s, Hooper was also the in-charge at All Saints' Church. Reverend Hooper had been a Boden Sanskrit Scholar at Oxford University, principal of St Paul's Divinity School in Allahabad (1881–1887) and, most famously, author of Hebrew–Urdu and Greek–Hindi dictionaries and many other works.[16] From 1890 until his death, Hooper resided in Mussoorie, officially as examining chaplain to the bishop of Lucknow, but also much involved in his own writings. There is a hall named in Reverend Hooper's honour at Wynberg Allen School. Today, neither Hooper nor Redemption is functioning as a house of worship. In 1979, the Church of the Redemption became part of the Hill Bird School (Eileen M. Rayner's Memorial Home). There was also an Anglican chapel on the grounds of Maddock's School, but the building no longer exists (see picture in Chapter 5).

Hooper Church near the Lal Bahadur Shastri Academy (L) and the Church of the Redemption in Barlowganj (R) were both small, community Anglican chapels. Neither Hooper nor Redemption is any longer functioning as a church, although both buildings still exist.
(Photos kind courtesy of Mela Ram & Sons, Mussoorie)

The Hindustani Church[17] was established in 1876 by the Ludhiana Presbyterian Mission to serve primarily the Indian Christian workers at Woodstock School, which it does to this day. In 1920, the church started a small school for the children of Woodstock workers. In 1961, this school was taken on by the City Board of Mussoorie and moved to a new building, below Tehri Road and not far from the church itself. It continues to function as a government-run, neighbourhood primary school. The current Hindustani Church building, including a ground floor parsonage, was completed in 1956 on a site levelled for the purpose on the Woodstock campus (previously, the Hindustani congregation had met in a room above servants' quarters on the Woodstock campus).

Of all the early supporters of the Hindustani Church, the one most often remembered, even today, is Miss Edith M. Jones, nicknamed 'Jonah' by her students, who for many years and until her retirement in 1944 was the Hindi/Urdu teacher at Woodstock School.

Miss Edith Jones, in particular, faithfully visited the sick, took meetings and… classes with the servants' wives and was well-loved by the servant community… On Good Friday, April 19, 1946 Miss Jones of the North India Mission, who had retired from Woodstock in January 1944, died at the Coronation Hospital in Dehra Dun. Her body was brought to Mussoorie and on Easter Saturday a funeral service took place in Parker Hall…Miss Jones had asked to be buried in the Indian Christian Cemetery below the College (Midlands). The funeral procession stopped at the Indian [Hindustani] Church, where a second service was held in Hindustani. After the service, the servants of Woodstock School carried the body of their well-loved friend to its last resting place.[18]

Miss Edith M. Jones, for many years the Hindi and Urdu teacher at Woodstock School, was a faithful supporter of the Hindustani Church on the campus of Woodstock School. This photograph of Miss Jones hangs to this day in the church. At her request, she was buried in the cemetery below Midlands and the Hindustani Church. *(Photo from Jones, Edith, Caroline Wilkie and Mary I. McGee,* Woodstock School, the First Century, *Landour: Woodstock School, second printing, 1999 [first printing, 1954])*

The Landour Union Church was formally established on 16 September 1868. A year later, in 1869, it was renamed the Mussoorie and Landour Union Church. This was an inter-denominational church, which in the early days was sometimes called 'non-conformist', in that it did not follow Church of England teachings. Initially, its members met '…for the Season…' in what was to become the municipal building and, later, they met at Mullingar, the house that Frederick Young had built. Home-based meetings were conducted during the winter months for the few parishioners who resided permanently in Mussoorie. In 1871, a committee body of the church met to negotiate the purchase of the land on which Union Church now stands. The land was bought from the estate of Mr Charles Grant, a major landowner in Mussoorie.[19] The deal was signed on 21 October 1872 and on 16 December 1872, the foundation stone for a new, permanent church building was laid by Sir William Muir, the lieutenant governor of the North West

Provinces. The first service in this new building was held on 1 October 1874, led by the church's first minister, Reverend Julius Frederick Ullman. Located at the foot of what was then called Club Hill in Kulri Bazaar, this building continues today as a Christian house of worship. In 1988, the church opened Hebron Elementary School, which now caters to approximately 300 local students. In 1997, Ms Ruth Unrau wrote:

> During our time, a large congregation of Indians, Anglo-Indians, and Westerners attended [Union Church]. Wynberg Allen students in their green and gray school uniforms filed in to occupy the front section of the church. We saw the congregation build a balcony to accommodate the standing-room-only assembly. Congregational health changes with the times and the personnel involved. When church attendance of students was no longer compulsory and a popular pastor retired, attendance dwindled, but now the congregation is again vital with an Indian pastor and a strong program.[20]

It is recorded that in the church's fiftieth Jubilee Year (1918), William Carey, the great-grandson of William Carey who was the pioneer Baptist missionary to India, became the pastor of Union Church.[21] George Müller, a nineteenth-century Briton famous for establishing orphanages around the world, also once ministered in this church (the George Müller Charitable Trust still operates out of the United Kingdom). The last foreign pastor of the church was an American, Reverend Charles Warren, who is credited with improving the church building and greatly expanding its ministry to the needy. The present-day pastor, Reverend G. Cornelius, who began his tenure in February 1976, was the first Indian pastor to lead Union Church.

Also in Landour, near the crest of Landour Hill, is Kellogg Church, established in 1903 with Presbyterian Mission Board and (mostly) local support. It is the last church in Mussoorie to be built by foreigners. The church was named after Dr Samuel H. Kellogg, a Presbyterian missionary, theologian and linguist from Canada, who famously wrote *A Grammar of the Hindi Language,* first published in 1875 (and still available). Kellogg met his death in Landour from a fall.[22] From 1931 onwards, the church has been non-denominational in character. In 1997, Unrau wrote about this church:

An 1880s photograph of the Union Church building, which was constructed in 1872–1874. Its activities today include running the Hebron Elementary School for local children.
(Courtesy of the Alkazi Collection of Photography, New Delhi)

The Kellogg Church building might be the replica of a small-town Midwest [USA] church, except that it sits on a knoll above the street with a long flight of steps leading to its front door. For a five-month season, Kellogg Church offered a complete program with a full-time minister, a choir, a pipe organ, and Sunday school classes, with a service in English, respite from the Indian village church where missionaries preached in a language other than their mother tongue.

[Now] the era of the Western missionary-in-charge is over. The long-sought indigenization of the church happened. Now Kellogg Church serves an Indian congregation [non-denominational] with an Indian pastor preaching in Hindi.[23]

Kellogg is also home to the Landour Language School, which was established in the late 1800s to teach Hindi to newly arrived missionaries. Today, the school's clients are mostly university students from around the world, focusing on one or another aspect of Indian studies.

An early postcard photo of Kellogg Church, founded in 1903 and named after Dr Samuel H. Kellogg, a Presbyterian missionary. Kellogg met his death in Landour from a fall which, unfortunately, is still not an uncommon event on the steep hillsides of the Station.

(Kind courtesy of the late H. Michael Stokes, Kent, United Kingdom)

Yet another Protestant denomination, the Methodists, have been active in Mussoorie from its early days.[24] One of their churches was called Mension Memorial Hall. Located in Landour Bazaar, it fell into disuse and was taken over in 1962 for commercial purposes. Presumably, this church hall served not only local Methodist families but also the faculty and students of Philander Smith School at Mullingar, a Methodist-inspired institution (see Chapter 5). The only Methodist church in the Station today is Central Methodist, built on land also purchased—for Rs 5,000—from the Grant family. (The Grant family also owned the adjoining land on which stands the current Brentwood Hotel.) Completed in May 1885, the church was originally called the Osborne Memorial Church, having been founded by Reverend Dennis Osborne and designated 'memorial' after his deceased daughter, Lily. A marble plaque at the entrance of the church reads simply, 'Our Lily'. The nave of the original structure was decorated on all four sides by clocks, which were lost during the 1905 earthquake. On the grounds of this church is a plaque noting the centre of the Station, a contribution from Survey of India experts (the text on the plaque reads 'The height of the top of this pillar is 6,570.026 feet [2,003 metres] above the mean level of the sea').

An early postcard photo of Central Methodist Church on the Kulri Hill. Founded in 1885, it was formerly called the Osborne Memorial Church, named after the deceased daughter of its founder, Reverend Dennis Osborne. In the grounds of this church is a Survey of India-installed plaque, noting the exact altitude at the centre of the Station.
(Kind courtesy of the late H. Michael Stokes, Kent, United Kingdom)

St Peter's Church near the top of Landour Hill is the oldest Catholic house of worship in the Station, put up at about the same time as St Paul's (early 1840s), primarily to serve the spiritual needs of British (Catholic) soldiers in the cantonment. Constructed on land provided by Frederick Young, St Peter's is the only structure in Mussoorie and Landour that is built in the classical Greco–Roman architectural style; and certainly, it is one of the few similarly styled buildings in any of the Indian hill stations. St Peter's stood unused for many years after the departure of the British, but has recently been renovated as a worship and pilgrimage centre.

St Peter's Church in the snows. St Peter's was built in the early 1840s to serve the spiritual needs of British Catholic soldiers. It was closed for many years but in 2009, was renovated and reopened as a worship and pilgrimage centre (this picture pre-dates the renovation).
(Kind courtesy of Ajay Mark, Landour)

In response to civilian worshippers who found the long trek up to St Peter's difficult, St Emilian's[25] Church was built in 1903 on what was then called Model Hill in Landour, on property donated by a wealthy local Catholic, David Emile. The original church building was destroyed in the 1905 earthquake, but rebuilt in 1908 on a smaller scale. The current parish hall house was David Emile's boarding house. St Emilian's, now named Sacred Heart Church, continues to serve as the parish church for most Catholics in the Station, although there is also Rosary Church at St George's in Barlowganj for the Catholic workers at the school, as well as St Michael's Parish Church on St George's campus.

These, then, are the oldest of the Christian houses of worship for the more-or-less permanent residents. Over time, some churches have closed their doors and others have opened or reopened. Today, new congregations are sprouting up—or probably more likely, old ones are regrouping—as the local Christian minority sorts out its theological and liturgical preferences.

A recent interior view of Sacred Heart Catholic Church, looking towards the rear. The church was built in 1903, destroyed in the 1905 earthquake and rebuilt in 1908 on a smaller scale than the original. It continues to serve as a house of worship for Catholics in the Station.

(Photo kind courtesy of Mela Ram & Sons, Mussoorie)

However, there are also several chapels on the various Catholic-founded school campuses, built specifically to serve the faculty, staff and students at the institutions where they are located. The Anglican chapel on the campus of what was Maddock's School no longer exists (see Chapter 5), but several Catholic school-related chapels are still in use. At Waverley Convent School, there is a recently renovated historic chapel, contained within a larger multi-use building. Similarly, there is a chapel at Hampton Court School. Both the Waverley and Hampton Court chapels are used primarily by the sisters of Jesus and Mary who manage these institutions. At St George's College in Barlowganj, there is not only St Michael's Parish Church, but also a smaller chapel in the St Francis Monastery, both founded in 1871. There is also a chapel for the use of nuns at St Clare's Convent School in Landour.

The interior of the chapel at Waverley Convent School, circa 1925. The inscription above the altar, 'Hæc Est Domus Dei Et Porta Cœli', translates: 'This is the House of God and the Gate of Heaven'. All the Catholic schools in Mussoorie include historic chapels, used for worship by staff and any Catholic students. *(Photo kind courtesy of the Congregation of the Religious of Jesus and Mary, Rome)*

Because Mussoorie and Landour were founded by the British with their interests, preferences and concerns utmost in mind, the Station's Christian churches were—and still are—architecturally prominent landmarks. However, the Station has always had Hindu temples, Muslim mosques and Sikh gurdwaras.

One of the most prominent Hindu temples is the Kateswar Temple to the west, near the Lal Bahadur Shastri Academy. This temple was built by Ugrasen Verma, who also built the recently razed Clock Tower in Landour.

The entrance to the St Francis Monastery on the campus of St George's School. The monastery was established in 1871 by Capuchin missionaries. *(From the authors' collection)*

The Kateswar Temple near the Lal Bahadur Shastri Academy of Administration, built by Ugrasen Verma.
(Kind courtesy of Mela Ram & Sons, Mussoorie)

One of the most beautifully situated Hindu houses of worship is the Jwalaji Temple atop Benog Hill, to the west of the Mall. Dedicated to Lord Krishna, it offers the visitor a spectacular view of the Himalayas. Also situated on the western side of Mussoorie, about 15 miles from the library, is the Bhadraj Temple, dedicated to Lord Bal Bhadra, brother of Lord Krishna. From here, there are commanding views of the Dun Valley and Chakrata hills. Similarly excellent views of the Dun and Mussoorie may be had from the ancient Nag Devta ('snake god' i.e., Lord Shiva) Temple located on the Mackinnon Cart Road about 3.7 miles (6 kms) from Mussoorie on the way to Dehra Dun. Much further away from the Station is the Surkhunda Devi Temple, 22 miles (35 kms) to the east, past Danaulti.

There are many other places of Hindu worship in the Station, most of them more recently constructed. These include the Laxmi Narayan Temple (library), the Radha Krishna Temple (Picture Palace) and the Sanatan Dharam Temple (Landour). Also, there is an Arya Samaj Temple (Landour), a Sai Baba Temple (Kulri) and the Shri Digambar Jain Temple (Landour).

The Station has four mosques. There are two Jama Masjids (one in Kulri and another in Landour), the Masjid Bucharkhana (Landour) and the Masjid Amania (library). There is also the Babu Bulleh Shah Mazar cenotaph below Wynberg Allen School. This is a 'symbolic tomb' of the Sufi saint, mystic and poet Babu Bulleh Shah (b.1680–d.1758), who was actually buried in Kasur, near the Indo–Pakistan Wagah border site (famous for its daily flag-lowering ceremony).

There are three Sikh gurdwaras in the Station, the Gurdwara Sahib Trust (Landour), the Gurdwara Sahib Trust (Mussoorie) and the Gurdwara Sri Guru Singh Sahib (Landour). The well-known Guru Nanak Fifth Centenary School located on the Vincent Hill Estate (see Chapter 5) has a gurdwara on campus, available for students and teachers.

More recently, with the arrival of Tibetans, there is the lovely Shedup Choephelling Temple in Happy Valley, near where the tennis courts were in earlier times. This Buddhist temple, distinguished from a 'monastery', which has religious educational facilities, was built by the Tibetan Homes Foundation in 1959 and is believed to be the first Tibetan Buddhist religious house built after the exile of His Holiness, the Fourteenth Dalai Lama. The temple houses a library of 102 volumes of Buddhist teachings, tomes carried out of Tibet by refugees and presented to the temple's library by the Dalai Lama when he was visiting Mussoorie in 1959.[26] The first floor of the temple includes a special chamber, attached to a prayer room, which serves as the Dalai Lama's quarters whenever he visits Mussoorie. The temple is maintained by the Tibetan Homes Foundation, and run on a daily basis by two monks who organize and lead all religious activities.

(Above) A view of Jama Masjid, Landour, from the road heading up to Sisters' Bazaar. *(Kind courtesy of Mela Ram & Sons, Mussoorie)*

(Above) The interior of one of the Station's most prominent gurdwaras, the Mussoorie Gurdwara Sahib Trust, located at the entrance to Library Chowk.
(Kind courtesy of Mela Ram & Sons, Mussoorie)

(Left) An interior view of the Shedup Choephelling Temple in Happy Valley.
(Kind courtesy of Mela Ram & Sons, Mussoorie)

As part of a discussion of religious edifices in the Station, it is appropriate to mention the several cemeteries that are supported by their religious communities. Most of these cemeteries are still in use, despite certain difficulties, as noted by Theon Wilkinson in his 1976 book, *Two Monsoons*:

> At hill stations, such as Mussoorie, where the ground was so rocky that it took two days to prepare a grave, there were always two spare graves dug ready for the next burial, and the practice has continued to this day.[27]

The Camel's Back Cemetery is supervised by the Mussoorie Cemetery Association, whereas the Landour Cemetery is overseen by a committee made up of representatives from Kellogg Church, the Roman Catholic Church and the Church of North India. However, the very earliest European grave in the Station is actually not in one of these or any other cemetery compound but rather, stands as a solitary memorial in Jharapani.

'The Rambler' related this story in 1936:

> Located near the former Halfway House, was the burial site of a sick officer on his way to Landour, '…whither he was repairing as a last hope…'
>
> It was not till April 1829 that regular batches of invalids began to come to Landour to recoup, but a few isolated cases were sent up earlier, one of whom died before reaching Landour, and his is the first European grave in the Station if we accept Jharipani as part of the Station, for that is where his remains lie. His resting place is by the side of the Rajpur-Mussoorie Bridle Path, to the left of the 'Halfway House', and used to be covered by a crumbling and fast disappearing obelisk which once bore a tablet which read: 'Sacred to the memory of Sir Charles Farrington, Bart. Captain of Her Majesty's 35th [sic, actually 31st] Regiment, who departed this life on the [sic] 28th March 1828. Aged 35 years.' The obelisk has now not only been rebuilt, but has also been moved into the Oak Grove School's estate.[28]

The story of this lone grave marker picks up again fifty years later, for in 1988 it moved again, disappearing down the hillside during a landslip. Subsequently, a number of accidents occurred on the Oak Grove campus (an ambulance fell off the road, a student died) and these unfortunate incidents were connected with the 'good luck marker' no longer there. Thus, it was re-erected but alas, without the original inscription. Recent restoration efforts by the Farrington family and Oak Grove friends reset the original inscription.[29]

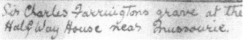

(L) A 1907 photograph of the gravesite of Captain Charles Farrington near Oak Grove School, the oldest grave in the Station (1828). Captain Farrington, the second baronet of Blackheath, died en route to the then recently opened convalescent depot for soldiers in Landour, '…whither he was repairing as a last hope…' (R) The memorial was restored in 2011. The plaques read:

'Sacred to the Memory of Sir Charles Henry Farrington Bart
Late Captain HMS 31st Regiment who Departed This Life 26th day of March 1828
In the 35th Year of his Age'

'Restored in 2011 by
Oak Grove School, Friends and the Farrington Family'
(Kind courtesy of Sue Farrington, England, and Robert Butler, Albania)

Besides Sir Charles Farrington's lone gravesite, there are, amidst the tall deodars on mossy hillsides, the several Mussoorie and Landour cemeteries that stand as silent reminders of the station's history, for:

> … what of those who are with us forever – those who sleep under the crosses that dot the eastern slope of Landour and of Camel's Back? Even in these prosaic times there is, for the diligent seeker, a lavish store of knowledge in a quiet walk through our cemeteries.[30]

But '..those who sleep...' were not all '...under the crosses...', for the Station has had from its earliest days both Muslim and Parsi cemeteries as well (the latter is not used now, as there is no longer a permanent Parsi community in the Station). Nonetheless, the Christian cemeteries are the oldest. Bishop Wilson consecrated the Landour Cemetery on 4 May 1840 and the Camel's Back Cemetery on 11 May 1840 (on this same visit, the bishop consecrated St Paul's Church). The earliest grave marker is that of Captain George Bolton. He died just three months after Sir Charles Farrington. Captain Bolton is buried in the Protestant section of the Landour Cemetery with this inscription:

Sacred to the Memory of
CAPTAIN GEORGE BOLTON
H.C.'s [Honourable Company's] 2nd European Regi[ment] who after some
Months of painful suffering, departed this
Life on the 13th of June in the year of our
Lord 1828. Aged 40.
His virtuous and amiable disposition
Rendered him generally beloved
In life and lamented in death.
This Memorial is erected by his affectionate Widow as the last
Earthly tribute of affection &
Respect to an indulgent &
Affectionate Husband.

I am the Resurrection & the
Life saith the Lord, he that
Believeth in me though he were
Dead yet shall he live.
Whosoever believeth
In me shall never die.
John 11.25-26

The Landour Cemetery is on what used to be called the Landour Mall, or Upper Chakkar/Upper Circular Road, with the Protestant section on the upper side and the Catholic section below, though that distinction is no longer maintained. Within the cemetery grounds, there is a deodar tree planted in 1870 by Alfred, duke of Edinburgh, which the Princess of Wales visited in the winter of 1906:

> Landour was covered with more than a foot of snow, and some of the roads were impassable. However a path was dug to the cemetery where the tree planted by [Alfred] the Duke of Edinburgh was seen to be flourishing exceedingly.[31]

(L) The lych gate at the Landour Cemetery, which originally had its Catholic and Protestant sections.
(Courtesy of Mela Ram & Sons, Mussoorie)
(R) The lych gate of the Camel's Back Cemetery, wherein are buried the remains of some of Mussoorie's most notable historic figures.
(Kind courtesy of the late H. Michael Stokes, Kent, United Kingdom)
Both cemeteries continue to be used by the Mussoorie–Landour Christian Community.

The Camel's Back Cemetery is on the north side of Camel's Back Road, and alongside it is the Parsi Cemetery. Within the Christian cemetery, there is a small Jewish section where some members of the Hakman family (of hotel fame) are buried. There are several other notables buried here, including Sir Henry Bohle (b.1783–d.1851) who established the first brewery in the Station. Perhaps reflecting his standing as a brewer with solid finances, his tombstone is the most imposing in the entire

The largest and most imposing headstone in the Camel's Back Cemetery is that of Sir Henry Bohle who started two breweries in Mussoorie, the Old Brewery and Bohle's Brewery.
(Photo kind courtesy of Mela Ram & Sons, Mussoorie)

Camel's Back Cemetery. Other 'worthies' buried here include John Lang (d.1864), the first Australian-born novelist who wrote for Charles Dickens's *Household Words* (see Chapter 10), John A. Hindmarsh (d.1890), one of the few survivors from '…the jaws of Death…' at Balaclava during the Crimean War (1853–1856)[32], and Frederick ('Pahari') Wilson and his second wife Gulabi (see Chapter 10).

There are also two Christian cemeteries on the grounds of St George's School, one next to St Michael's Parish Church, where former priests and brothers are buried, and another some distance away down the hillside. On the Woodstock School campus there is the Indian Christian Cemetery where Edith M. Jones is buried.

There are two Muslim cemeteries in town, under the management of the local mosques. The older is located on the Tehri Road below Woodstock School. A newer cemetery, Shergarhi Kabristan, was established within the last ten years and can be seen on the Mussoorie–Dehra Dun road below Kincraig.

These houses of worship and sacred burial sites clearly link to Mussoorie's past, yet they also reflect aspects of life in the Station for many of today's residents. Truly, whether '…eyes to the hills…' in worship or '…with us forever…' in cemeteries, these edifices stand as witnesses of both the past and present.

Notes

1.   Northam, John, *Guide to Masuri, Landaur, Dehra Dun and the Hills North of Dehra*, Calcutta: Thacker, Spink and Company, 1884 (reprinted by Pagoda Tree Press, Bath, 2007: 26).

2. Morris, Jan, *Stones of Empire*, Oxford: Oxford University Press, 1983: 158.

3. '...After 1857 the British Raj shifted its policy from lukewarm support for the missionaries to outright disapproval' (Luce, Edward, *In Spite of the Gods*, London: Abacus, 2007: 310). Until the Charter Act of 1813, the East India Company actually blocked the entry of missionaries into India, so it was only between the years of 1813–1857 that there was company-sanctioned 'lukewarm support' for foreign missionaries. In any case, before and after company rule, missionaries were usually looked down upon by the status-conscious British ruling class in India.

4. Bateman, Josiah, *The Life of the Right Rev. Daniel Wilson, D.D., Late Lord Bishop of Calcutta and Metropolitan of India*, London: John Murray, 1860: 108-109.

5. Ibid, p. 109.

6. Information from *Crockford's Clerical Directory for 1860, being a Biographical and Statistical Book of Reference for Facts relating to the Clergy and Church*, London, 1860.

7. King, Mrs. Robert Moss, *The Diary of a Civilian's Wife in India, 1877-1882*, London: Richard Bentley & Son, 1884: 144-145.

8. Williams, C. ('The Rambler'), *A Mussoorie Miscellany*, Mussoorie: Mafasilite Press, 1936: 18.

9. Unrau, Ruth, *Hill Station Teacher*, Kansas: Kidron Creek Publishers, 1997: 47-48.

10. The restoration of the Christ Church windows was undertaken during 2002–2003 by M.N. Manikandan of Thrissur, Kerala, assisted by a team of other young artisans, also from Kerala. Manikandan was first introduced to the art of restoration and conservation at the Indian National Trust for Art and Cultural Heritage (INTACH), New Delhi. He is a protégé of the world-renowned stained-glass artisan, Alfred Fischer, who recently created the Golden Jubilee window in Queen Elizabeth II's chapel at Buckingham Palace.

11. Christ Church became a part of the Church of North India on 29 November 1970 (the first Sunday in the pre-Christmas 'Advent' season), when the CNI was formed from the ecumenical union of six Protestant denominations: Church of India, Pakistan, Burma and Ceylon (Anglican); United Church of North India (Presbyterian and Congregational); Methodist Church (British and Australian Conference); Church of the Brethren; Church of the Disciples of Christ; and Council of the Baptist Churches in Northern India. Today, Christ Church is part of the CNI's Diocese of Agra. Its style of Christian worship remains similar to what it always was, although with more inclusive aspects.

12. King, Ibid, p. 144.

13. Christopher William Corbett, a widower and Assistant Apothecary with the Horse Artillery Regiment, was posted to Landour in the 1850s. As recorded in the register at St Paul's, he married Mary Janet Doyle, also widowed, at the church on 13 October 1859. It is their son, Jim, after whom the Jim Corbett National Park is named. Having managed to escape from the Agra Fort in 1857 with her three children born from her first husband who was killed at the Battle of Harchandpur (Rae Bareli, Uttar Pradesh state) in 1858, Mary and family had taken refuge in Mussoorie, which was relatively safe during this 'Mutiny' period. After Mary and Christopher had married, both for the second time, Christopher left the military

and joined the postal service in Mussoorie. In 1862, he was transferred by the postal service to Nainital, where Mary established a successful house rental agency and where, years later, their son Jim made his reputation as a big-game hunter, naturalist, landlord and author.

14. Williams, C. ('The Rambler'), Ibid, p. 36.

15. '...The material from All Saints' Church was brought over [to the Woodstock campus] at a cost of Rs 2,000/-, and stored on the site' (information from an unpublished booklet, *Woodstock Hindustani Church, Early History*, apparently anonymously written circa 1970).

16. Reverend William Hooper, DD (Doctorate of Divinity) authored many publications besides his dictionaries, among them *Christian Doctrine in Contrast with Hinduism and Islam*, 1891; *Helps to the Attainment of Hindustani Idiom*, 1901; *The Doctrine of Salvation as set forth in Christianity, Hinduism, and Islam*, 1906; and *The Hindustani Language*, 1917.

17. Originally called the Hindustani Church, the name was changed in the 1950s to Landour Memorial Church, in honour of the four persons who had particularly promoted the welfare of the church: Miss Edith M. Jones, for many years and until 1944 the Hindi/Urdu instructor at Woodstock School; Rev. Allen E. Parker, Woodstock co-principal with his wife during the inter-war years (1922–1939); Rev. Samuel David, Woodstock employee and senior member of the church, who upon retirement from Woodstock School in 1946 and until his death in 1950 served as pastor at the church; and Dr D. Emmet Alter, Woodstock principal (1932–1933 and 1940–1943). In 1966, at the request of the congregation, the name was changed back to the original 'Hindustani Church'.

18. Information about the Hindustani Church was taken from an unpublished booklet, *Woodstock Hindustani Church, Early History*, 1970. A copy of this booklet from the Woodstock School archives was provided to the authors by Ms Judy Crider, community relations officer, Woodstock School. Direct quotes from the booklet are from p. 4, 6 and 9.

19. Charles Grant, Senior (b.16 April 1746–d.31 October 1823) of Inverness, Scotland, came to India in 1767 to take up a military position and rose in the ranks of the British East India Company, becoming superintendent over Bengal-related trade. In 1787, Lord Cornwallis appointed Grant as a member of the East India Company's Board of Trade. Grant purportedly lived a profligate lifestyle as he climbed the ranks of the company, but after losing two children to smallpox, he underwent a religious conversion, becoming a staunch evangelical Anglican. He later served as chairman of the British East India Company, and as a member of Parliament.

His eldest son, Charles Grant Junior (b.26 October, 1778 in Kidderpore, near Calcutta–d.23 April 1866 in Cannes, France) was the first baron of Glenelg. Grant Junior served as a Scottish politician and colonial administrator, and member of Parliament. Educated at Magdalene College, Cambridge, he was called to the bar in 1807. At one point, Grant served as president of the Board of Control, where he was primarily responsible for the Act of 1833 that altered the Constitution of the Government of India. It is most likely that in the settlement of the Grant estates, well after the death of Grant Junior, some of the family's Mussoorie lands were sold to the Non-conformists (Union) and Methodist churches. The

Glenelg Estate itself, nearby to Bassett Hall, came into the possession of the maharaja of Nabha.

20. Unrau, Ibid, p. 48.

21. Information about Union Church was taken from personal interviews and a small souvenir brochure *Union Church, 1869-1994, 125 Years.*

22. Allison, Walter Leslie, *One Hundred Years of Christian Work of the North India Mission of the Presbyterian Church, USA*, Mysore: Wesley Press and Publishing House, circa 1937: 147.

23. Unrau, Ibid, p. 48.

24. 'Methodism' was started in the eighteenth century as an evangelical revival movement within the Anglican Church, inspired by the Reverend John Wesley. Later, the movement formed its own denomination.

25. St Emilian was an eighth-century Catholic bishop of Nantes, France. He is particularly remembered for saving the city of Autun from an attack by the Saracens (Muslim invaders) who had entered France by way of Spain. St Emilian died in battle on 22 August 725. This day is marked each year as St Emilian's feast day. Autun, a city rich in abbeys and monasteries, is located in what is today the modern French administrative region of Bourgogne (Burgundy).

26. Information obtained from an undated pamphlet, *Tibetan Buddhist Temple, Mussoorie (U.P.) India*, produced by the Tibetan Homes Foundation.

27. Wilkinson, Theon, *Two Monsoons, the Life and Death of Europeans in India,* London: Duckworth, 1976: 13.

28. Williams, C. ('The Rambler'), *A Mussoorie Miscellany*, Mussoorie: Mafasilite Press, 1936: 14. Captain Thomas Skinner, who wrote about his 1828 excursions in the Himalayas, was at the halfway point up to Mussoorie from Rajpur on the night that his fellow officer in the 31st Regiment, Captain Charles Farrington, died there. 'This ground [halfway up the hill to Mussoorie] is generally chosen as the first day's halting-place for the invalids, who are ascending the hills in pursuit of the health they lost in the plains. Many, no doubt, will have cause to bless it, for the air is pure and delicious. It has already, however, been marked as the last stage on earth for one whose race was closed last night. There is something extremely melancholy in the desolation of the spot, where one, who had passed so many scenes of danger, had come to die at last. He had been in nearly every battle from Talavera to Waterloo: and but a short time ago had escaped from the most appalling calamity, – for he was on board the Kent East Indiaman, when she was burnt, – to be buried where no Christian ever lived, and none before him ever died! When Napoleon, however, lies on the rock of St. Helena, it is unnecessary to moralize on the fate of a British Captain!' In a footnote, Skinner continues: 'Captain Sir Charles Farrington, 31st Regiment. I hope I may be excused this passing tribute to the memory of a brother officer, whose tomb, if erected as it was intended, will, in all probability, give his name to the spot' (Skinner, Thomas [Captain in the 31st Regiment], *Excursions in India; Including a Walk over the Himalaya Mountains, to the Sources of the Jumna and the Ganges* [2 vols.], vol. 1, second edition, London: Richard Bentley, 1833: 206-207).

29. This information was provided by Professor Rekha Sangal of Oak Grove School. A descendant of the deceased, Ms Sue Farrington of England, undertook, with the help of others, the replacement of a replica plaque on the already re-erected marker. Ms Farrington is a very active member of BACSA, the British Association of Cemeteries in South Asia, and an expert on the Raj-era graveyards of the subcontinent.

30. Williams, C. ('The Rambler'), Ibid, p. 110.

31. Reed, Stanley, *The Royal Tour in India, A Record of the Tour of T.R.H. The Prince and Princess of Wales in India and Burma, from November 1905 to March 1906*, Bombay: Bennett, Coleman & Co., 1906: 412.

32. Alfred, Lord Tennyson memorialized the Battle of Balaclava in his poetic rendering, 'The Charge of the Light Brigade' (1870). Here is an excerpt:

> Cannon to right of them,
> Cannon to left of them,
> Cannon in front of them
> Volley'd and thunder'd;
> Storm'd at with shot and shell,
> Boldly they rode and well,
> Into the jaws of Death,
> Into the mouth of Hell
> Rode the six hundred.

Members of the Himalaya Club in 1884. The club was founded in 1841, with Frederick Young as its first president. Strictly European and all male, the club's existence was threatened in the early 1900s when the popular Happy Valley Club opened to the west; whereupon, in order to make the Himalaya Club more viable, management decided to open the residential quarters to married members. Shortly after the First World War, elitism put paid to the club and, today, the much altered building is the Himalaya Club Hotel.

(Kind courtesy of Hugh Ashley Rayner, United Kingdom)

7

COMMUNITY LIFE IN THE CLOUDS

A burning sun in cloudless skies
And April dies,
A dusty Mall—three sunsets splendid—
And May is ended,
Grey mud beneath—grey cloud o'erhead
And June is dead.
A little bill in late July
And then we fly.
~ Rudyard Kipling, Verses on the Charleville Hotel[1] ~

Joseph Rudyard Kipling, celebrated poet and teller of tales about British India, may have 'fled' Mussoorie in late July but, in fact, the Season extended from April through October, the six months when the heat of the plains inspired any Europeans to bundle off to the hills. And in Mussoorie, like in other hill stations, numerous institutions were established that became central to the lifestyle of the Europeans (mostly British) and some Indians (many of them royalty), who had the means to spend the Season in the bracing, alpine climate of the Himalayas. Mussoorie had its many schools, churches, the cantonment, its ever-improving civic infrastructure and of course its bracing air, but entertainment was also required in the Station to assure an enjoyable sojourn in the hills.

Foremost among the institutions that emerged to entertain this elite clientele were the clubs, which provided its members with a relaxed yet exclusive environment. Anthony Wild in his book, *Remains of the Raj*, put it this way:

[Clubs in India were] a home from home and daily reaffirmation of the virtues of fair play and honourable behavior, and the ultimate expression of the Empire builders' apartheid mentality. The reassuring rustle of newspapers and chiming of a well-wound clock spoke of permanence, standards and an unswerving Britishness... [the hill station clubs, in particular] were specifically designed to re-create an ideal of Englishness.[2]

This 'ideal of Englishness' excluded Indians, particularly in the early years. Such racism did, in fact, begin to change towards the end of the Victorian period, although some clubs remained steadfastly British until Independence, when they closed. Clubs were also sexist, especially by today's terms. Women were excluded as members, although sometimes provided with separate facilities. But the discrimination didn't stop there, for certainly not just any Englishman could enter. As 'The Rambler' put it in 1936, with regard to Mussoorie's top drawer Himalaya Club:

> It [the Himalaya Club] was a terribly 'select' institution and while merchants were permitted entry mere tradesmen were taboo! Such a vast distinction was, perhaps, adjudged on whether one sold tin cans or tin cars.[3]

An 1866 photograph of the exclusive Himalaya Club, which was located on Club Hill in Landour. Note the thatched roofs that were later replaced by galvanized tin. The round building (lower centre) was the ice house. An original of this photograph hangs in the Oriental Club in London.

(Kind courtesy of the Oriental Club, London; David Swain, secretary)

The Himalaya Club was the apex of Station society for eight decades. Founded in 1841 on what was then called Club Hill, it started with 148 members. By 1907, there were 775 temporary and permanent members. Membership was by balloting and '...one black ball in six excludes.' The entrance fee was Rs 100 but could be paid in monthly instalments of Rs 10 per month. The first president of the Himalaya Club was Colonel Frederick Young (see Chapter 1), although the initial organizing of the club '...was in great measure due to Lieutenant (now General) Showers.'[4] The vice president was George Bacon and the honorary secretary was Captain F. Angelo.

In 1907, the Himalaya Club facilities were thus described:

> There are thirty-two sets of quarters in the Club buildings for bachelors, and in 'the Oaks'—a large house with two detached cottages, charmingly situated in a bright, sunny spot, with a lovely view, not far from the Club—there are eight suites for married people, one more in the small cottage and two in the large one, making elevens suites in all available for ladies. The Oaks stands in fine large grounds, and there is a good tennis court. Residents of the Oaks have the use of the rooms in the Club set apart for ladies, i.e., the ladies dining room and reading room; there is also a small library. The ladies dining room is available during the Season for luncheon and dinner parties....A 'Sticke' Court[5] was added to the Club in 1906, which is placed at the disposal of the members free of charge.[6]

Northam said in 1884 that the Himalaya Club was one of the best in India[7] and similar reports by others abound in historical records. However, the changes wrought by the Great War, including easier travel to Britain for holidays as well as the impact of the Independence movement on such an elitist facility, put paid to the club, and it ceased to function soon after the First World War. The property, or at least part of it, is now the Himalaya Club Hotel.

The second major club in Mussoorie was in Happy Valley to the west. The Happy Valley Club was a relative latecomer to the Station's social scene, but it proved to be extremely popular. Even the 1911 *Gazetteer* was enthusiastic: 'It is difficult now-a-days to imagine how Mussoorie in the old days contrived to exist without it.'[8] The Happy Valley property was owned by Bengal Civil Service and superintendent of Dehra Dun, Mr Henry Vansittart, in the 1840s, and used as a racecourse. In 1904, Mr Vincent A. Mackinnon, co-owner of Bohle's Brewery and son of John Mackinnon who founded Mussoorie Seminary, purchased the property and, subsequently, a meeting was held at the library to decide the best means of managing it. The decision was strongly in favour of an 'amusement club'—subscriptions and terms for membership were fixed, and a managing committee elected. The first managing committee had as its president Major General Henry. A family membership for the Season was set at Rs 60, with cricket, hockey, badminton and tennis facilities marking it as primarily a sports club. The Club House also had a reading room, library, card room and billiards room.

The Happy Valley Club has been most successful, and has proved a great boon, not only to the residents at the west end of Mussoorie, but to visitors generally. Organized something on the lines of the Darjeeling Amusement Club, chiefly as a place for meeting and for recreation, the games available, the books and papers, make it a favourite resort; which the fact that it is a Club, the members of which must be duly elected by the Committee, gives sundry advantages which need not be enlarged upon.[9]

A Thomas Alfred Rust photograph of the Happy Valley in 1900, prior to the Happy Valley Club being established. Before the founding of the club in 1904, this ground was used as a racecourse and for sports generally. The Charleville Hotel is seen to the right.

(Courtesy of the National Army Museum, London)

These 'sundry advantages' no doubt included keeping out 'undesirables'. However, the Happy Valley Club was never as segregated an institution as the Himalaya Club. Raj Chatterjee, a Delhi resident who spent his summers in Mussoorie as a child, recorded these memories in 2003:

Below the [Charleville] hotel sprawled the grounds of the Happy Valley Club, one of the very few clubs in India which, at the time [1920s], was open to Indians. The club had a dozen tennis courts, and a practicing wall much used by me.

My parents, who summer after summer rented a house in Happy Valley, the most attractive part of Mussoorie, were members of the Club and I was allowed to play tennis there and borrow books from the library.

Every summer the Club held a tennis tournament which was popular with visitors from all over the country. On one occasion, at the age of 13, I extended the local champion to three sets. In all honesty I should add that my handicap was plus 30 and his minus 30. The tournament provided me with some extra pocket money. I always watched the finals of the various events with my box Brownie at the ready, snapping the winners as they came off the courts mopping their brows with bits of toweling and shouting to the *abdar* [waiter] for a drink.[10]

The Happy Valley Club, founded in 1904, was popular from the outset as a social and sports club. It had twelve tennis courts and also offered cricket, hockey, badminton and billiards, as well as a library, reading room and refreshments. *(Kind courtesy of the late H. Michael Stokes, Kent, United Kingdom)*

Nonetheless, despite its popularity, the Happy Valley Club too succumbed to changing times. It closed in the mid 1930s and, by 1948, it was declared a deserted property. Today, the Happy Valley is associated with Tibetans who first started settling in Mussoorie as refugees, following the Dalai Lama's 1959 departure from his homeland. The grounds now include a beautiful Buddhist temple (see Chapter 6) and the Central School for Tibetans.

Another sporting venue was a racecourse and polo ground that, according to the *Gazetteer*, was carved out of a hillside in 1904 about a half mile (0.8 kms) below Herne Dale and to the northwest of Happy Valley. Earlier, there had been a racecourse on the Vansittart property but when that was sold and made into the Happy Valley Club, a new location had to be found.[11] To the east, there was Taylor's Flat in Landour, which was used for cricket and hockey (see Chapter 4). The racecourse and polo ground was deserted by 1948, but Taylor's Flat is still used as a playing field.

In 1904, a new racecourse and polo ground was carved out of a hillside to the northwest of Happy Valley, as a replacement for the racecourse that had been situated on the property taken over for the Happy Valley Club. Today, this property belongs to the Lal Bahadur Shastri National Academy of Administration. The academy uses it as a helipad for important visitors, and it is also used by local groups as a playing field. *(Kind courtesy of the late H. Michael Stokes, Kent, United Kingdom)*

There was also a Dehra Dun Fishing Association formed in Mussoorie in 1887. The association leased from the Siwalik Divisional Forest Officer parts of the Song, Suswa and Asan rivers for the use of its members, who paid an annual subscription of Rs 15.[12]

Yet another major sporting and entertainment facility in the Station was the Rink, which was used not only for roller skating but also as a concert hall and theatre. The Rink was built as an investment by Mr Joseph Miller, a dental surgeon in the town. Miller was the sole proprietor until 1890, when the Mussoorie Skating Rink and Amusement Club Ltd was formed. The first day-to-day manager of the Rink was a Mr Keelman, who also established the first skating rink in Calcutta. In 1894, Charles Wilson, son of Frederick 'Pahari' Wilson, became the sole proprietor. Wilson's first manager, Mr George Leslie, succeeded in making it into a major attraction with not only roller skating but also performances by the Mussoorie Amateur Dramatic Club and others but, nonetheless, the property came into the possession of the Bank of Upper India. During the First World War, Fitch & Co. leased the Rink from the bank, and it was then reputed to have returned the largest profit in its history. After the First World War, it was sold to the Mussoorie Development Co. Ltd. Boasting a skating floor that was said to be '...one of the finest in the East' the Rink featured private boxes for use during entertainments, bars and tea galleries, a billiards saloon and tennis courts. During the Roaring Twenties, Maurice E. Bandman and the Bandman Comedy Company, managed by Stephen Lopez, toured India with Mussoorie—and the Rink—as one of its stops. Their shows were typical of the entertainments brought to the Station during the Season. In 1922, the All India Boxing Tournament was held at the extensive facility. The Rink Amusement Club, which may be considered the third of the three clubs in the Station,[13] provided members with special and sometimes private access to Rink facilities. The Rink is said to have enjoyed its most prosperous days '...before the [live] theatre in India was suppressed by the talkies.'[14] It is now owned by Mr Rajesh Agarwal, a well-known Delhi resident with significant holdings in Mussoorie, and is still functioning, but much reduced in terms of facilities and amusements.

In addition to these clubs, masonry—the Freemasons—also found a niche in the social structure of the Station, and of all the membership social organizations of early Mussoorie, this is the only one to have survived to the present time. The Freemasons were an important institution in the Empire, and the various local lodges (branches) exercised significant unofficial power in military, business and government from

A June-1900 Thomas Alfred Rust photograph of the Rink amusement centre. The Rink opened in the 1880s with, it was said, one of the 'best roller skating floors in the East'. But its fame went well beyond skating and skating tournaments. Over the years, the Rink hosted boxing tournaments, fashion parades, flower shows, dog shows, seasonal festivals, ballroom dances, theatrical performances and, with the arrival of electricity, cinema pictures. It is still functioning, but on a much reduced scale.

(Courtesy of the National Army Museum, London)

This 1922 photo shows the winners of the All India Boxing Tournament of that year. The tournament was held at the Rink in Mussoorie.

(Courtesy of the Record Office for Leicestershire, Leicester & Rutland, United Kingdom)

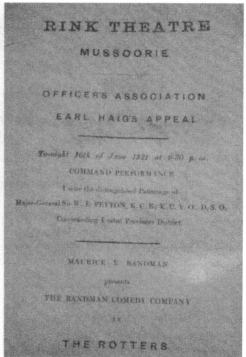

(L) This playbill advertises an Oscar Wilde play performed at the Rink by the Mussoorie Amateur Dramatic Club. This thespian club was a major source of entertainment and diversion during the Season, with ticket profits often going to charity. *(From Mrs William Cuppage's collection of programmes, broadsides and newspaper cuttings relating to amateur dramatics and concerts, British Library)*

(R) This programme shows a typical theatre entertainment brought to the Station during the Season. Maurice E. Bandman and the Bandman Comedy Company, managed by Stephen Lopez, toured India in the 1920s, with the Rink in Mussoorie as one of its stops. *(Kind courtesy of Vanessa Lopez, Bath, England, granddaughter of Stephen Lopez)*

whence its membership was drawn. Members supported each other and, in addition to its secretive aspects, Freemasons also participated in many civic and charitable activities. The Mussoorie branch—called Lodge Dalhousie—was constituted in 1854 when the earl of Dalhousie was governor general, the first 'Master' being Reverend T. Cartwright Smythe. Subsidiary branches—the Royal Arch St John the Baptist chapter, the Mark Lodge Adonhiram chapter and the Lodge Caledonia chapter—were added in 1855, 1875 and 1881 respectively.[15] These subsidiary branches no longer operate. The building of the still-functioning Lodge Dalhousie can be seen on the road from Kulri leading down to Dehra Dun. Along with it, there are two other post-Independence clubs that are active, Rotary International and the Lions Club International.

A 1960s photo showing St George's cadets standing at attention. For many years, St George's had close military connections, in that it admitted orphans from military families and, in the very early period, received a military subsidy. The St George's corps was raised in the 1880s.

(Courtesy of the Delany Archives, Carlow College, Ireland)

A rifle corps—the Masuri (Mussoorie) Volunteer Rifle Corps—was raised in 1871 and grew to four and eventually seven Station-based companies. The original four companies were the Station Company, Masuri School (Mussoorie Seminary) Cadet Company, St George's College Cadet Company and the Dehra Company. In total, there were some 200 officers, non-commissioned officers and volunteers.[16] These quasi-military units were raised not just in India but across the British Empire, to assist in the case of any sort of local emergency. In the Station and in Dehra Dun, where so many retired military personnel resided, there was a ready pool of volunteers as well as active officers to organize and lead these units. As the names suggest, two of the original corps in Mussoorie were made up of student volunteers cadets, while the Station Company was formed by volunteers from among the retired military residents and from the European business community. By the Second World War, there was an Indian Army Reserve in the Station, which was active in assisting Landour Muslims seeking refuge and transport to Pakistan. The closest modern equivalent to these volunteer units would seem to be the National Cadet Corps, which is made up of high school and college volunteers, who are introduced to basic military training, discipline and parade (NCC officers and cadets are not obliged to enter active military service once they complete their course).[17]

AN EXCERPT FROM *THE FRIEND OF INDIA*, CALCUTTA 26TH OCTOBER 1899 (FROM OUR CORRESPONDENT)

Mussoorie, 17th October. The annual inspection of the Mussoorie Volunteer Rifle Corps was held in the Happy Valley on Thursday by Major-General Sir Bindon Blood. The Battalion, consisting of seven companies, assembled at 10.30 and the General with his Staff arrived on the ground punctually at 11.00 AM, being received with a general salute. The Battalion marched past in column and quarter column, wheeled to the right and deployed into line. The manual and firing exercises having been performed, battalion drill and afterwards company drill by company officers were gone though. The Battalion being then re-formed, wheeled into line and advanced in review order. On completion of the inspection, the Officers having been called to the front, Sir Bindon Blood address them as follows: "Colonel Beer and Officers of the Mussoorie Volunteer Rifles,—I have been very much pleased today with all I have seen on parade, and with the steadiness with which the various movements have been performed, and when I bear in mind the difficulties you labour under, especially in the matter of a suitable drill ground on which to drill the seven companies on parade today, I think it reflects the greatest credit on all concerned. I shall have great pleasure in making a very favourable report of my inspection to Government." The Volunteers were marched off to their well-earned tiffin (two of the companies had marched five miles uphill to the ground), and the General Staff was entertained at luncheon by Colonel Beer and Officers of the Corps. The Volunteers, exclusive of the company at Meerut, are over 400 strong, and doubtless when, as is most certain to be the case, the number of students at the various local schools is largely increased, consequent on the opening of the railway to Dehra next March, their strength will receive additions. The want of a level space of ground sufficiently large to admit of Battalion drill being carried out has been a matter of much anxiety to the Commandant, Colonel Beer, but, it is hoped, the difficulty will be removed, if the project under consideration of the Municipality to level the Botanical Gardens, for this and other purposes, receives the sanction and necessary financial assistance from Government. The annual shooting of the Corps will take place on the 16th and the athletic sports on the 26th of this month.

This notice regarding the inspection of the Mussoorie Volunteer Rifle Corps appeared in *The Friend of India*, a Calcutta newspaper. The levelling of the Botanical Gardens to provide the corps with a parade ground was fortunately never carried out.
(Courtesy of British Library)

Mussoorie, perhaps more than any other hill station, is said to have had a reputation for frivolity, fun and flirting, made possible to a large extent because the Station was not a summer capital with all the attendant formality and restrictions. It was a resort where one went for holiday strictly to enjoy oneself. Local resident Hugh Gantzer, an Indian naval officer (retired) and native of Mussoorie, put it this way:

> It was difficult for people to let their hair down in Simla, the official summer capital; you had to do all that card-calling and be terribly stiff and starchy. So they decided to make Mussoorie free of administrators.[18]

Young soldiers on leave apparently had an eye for the 'grass widows', a term used during the Raj period to describe married women who went up to the hills for the hot weather, while their husbands remained on duty in the plains. Such wooing and winning was forever memorialized by the world-renowned travel writer, Lowell Thomas, who observed: 'There is a hotel in Mussoorie where they ring a bell just before dawn so that the pious may say their prayers and the impious get back to their own beds.'[19]

However, while Mussoorie's reputation as a freewheeling bolthole is no doubt deserved, it also has probably become a bit exaggerated over time. Byron Farwell, the military historian, who has written extensively about the lifestyle of officers and other ranks in the British Indian Army, had this to say:

> There was, of course, a considerable amount of philandering, particularly at the
> hill stations, though perhaps not as much as was imagined, for they were tight
> communities where all were watched and all were known. Too much attention
> to women was called 'poodle-faking' and the colonels of some regiments banned
> some hill stations which were famous for their frivolity. Still, hill stations filled
> with bored wives whose husbands were sweating with their regiments on the
> plains below presented some officers on duty or leave there with a combination
> of desire and availability they found irresistible.[20]

Writing of the Edwardian period (1901–1910), historian Valerie Pakenham adds:

> Subalterns' morals were supervised fairly strictly by their commanding officers.
> A trip to Kashmir to shoot sheep would be approved, but a subaltern asking
> for two months' leave in Mussoorie, notorious for its population of pretty girls,
> would almost certainly be turned down.[21]

In any case, many young soldiers managed to get their 'leave' approved and, no
doubt, helped a great deal in adding to Mussoorie's 'notorious' reputation.

A CODE OF MORALS*

Now Jones had left his new-wed bride to keep his house in order,
And hied away to the Hurrum Hills above the Afghan border,
To sit on a rock with a heliograph; but ere he left he taught
His wife the working of the Code that sets the miles at naught.

And Love had made him very sage, as Nature made her fair;
So Cupid and Apollo linked, per heliograph, the pair.
At dawn, across the Hurrum Hills, he flashed her counsel wise—
At e'en, the dying sunset bore her husband's homilies.

He warned her 'gainst seductive youths in scarlet clad and gold,
As much as 'gainst the blandishments paternal of the old;
But kept his gravest warnings for (hereby the ditty hangs)

*From Kipling, Rudyard, *Barrack Room Ballads and Departmental Ditties*.

That snowy-haired Lothario, Lieutenant-General Bangs.

'Twas General Bangs, with Aide and Staff, who tittupped on the way,
When they beheld a heliograph tempestuously at play.
They thought of Border risings, and of stations sacked and burnt—
So stopped to take the message down—and this is what they learnt—

'Dash dot dot, dot, dot dash, dot dash dot' twice. The General swore.
'Was ever General Officer addressed as "dear" before?
"'My Love,' i' faith! "My Duck," Gadzooks! "My darling popsy-wop!"
'Spirit of great Lord Wolseley, who is on that mountaintop?'

The artless Aide-de-camp was mute; the gilded Staff were still,
As, dumb with pent-up mirth, they booked that message from the hill;
For clear as summer lightning-flare, the husband's warning ran:—
'Don't dance or ride with General Bangs—a most immoral man.'

[At dawn, across the Hurrum Hills, he flashed her counsel wise—
But, howsoever Love be blind, the world at large hath eyes.]
With damnatory dot and dash he heliographed his wife
Some interesting details of the General's private life.

The artless Aide-de-camp was mute, the shining Staff were still,
And red and ever redder grew the General's shaven gill.
And this is what he said at last (his feelings matter not):—
'I think we've tapped a private line. Hi! Threes about there! Trot!'

All honour unto Bangs, for ne'er did Jones thereafter know
By word or act official who read off that helio.
But the tale is on the Frontier, and from Michni to Mooltan
They know the worthy General as 'that most immoral man'.

"Herne Dale": June. '88.
"Hereby the photo hangs.
"That snowy-haired Lothario, Lieutenant-General Bangs"

In the album containing this photograph, Rudyard Kipling captioned it as:

'Hereby the photo hangs,
That snowy-haired Lothario,
Lieutenant-General Bangs'

In 1881, Mrs Samuel (Edmonia) Hill and her husband spent the summer at the Charleville Hotel, as did Rudyard Kipling. Many years later, in 1921, she remarked that this poem, 'A Code of Morals', was penned by Kipling as a spoof on the then resident of Herne Dale bungalow. Herne Dale is located in the northwest of the Station, beyond Happy Valley. This humorous poem could only have added to Mussoorie's 'racy' reputation.
(Photo by Mr and Mrs S.A. Hill from the Ballade of Photographs, 1888, captioned by Rudyard Kipling, Rare Book and Special Collections Division, Library of Congress)

And it was the Savoy Hotel, more than any other, which provided a happy playground for visitors, although the poor rank-and-file soldiers usually found no welcome at this posh—and expensive—establishment that was named after the Savoy Hotel on the Strand, London, itself the first luxury hotel in Britain, built in 1889. The Mussoorie Savoy has recently been completely renovated and reopened.

When the Mussoorie Seminary (later called Maddock's School) closed in 1900, this prime twenty-acre property just above the Mussoorie Library was purchased by Cecil D. Lincoln, an Irishman and barrister in Lucknow, who constructed a palatial six-building facility that included superb dining and public rooms, as well as a bar, much later called the Writers' Bar, a sprung dance floor, a glass-enclosed verandah room and even a café on the second floor of the library building for better enjoyment of the performances in the bandstand. There was a gymnasium and racquet, tennis and badminton courts nestled amidst the ancient deodars. And, of course, on clear days the views of the snow-capped mountains were stupendous. The hotel started with sixty-four suites of rooms. It was closed for a time after the 1905 earthquake, but all damaged structures were soon rebuilt and the hotel reopened.[22] Support facilities included an orchard with trees imported from France, a vegetable garden, a dairy, an 'up-to-date piggery with English pigs', a poultry farm and a special structure for keeping quails.[23] Nothing was lacking, and the service was impeccable. The whole affair was managed for many years by hotel manager Mr F. Schmuck.

Soon after it opened in 1902, as the largest purpose-built hill station hotel in India,[25] the Savoy acquired India-wide and, indeed, international fame. During the April through October season[26], the piano keyboard tingled, the orchestra played, dancers took to the floor, champagne flowed, uniformed servants moved about quietly and efficiently, and regal spreads were heaped on groaning tables in the imperial dining room.

Even deadly intrigue was played out in the 1911 murder of a Savoy guest, Miss Frances Mary Garnett Orme. Miss Orme was found to have been poisoned and, while the case was never solved, the murder is said to have inspired Agatha Christie's first novel, *The Mysterious Affair at Styles* (alas, set in Britain). Some believe to this day that Miss Orme's ghost still wanders the halls. It all adds to the mystique of the Savoy.

During the Season, military bands played from the bandstand, which is still located at Library Chowk (also called Gandhi Chowk, as there is now a statue of the Mahatma at the busy intersection). Recently restarted, musical events are again being staged at the bandstand on an occasional basis.

(Kind courtesy of the late H. Michael Stokes, Kent, United Kingdom)

The Savoy Hotel was one of the grandest in India and, indeed, in the entire East, favoured by the rich, royal and famous from its opening in 1902 until the Second World War. It has recently been restored to its former splendour.

(Kind courtesy of the late H. Michael Stokes, Kent, United Kingdom)

The Charleville Hotel had bachelors' quarters overlooking the Happy Valley, especially available for non-married officers and civilians. The presence of these unattached young men during the Season no doubt added greatly to the 'frivolity' for which Mussoorie was famous. *(Courtesy of British Library)*

A postcard of the Savoy Café, which was situated on the balcony of the library. In the early twentieth century, the Criterion and the Savoy restaurants at Library Chowk did roaring business during the Season. The two-storey Criterion Restaurant (and hall) was an extension of Wutzler's Charleville Hotel and, as its name implies, the Savoy Café was run by the Savoy Hotel. In 1907, Bodycot commented on these watering holes: 'The Criterion and Savoy restaurants, the latter on the upper floor of the Library, are…a boon and blessing to man, and women too. Ices, cakes, coffee, cold drinks, and cigarettes add considerably to the charm assigned to music "to sooth the savage breast"; and where the charm of lovely woman [sic], and the privilege of paying for the particular fancy in creams or confectionery of your own—or someone else's—best girl, is added, life becomes indeed worth living.'[24] *(Courtesy of British Library)*

The 1920s–1940s was the heyday of the Savoy Hotel, particularly the Roaring Twenties and during the Second World War, when Mussoorie became a frenetic playground for British officials, American military personnel and Indian royalty prevented by the war from travelling to Europe. Professional entertainers were brought it from other parts of India and from abroad, including the famous Maurice Bandman and Stephen Lopez shows.[27]

> Each day there was a tea dance, a cocktail dance and a dinner dance [at the Savoy and other leading hotels], and people rushed from one to the other, often having to switch to formal evening wear for dinner. The starched formality of the dinner suit soon gave way to the more comfortable *sherwani* and Jodhpur jacket. Ladies wore sensible shoes for walking from one place to the other, but carried more delicate slippers and sandals for dancing.[28]

In 1946, the Savoy was purchased by Kripa Ram Jauhar, whose son Anand Kumar ('Nandu') Jauhar held control for many years. Over time, the hotel gradually fell into serious decline as Mussoorie itself went through an economic downturn, but it has now been renovated by its new owner and recently reopened.[29]

However, the Savoy was not where Mary of Teck, HRH the Princess of Wales, stayed on her impromptu visit to Mussoorie in 1906 (see Chapter 9). That honour was reserved for the Charleville Hotel, located to the west of the library on the grounds now occupied by the Lal Bahadur Shastri National Academy of Administration for training of IAS (Indian Administrative Service) officers, established in 1959. The fact that Her Royal Highness stayed at the Charleville, rather than the Savoy, gives credence to the claim that the Charleville was at the time '...the leading hotel in this charming hill station.'

The original Charleville building dates back to 1842, although the main building is said to have been constructed in 1854 by General Wilkinson, on land he had purchased from the mahant (headman) of Dehra. In 1857, one of the buildings on the property was apparently used as a girls' school; this was probably a temporary extension of the Waverley Convent School which, during the First War of Independence, housed many 'refugees' from the plains. In 1861, Wilkinson sold the property to Mr Hobson, the manager of the Mussoorie Bank and also proprietor, at the time, of the Happy Valley Estate. However, it was not until 1877 that Hobson opened the Hotel Charleville, a portmanteau of his two sons' names, Charlie and Willie, although the Charleville came to be pronounced as 'Sharlyville'. In 1880, Hobson died and the hotel was then run for approximately two years by the Mussoorie Bank, with Mr Treherne as manager. In 1884, the Mussoorie Bank leased the property to Messrs T. Fitch and C. Stowell, who operated it in conjunction with Mr Henry Wutzler as managing partner. In 1887, the enterprising Wutzler purchased the hotel from the bank. Wutzler later formed a limited liability company—Wutzler Ltd—that included not only Hotel Charleville but also the two-storied Criterion Restaurant on the Mall opposite the bandstand and near the library, as well as the Royal Hotel in Lucknow.[30]

In 1884, Charleville had some forty rooms, but by the turn of the century there were 112 rooms; it was said to be the largest hotel in India outside of Bombay. Just how lavish the Charleville was can be gathered from Bodycot's 1907 comments:

CHARLEVILLE HOTEL, MUSSOORIE.

A sketch of the famous Charleville Hotel.
(From *Cyclopedia of India,* Calcutta: Cyclopedia Publishing Company, 1908.)

office of the Charleville Hotel.

*and there were men with a thousand wants
And women with babes galore —
But the dear little angels in Heaven know
That Wutzler never swore.*

The Hotel Charleville, which was on the grounds of what is now the Lal Bahadur Shastri National Academy of Administration, was a very popular hotel and a degree more exclusive than the Savoy. Rudyard Kipling stayed there in 1888 and spun this verse about guests and the German-born manager (Henry Wutzler):

'And there were men with a thousand wants
And women with babes galore—
But the dear little angels in Heaven know
That Wutzler never swore.'

*(Photo by Mr and Mrs S.A. Hill from the Ballade of Photographs,
1888, captioned by Rudyard Kipling, Rare Book and Special Collections Division, Library of Congress)*

The public rooms are a large dining room, a children's dining room, ballroom, public drawing room, smoking room and card room, a fine billiard room with two tables, and a ladies cloak room for ball nights. The linen room is in charge of a European housekeeper, and in addition to the finely appointed kitchen, there is a bakery and a confectionery. There are two tennis courts and a badminton court. There is out-office accommodation for 400 servants, stabling for 50 horses, a piggery, a poultry yard and extensive fruit and vegetable gardens. The area of the estate is twenty-five acres.[31]

The main building of the Charleville burned down in 1984, yet the hotel lives on in local lore and in Kipling verse.[32]

Besides the Charleville, John Northam mentioned several other Mussoorie hotels in his 1884 guidebook, although noting that '…to extol or disparage, in the case of, in a sense, rival institutions, would be quite out of good taste in a book of this sort.'[33] So, without much commentary on the quality of facilities or services, Northam goes on to mention the Himalaya Hotel, which opened in the Himalaya Bank building, now housing the State Bank of India; the Masuri (Mussoorie) Hotel, informally called 'Bobby Sahib ka hotel' in the bazaar, Bobby Hesseltine being the manager of this hotel, which later became part of the Wynberg Allen School; and the Woodville Hotel in lower Landour. Northam does not mention the Calcutta Hotel, which was on the grounds of what is now Hampton Court School, as this would already have closed by 1884 (see Chapter 5).

Bodycot's 1907 guidebook fails to mention the Masuri Hotel or the Woodville Hotel; however, he did make two additions that were not in Northam's earlier guidebook: the Waverley Hotel, near the library on the way to Happy Valley, and the Hotel Cecil, on the hill to the east of the library. The Waverley was in what was originally called Oxford House, a large property that for a time had been rented to the raja of Jind. In 1908, the Waverley became the Alexandra Hotel, run by Mrs Lee Richards in conjunction with a hotel of the same name in Dehra Dun. Later still, it became the Union Hotel. The Hotel Cecil opened in 1907 in premises built for the purpose by Mr C.M. Gregory, a well-known graduate of Maddock's School who was also responsible for building many railway bridges around India. The Hotel Cecil is now called the Prince Hotel.

Our drawing-room at the Charleville.

Both the Charleville and Savoy hotels had very elaborate suites for their guests. A story is told about an elderly couple who were shown the Savoy's bridal suite when the hotel was otherwise full. The old man said, 'What will we do with this?' Whereupon the manager responded, 'Sir! If you're shown the ballroom, you don't have to dance!' *(Photo by Mr and Mrs S.A. Hill from the Ballade of Photographs, 1888, captioned by Rudyard Kipling, Rare Book and Special Collections Division, Library of Congress)*

Capt King   Mr Tweedie   *A group at the Charleville.*   Mr Palin
       Capt Weir   Capt Jennings   Mrs March.
    Mrs Tweedy   Mrs Digby.
       Mr Logan.   Mrs Beresford. (erct)

"Where a now the merry party
  I remember long ago?"

An 1888 group at the Charleville Hotel, with Kipling's caption: 'Where is now the merry party I remember long ago?' *(Photo by Mr and Mrs S.A. Hill from the Ballade of Photographs, 1888, captioned by Rudyard Kipling, Rare Book and Special Collections Division, Library of Congress)*

Himalaya Hotel, Mussoorie.   May. 19. 1904.

you have stayed in many Hotels, but not one like this, I think. I am staying at a Clergy Rest House, which reminds me of Mentone. we are 3 at present. There are shows here, as at Montreux. What [news] of Harold? Did I tell you I met a soldier in Calcutta who had been his servant in S.A.? much love from your affectionate nephew J.H. Jennings

The Himalaya Hotel was one of Mussoorie's premier hotels in the late nineteenth and early twentieth centuries. The building started out as the Himalaya Bank, became the Himalaya Hotel and then the home of the Bank of Upper India, which became part of the Imperial Bank of India (now the State Bank of India). The note on the postcard, dated 19 May 1904, reads: 'You have stayed in many hotels, but not one like this, I think. I am staying at a Clergy Rest House, which reminds me of Mentoue [sic, Mantoue, Italy]. We are three at present. There are shows here, as at Montreux [on Lake Geneva, Switzerland]. What news of Harold? Did I tell you I met a soldier in Calcutta who had been his servant in S.A. [South Africa]? Much love from your affectionate nephew, J.H. Jennings.' The 'Clergy Rest House' where Jennings was staying may have been Bassett Hall, now Kasmanda Palace Hotel. T.A. Rust, the well-known photographer whose name is noted on this postcard, had a studio in Regent House, Kulri, Mussoorie. *(Postcard photo from the private collection of the late H. Michael Stokes, United Kingdom)*

'The Rambler's' 1936 guidebook advertised thirteen hotels, not least of which was the Hakman's Grand Hotel on the Mall. The Grand boasted of '…the finest ballroom in Mussoorie', tea dances, spacious and airy rooms, all on moderate terms. There were regularly booked cabaret dancers and orchestras at the Grand and at the Savoy and Charleville; but, alas, it is said that exorbitant entertainment taxes put paid to live entertainments in Mussoorie after the 1970s.[34]

A postcard view of the Hotel Cecil on the hill to the east of the library. The Cecil opened in 1907 in premises built for the purpose by Mr C.M. Gregory, a well-known graduate of Maddock's School who was also responsible for building many railway bridges around India. *(Courtesy of British Library)*

But, in the longer run, that didn't slow the hotel industry overall. A 1990 Survey of India map listed forty hotels in Mussoorie. Today, there are as many as two hundred!

Besides the entertainment provided in the leading hotels, there was Stiffle's Restaurant and Ballroom on the Mall, where the Garhwal Terrace Hotel now spreads. Stiffle's had a popular restaurant and tea room on the ground floor and a huge ballroom on the first floor. After Independence, the ground floor of the Stiffle's building was rented out to shops and the first floor became the Standard Skating Rink. When the building burned down, the Garhwal Mandal Vikas Nigam bought the gutted building, demolished it, and built the Garhwal Terrace.[35]

In the early twentieth century, Stiffle's was certainly a place to 'see and be seen' and, in keeping with Mussoorie's reputation as a freewheeling watering hole, it figured in a scuffle or two amongst ranking visitors. In 1923, there was an amusing

The Hotel Cecil has become the Prince Hotel, but the historic transom above the door reminds today's guest of the earlier vintage. *(Kind courtesy of Mela Ram & Sons, Mussoorie)*

but apparently major dust-up involving the Baroda heir-apparent, Maharaj Kumar Dhairyashil Rao, who ran afoul of local authorities and the government when he '…went to Stiffle's and became uproarious with drink there…' and had to be removed. Later at the Rink, he got into a fisticuffs with a bandsman of the 16th Lancers. This, combined with running up debts on the Mall, was all too much for the authorities, and the thirty-year-old prince was removed from the Station and packed off back to Baroda.[36] It was grist for the gossip mill in Mussoorie and beyond. And in 1925, His Highness the raja of Mandi, Joginder Sen Bahadur, repaired to Stiffle's after having been denied admittance to Christ Church for refusing to take off his shoes and turban! His Highness had been invited to the wedding of the stepdaughter of his friend, Lieutenant Colonel C.A.G. Shoubridge, and vastly important to the occasion, was to have formally escorted the bride's mother down the aisle during the ceremony. For his part, the unperturbed raja, who apparently had attended weddings in Westminster and London churches where shoes and turbans were very much allowed, simply removed himself to Stiffle's to wait for the wedding reception to begin. He may have been bemused, but not so upset that he didn't join in the post-nuptial celebrations. However, according to the record, the outraged host, Lieutenant Colonel Shoubridge, elevated the rebuff in letters to the government and to Christ Church, so that the incident became a much talked of tempest-in-a-teapot 'Mandi Affair.'[37] The Roaring Twenties, Mussoorie style! But at the same time, such incidents also provide glimpses into the often ambivalent relations that existed between the ruling British and the ranking Indian aristocracy.

In Barlowganj, there was the palatial Tivoli Garden, which Lionel Douglas Hearsey carved out of his Maryville estate in 1882; it '…at once became a favourite resort of the Masuri public.' This playground was named after Tivoli, Italy, a stylish resort near Rome, famous for its scenic views and beautiful gardens. Tivoli Garden in

The Stiffle's, including a restaurant, tea room and ballroom, was a premier entertainment centre in the Station well into the twentieth century. The site is now occupied by the Garhwal Terrace Hotel and Restaurant. *(Kind courtesy of the late H. Michael Stokes, Kent, United Kingdom)*

Barlowganj was not a garden in the botanical sense, even though there were '…beds of choice flowers prettily laid out.' There was a dancing pavilion with dressing rooms, a dining saloon with kitchen attached, tennis and badminton courts and, for the kitchens, fruit trees and beds of strawberries on the road leading to Mossy Falls and Hearsey Falls.[38] The Tivoli Garden was seriously damaged in the 1905 earthquake and never reopened. In 1936, 'The Rambler' reported that the garden was in ruins and had returned to jungle.[39]

To add more entertainment, the 'electric pictures' arrived to enthusiastic crowds soon after hydro-electric power came to the Station in 1909 (see Chapter 3 and Appendix C). At one time, there were as many as six cinema halls in the Station. The first to arrive was the Electric Picture Palace in Kulri; later came the Jubilee on the lower level of the same building. Other early halls were the Majestic (subsequently called the Basant and, even later, the Vasu) on the Mall below Christ Church, the Capital located on the premises of Hakman's Grand Hotel, the Palladium below

Hakman's Grand Hotel, and the Rialto near Hamer's. Today, there are no longer any functioning movie theatres in town.

The Picture Palace in Kulri, flying the Union Jack. This was the first picture hall to open in Mussoorie, soon after electricity arrived there (1909). It wasn't long before picture halls dotted the Station but today, none remain. The Picture Palace building still stands but is no longer used for showing movies.
(Kind courtesy of John and Sonia née Payne Harriyott, England)

In Mussoorie, there was always plenty of beer to go around at the clubs, hotels and restaurants, and also in the cantonment and homes—all conveniently provided by the local breweries. The first brewery opened in Mussoorie in 1830. During this era in India, brewers headed straight away to the hills to pursue their craft, for hill stations were free of both excessive heat and the wild yeast strains, which were prone to frustrate attempts to brew beer in the plains.[40] These hill breweries—from Murree in the West to Solan near Shimla and on to Mussoorie, Nainital and Darjeeling—continued to prosper, until technology overcame the difficulties of brewing on the plains.

Prosper, yes, and the intrepid Fanny Parkes noted in 1838 that '...though it cannot be compared to Bass's or Allsopp's Pale Ale, [the local beer] is very fair, when you consider it is country made.'[41] No doubt Fanny had looked closely into this matter.

It was Mr Henry Bohle (later, Sir Henry Bohle) who established in 1830 the first brewery in Mussoorie, called the Old Brewery, to the west of the Station. It closed down two years later, possibly as a result of some trouble with Colonel Frederick Young. The difficultly seems to have been about supplying beer to soldiers who came down from the cantonment to the brewery with forged passes. Mr Bohle sold this property to a Mr Parsons who, in turn, sold it to Mr John Mackinnon as a site for his Mussoorie Seminary. However, Bohle did give brewing another go and, in 1838, he reopened 'Bohle's Brewery' to the north of the original site.[42]

In 1850, Mr John Mackinnon closed the school he had established in 1834 at the original Old Brewery site and took over Bohle's Brewery (see Chapter 5 for a discussion of Mackinnon's career in education). Henry Bohle was John Mackinnon's brother-in-law. Mackinnon and, later, his sons Philip Walter and Vincent Arthur Mackinnon greatly expanded the business and '...by their energy, backed by experience, they gave Mussoorie beer a reputation which enormously increased the demand'. On premises covering six acres, the Mackinnon brothers installed modern water-powered equipment, with brewing water coming from a nearby spring. The firm, Mackinnon & Co., had large contracts

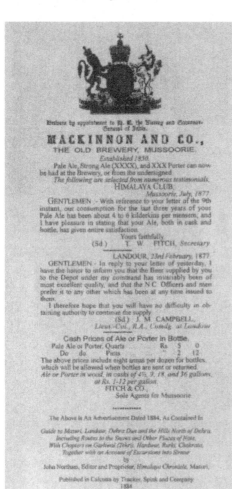

This Mackinnon and Co. advertisement appeared in Northam's 1884 guide to Mussoorie. The company's Old Brewery brand (reverting to the name of the first brewery in the Station) of beers and ales was sold throughout India, but Fitch & Co. was their sole agent in the Station. The Mackinnon Brewery closed in the early twentieth century, when technology allowed for quality brewing on the plains.
(Northam, John, Guide to Masuri, Landaur, Dehra Dun and the Hills North of Dehra, *Calcutta: Thacker, Spink and Co., 1884*)

for the supply of beer to the army and, with demand growing for their product, they opened another large brewery in Jubbulpore (Central Province, now Jabalpur in Madhya Pradesh state).

Miss Haig, Miss Hauser and Miss Blewitt enjoying an outing at the brewery in 1888. At this time, there were two breweries in Mussoorie, the Mackinnon Brewery to the west and the Crown Brewery in Barlowganj. It is not certain which of these breweries the young ladies were favouring with their presence, but the contents of their bottles, cups and glasses is not really in doubt.
(Photo by Mr and Mrs S.A. Hill from the Ballade of Photographs, 1888, captioned by Rudyard Kipling, Rare Book and Special Collections Division, Library of Congress)

John Mackinnon may be credited with establishing one of the leading families in the Station, for he was both a savvy businessman and a tireless civic leader, taking advantage of the nineteenth-century acceptance of brewers into 'society', even while publicans were very much lower down on the social scale.[43] This was the same attitude that had caused 'The Rambler' in 1936 to note the vast distinction observed, depending on whether one sold tin cans or tin cars.

Besides Mackinnon's involvement in education and brewing, he was the moving force behind the construction of the Mussoorie Cart Road, an undertaking that was obviously in the interest of all the commercial houses in Mussoorie. John Mackinnon died in 1870. His elder son, Philip Walter, served on the municipal board for over twenty years. His second son, Vincent Arthur, visited England several times in pursuit of the latest brewing technologies. Vincent too served on the municipal board, for several terms as vice chairman, and it was he who purchased the Happy Valley Estate in 1904 and promoted establishment of the popular Happy Valley Club (see above). In the early twentieth century, there also was a nine-hole Mackinnon golf

The Mackinnon family was perhaps the most renowned Mussoorie family of the colonial era. John Mackinnon (centre) brought his boarding school from Meerut to Mussoorie in 1834, but in 1850 dramatically switched careers when he took over a brewery that had once been owned by his brother-in-law Henry Bohle. Renowned for his involvement and influence in local affairs, John Mackinnon (d.1870) is credited with developing the Mussoorie Cart Road, which was an important economic fillip to the Station. His sons, Philip Walter (R, b.1849–d.1912) and Vincent Arthur (L, b.1852–d.1916) took over their father's brewery and ran it successfully for many years. Family interests moved beyond brewing to owning vast expanses of property, including the Park Estate earlier held by Sir George Everest, the Happy Valley Estate and much forest land. The brothers promoted development of the Happy Valley Club, a nine-hole golf course, and a racecourse and polo ground. Both brothers served on the municipal board. There are six memorial inscriptions in Christ Church remembering various members of the Mackinnon family.

(Photos of Philip and Vincent Mackinnon, British Library; photo of John Mackinnon from an original in the Mussoorie Library and courtesy of Robert Hutchison, Switzerland)

course on the Park Estate. Hole #5 was said to be on the site of Bachelors' Hall, which had been Survey staff quarters, but no trace of that any longer exists.[44] Both Mackinnon brothers were also directors of the racecourse and polo ground. Philip Mackinnon resided at Lynndale and Vincent Mackinnon at Kandi Lodge (named after a nearby village and now spelled 'Kandy'), both cottages being to the west in the vicinity of the brewery.

> They [the Mackinnon brothers] are extensive property owners in Mussoorie. The Bhilaru Estate, which contains some 550 acres, including some charming building sites, is their property; also the Park Estate of 500 acres, heavily timbered, and Snowdon, 220 acres of splendid forest. The brothers Mackinnon have an up-to-date forestry department, and huge quantities of timber have been cut from their estates since 1850, which has been more than replaced by new plantings.[45]

In Christ Church, there are six memorial inscriptions remembering this prominent local family. The oldest is in memory of Philip Walter, who died in 1912. For reasons unknown, there is not just one but two memorial inscriptions to him in Christ Church. The most recent Mackinnon inscription remembers Lillian Mary, who died in 1945.

A second brewery, the Crown Brewery, was established by Messrs Murch and Dyer in 1867 in Barlowganj.[46] However, it closed in 1869. In 1876, this property was taken over by Messrs Whymper and Co. and further enlarged. In 1884, a limited liability company was formed by Mr J.W. Whymper, managing director, and Mr A.M. Ker, whereupon further improvements were made.

In 1903, the two breweries employed a total of 131 men and made nearly half a million gallons of beer.[47] However, both the Mackinnon Brewery and the Crown Brewery eventually became victims of modern technologies that made it possible and certainly more convenient to brew in the plains, closer to major markets. Both breweries closed in the second decade of the twentieth century. The ruins of both breweries have been built over in the past five years.

But Mussoorie wasn't only about clubs, hotel entertainments and beer. Very early on in the history of the Station, the townspeople established a library for themselves, and this is one of the leading early institutions that continues to this day. The Mussoorie Library project was begun in 1843 with funds collected by private subscription, and the building at Library Chowk was completed in July

1844. Residents and visitors alike were eligible to join the library as members or temporary subscribers. This is still the case today. The affairs of the library have always been run by a designated committee.

In the early twentieth century, there was also a Reading Club of the Landour Community Centre. Although this book club is no longer functioning, it is particularly remembered for having published, in 1930, *The Landour Community Centre Cook Book*. This cookbook proved to be very popular and, as a result, has been reprinted several times. It is still available.

The Criterion Restaurant (building next to Mussoorie Library) was a major watering hole in late nineteenth and early twentieth-century Mussoorie.
The library, established in 1844, is shown on the left, below the Savoy Hotel.
(Early twentieth-century postcard photo, kind courtesy of the late H. Michael Stokes, Kent, United Kingdom)

Mussoorie also boasted several newspapers over the years and, indeed, was the first hill station to have its very own 'rag'. None of these early newspapers are in circulation today and very few copies of the original editions even exist.

The first paper to come on to the scene was *The Hills*, which was started in 1842 by the civic-minded John Mackinnon. Its first incarnation lasted until 1850. It was restarted ten years later in 1860 by A.S. Mackinnon ('...published at Mussoorie every Thursday, subscription for one year, in advance. Rs 20/-') but lasted only until 1865.[48] The next on the scene was *The Mussoorie Exchange Advertiser* in 1870, but this was said to be only a medium for advertisements. Next came *The Mussoorie Season*, started by a Mr Coleman in 1872. However, Mr Coleman's newspaper '... sometimes possessed a tendency to give needless offence...'[49] and it wound up in 1874 when Coleman himself left India. *The Mussoorie Season* partially re-emerged in 1875, when it was incorporated into the *Himalaya Chronicle*, started by Mr John Northam, author of the well-regarded 1884 guide to Mussoorie. For one short year (1884), the *Himalaya Chronicle* was published year round, but that effort failed. At the same time, Messrs Buckle & Co., contractors of bullock trains (see Chapter 2), started publishing *The Hill Advertiser*, first with only advertising but later with some local news included.

Both the *Himalaya Chronicle* and *The Hill Advertiser* ended publication in 1885, but that year saw Mr Hawthorne's *The Beacon* come on to the scene. For many years, there was also Mr Charles Liddell's *The Mafasilite* (sometimes spelled 'Mofussilite'), which Mr Norton took over in 1898 after attempting *The Eagle* for a short time. In 1901, Mr F. Bodycot, who also later compiled a Mussoorie guidebook (much quoted herein), bought *The Mafasilite*, keeping that name for job printing but renaming the newspaper *The Mussoorie Times*. Upon Bodycot's death in 1929, a syndicate bought up the business, which continued for some time under various owners. At one point, *The Mussoorie Times* was printed at the small Cambridge Bookstore print shop (the Cambridge Bookstore remains a venerable local institution, owned by Mr Sunil Aurora). In 1907, Mr T. Kinney, yet another guidebook author, started *The Echo* but that did not last beyond 1913. In 1924, Mr R.C. Gupta started *The Mussoorie Herald*, which was published during the years 1924–1927 and 1930–1933. By the middle of the twentieth century, Mussoorie had seen the last of its local rags, although today some national and regional newspapers do provide Mussoorie- and Dehra Dun-specific news and features.[50]

Mussoorie, 19th September. As naturally happens at the end of the Season, events are crowding upon us. For the next fortnight, rapid locomotion will be necessary in order to enable the same individual to be present at the various engagements set down for each day. Commencing on the heels of the last epistle, we had Signor Rampezzotti's vocal and instrumental concert at the Criterion Hall on Tuesday. As usual at the concerts given by the Professor, the music, both vocal and instrumental, was excellent. The audience was a lamentably scanty one, but there was good reason for the fact, as two other functions were taking place simultaneously, in the shape of "At Homes" given by the Maharani of Kapurthala and Mrs. DeGwyther [sic, D'Gruyther], both of which were largely attended. The reception at St. Helen's was, of course, barred to the male sex, but over a hundred ladies availed themselves of the Maharani's invitation, and thoroughly enjoyed their entertainment, the most striking feature in which was the singing of the first stanza of "Sister Mary Jane's Top Note," (from "The Gay Parisienne"), by the four sons of the Maharaja, who, exquisitely dressed as they always are, formed a most charming group. Recitations, in English and in French, were also given by the same youthful scholars. At 9.30 on the same day, a large company of relatives and friends of the Principal and students of the Modern School were invited to the "Rink" for the purpose of witnessing "She Stoops to Conquer." The play is a long one, requiring a lot of study but this had been given, and a big success was the result. Among so large a "cast" it is difficult, as well as invidious, to distinguish, but the male actors who came into most prominence, both from the nature of their parts and manner of sustaining them, were "Hardcastle" (Mr. T.M. Smith), "Marlow" (Mr. Quarry), and "Tony Lumpking" (Mr. H. Sinclair). That the graceful aid of the fair quartette of ladies who appear in the cast was fully appreciated, was amply testified by the profusion of gigantic and lovely bouquets showered at their feet. At the close of the performance, an interval was devoted to consumption of the liberal refreshments provided by the hosts. Then dancing set in and was vigorously carried on until well into the small hours. On Friday and Saturday the Crofton-

Wilmer Company made their appearance on the Rink stage in "The Liars." On Saturday also, the weather generously permitted the eleventh Gymkhana, already twice abortively announced to take place, and, though the spectators did not muster in record numbers, those who were present were truly glad to see the "gees" about once more. At night, a Skating Session was held and a match at hockey played, which was won by the side generalled by Captain Condon, R.A.M.C. The current week opened cheerily with an "At Home" (smoking concert), given by the Mussoorie Amateur Dramatic Club to their numerous friends, and most genial host and hostesses did the M.A.D.C. make. A portion of the Rink auditorium had been curtained in, carpeted, and furnished with tables, chairs, settees. The concert programme was a full one, and admirably executed, the various songsters and songstresses being warmly, and deservedly, applauded and encored, the band of the Connaught Rangers, under Mr. Gregory, playing selections in the intervals. The evening was bright and pleasant, the company present, among whom were Sir Bindon and Lady Blood and the Maharaja of Kapurthala, numbering about 170, all of whom thoroughly enjoyed themselves.

This social reporting at the height of the Raj gives a flavour of the period in Mussoorie. Obviously, the residents had a good deal of leisure time on their hands, and regular entertainments reinforced Mussoorie's reputation as a station built for fun and relaxation. *The Friend of India* was a popular Calcutta newspaper. *(Courtesy of British Library)*

Fortunately, many of the other early institutions in the Station did not suffer the same fate as the local newspapers. Despite the 'new look' of Mussoorie along the Mall, the town can still boast a number of historically significant sites; for example, Dalhousie Lodge, the Botanical Gardens, the library, the recently reopened Savoy Hotel, and many churches and schools. This continuity certainly adds to the treasure that is Mussoorie and gives a sense of permanence to 'community life in the clouds'.

Notes

1. Kipling, Rudyard, *Selected Poetry*, London: Penguin Books, 1992: 2.
2. Wild, Anthony, *Remains of the Raj*, London: HarperCollins, 2001: 196.
3. Williams, C. ('The Rambler'), *A Mussoorie Miscellany*, Mussoorie: The Mafasilite Press, 1936: 20.
4. Northam, John, *Guide to Masuri, Landaur, Dehra Dun and the Hills North of Dehra*, Calcutta:

Thacker, Spink and Company, 1884: 27. The organizer of the club referred to here was Lieutenant Charles Lionel Showers (b.1816–d.1895).

5. Sticke or sticke tennis is a racquet sport invented in the late nineteenth century, merging aspects of real tennis but played on a smaller, enclosed court.

6. Bodycot, F. ('compiler'), *Guide to Mussoorie with Notes on Adjacent Districts and Routes into the Interior,* Mussoorie: Mafasilite Printing Works, 1907: 138-139.

7. Northam, Ibid, p. 27.

8. Walton, H.G., ICS, *The Gazetteer of Dehra Dun,* Dehra Dun: Natraj Publishers, 2007 reprint (first printed in 1911): 247.

9. Bodycot, Ibid, p. 139-141.

10. Comments made by Raj Chatterjee in the 'Opinion' page of *The Times of India,* March 2003.

11. Walton, Ibid.

12. Walton, Ibid, p. 35.

13. In the 1930s, the Christian missionary community, specifically the United Presbyterian Church, built the Landour Community Centre, which was something like a club, in that membership was informally linked to Woodstock School and missionaries living on the hillside. The centre was closed in the 1970s, and the property was handed over to Woodstock School. Since 2001, the building has been and continues to be used as a student hostel for the school. (Information kind courtesy of Ms Judy Crider, community relations officer, Woodstock School)

14. Bodycot, Ibid, p. 142-143 and Wilson, Ibid, p. 41-42.

15. Bodycot, Ibid, p. 146 and Williams, Ibid., p. 36.

16. Northam, Ibid, p. 42.

17. The NCC is the post-Independence successor entity to the University Corps that was started in India during the First World War in order to have a pool of trained youth available for induction into the armed forces.

18. Hugh Gantzer quoted in *The Observer,* London, 18 August 2002.

19. Thomas, Lowell Jackson, *India, Land of the Black Pagoda,* New York: Garden City Publishing Company, 1933: 263-264. The entire quote, preceding the section written in-text and all Thomas ever said about Mussoorie is as follows: 'Mussoorie and Murree are both banal to a degree, but the former is probably the pleasanter of the two, being less official. There is a hotel…' It is usually assumed that Thomas was talking here of the Savoy Hotel.

20. Farwell, Byron, *Armies of the Raj, from the Great Indian Mutiny to Independence: 1858-1947,* New York: W.W. Norton & Company, 1989: 140.

21. Pakenham, Valerie, *The Noonday Sun, Edwardians in the Tropics,* London: Methuen London Ltd., 1985: 170.

22. The earthquake of 4 April 1905 shook Mussoorie and Landour, starting at 6.22 a.m. with continuing shocks throughout the morning. The quake severely damaged not only the Savoy and other hotels but also St Emilian's Church, Waverley Convent and other schools, as well as numerous private houses. Mussoorie remains seismically vulnerable.

23. Kinney, T., *The Echo Guide to Mussoorie*, Mussoorie: Echo Press, 1908: 93.

24. Bodycot, Ibid, p. 11.

25. Wild, Antony, *Remains of the Raj*, London: HarperCollins, 2001: 186.

26. The Savoy was open each year from 1 April to 31 October, closing for the winter, according to *The Echo Guide to Mussoorie* (1908: 93).

27. Many of the entertainers brought to Mussoorie from other parts of India were Anglo-Indians, who could combine their talents with a good and sympathetic understanding of British culture. In fact, two modern-day entertainers come out of this mould. Harry Webb, who entertains as Cliff Richard, is a British singer with Indian roots (he was baptized at St Thomas Church in Dehra Dun). Jerry Dorsey, popularly known as Engelbert Humperdinck, was raised in Madras (Purcell, Hugh, *After the Raj: The Last Stayers-On and the Legacy of British India*, Gloucestershire: The History Press, 2008: 125).

28. Pillai, K.K. *A Gathering of Princes*, from the brochure of the Mussoorie Winter Festival, Millennium Carnival 24 December 1999–1 January 2000, p. 8.

29. In 2005, Anand Jauhar sold the property to R.P. Singh, a Kanpur industrialist. The Savoy Hotel is now open under the management of Fortune Hotels, part of the ITC Welcomgroup Hotels.

30. Williams, Ibid, p. 67 and Kinney, Ibid, p. 90-92.

31. Bodycot, Ibid, p. 158.

32. The Karmshila Building, which houses a library, dining halls, lounges and conference halls of the Lal Bahadur Shastri National Academy of Administration, now occupies the site of the destroyed main building of the Hotel Charleville.

33. Northam, Ibid, p. 47-48.

34. The Hakman's were a Jewish family, some of whose members are buried in a small Jewish section of the Camel's Back Cemetery.

35. Information on Stiffle's kindly provided by Hugh Gantzer, Mussoorie.

36. 'Removal of Maharaj Kumar Dhairyashil Rao, son of the Gaekwad of Baroda, from Mussoorie', records of the Foreign and Political Department. (British Library)

37. 'Mandi Affair, incident at the wedding of the daughter of Colonel S G Shoubridge in Mussoorie at which His Highness the Raja of Mandi was a guest'. (British Library)

38. Northam, Ibid, p. 39.

39. Williams, Ibid, p. 43.

40. Wild, Ibid, p 185.

41. Parkes, Fanny, *Wanderings of a Pilgrim, in Search of the Picturesque, during Four-and-Twenty Years in the East; with Revelations of Life in the Zenana*, London: Pelham Richardson, 1850: 257 in vol. 2.

42. Bodycot, Ibid, p. 32.

43. Charles Dickens made this point in one of his novels: 'Her father…was a brewer. I don't know why it should be a crack thing to be a brewer; but it is indisputable that while you cannot possibly be genteel and bake, you may be as genteel as never was and brew. You

see it every day. Yet a gentleman may not keep a public house, may he?' (Dickens, Charles, *Great Expectations*, first published in 1860-1861, London: Penguin Group, 1996: 180)

44. Smith, M.R. *Everest: The Man and the Mountain*, Caithness, Scotland: Whittles Publishing, 1999: 154.

45. Kinney, Ibid, p. 96.

46. Edward Dyer was the father of Reginald Edward Harry Dyer. Reginald ('Rex') became infamous as the 'Butcher of Amritsar', following the 13 April 1919 Jallianwala Bagh Massacre.

47. *Imperial Gazetteer of India,* 1908: 267.

48. *The Hills,* 12 December 1861. Of all the Mussoorie newspapers published over the years, this is the only one—and that too for only a single day in 1861—that is available at the British Library, London.

49. Northam, Ibid, p. 27.

50. Interestingly, there was also a school magazine, *The Maddock*', published by Maddock's School between 1894 and 1899, but sadly no copies have come to light (Craig, Hazel Innes, *Under the Old School Topee*, Putney, London: BACSA, 1990: 35).

Contrary to the belief that houses in Mussoorie inappropriately mimicked the architecture of the plains, many of them were, in fact, very comfortable and appropriate to the climate.

(Kind courtesy of Mela Ram & Sons, Mussoorie)

8

AT 'HOME' IN THE HIMALAYAS

He has a wife, three daughters fair,
One little boy, his son and heir,
A nice snug house round Camel's Back,
What more then can my hero lack?
~ 'May'[1] ~

he British were very much at home in Mussoorie, because it reminded them so much of 'Home'. It was cool, it was green, it was quiet, it was comfortable, it was chock-a-block with fellow countrymen and it was relaxing.

Until 1919, time was marked in this relaxed Station by a high noon blast from the Cossipore cannon, set atop Gun Hill. The cannon had been supplied to the Station by the Cossipore arsenal[2] shortly after the First War of Independence, and it continued its noonday booming until 1919, when it was relieved of duty. It is said that the cannon was silenced in a 'great economical push'[3]; however, the advent of watches, then called timepieces, and the inconvenience caused by vibrations that loosened plaster and wandering 'shot' that occasionally spattered passers-by may have had more to do with the decision to stop the ritual. Gun Hill, encircled at the base by Camel's Back Road, is still called by that name. A water reservoir for the Station is located here, close to 'dress-me-up' photo shops with cameras aimed at the tourists. Today, Gun Hill—the second highest peak in Mussoorie proper after Blucher's Hill (west end)—can be accessed by foot, pony or a 1,310-foot (400-metre) ropeway that was constructed in the late 1960s.[4]

Shortly after the First War of Independence, the Cossipore arsenal, properly called the Gun Carriage Agency, supplied Mussoorie with a cannon that was set off each day at high noon. The cannon fell silent in 1919. (*Kind courtesy of John and Sonia née Payne Harriyott, England*)

For the Station's residents and visitors, the day normally started early and very much before the Cossipore cannon was let off. Of course, it must be remembered that 'visitors' in those days did not come for just a day or two. In fact, many came up for the entire Season from April to October. These seasonal visitors included 'grass widows,' often with small children, whose husbands would join them from the plains for only a short part of the Season; retired military and civilian officers who would be in Mussoorie for the hot weather and then trundle down to Dehra Dun or elsewhere on the plains for the winter months; and, of course, the invalided soldiers and officers of the cantonment, as well as those on leave. Other part-time residents included shopkeepers, hoteliers, teachers and students, for in the early years shops, hotels and schools were closed during the coldest months, generally from November to March (today, only the schools follow this winter break).

For these and for the relatively few year-round residents, everyday life was often not particularly exciting but still, pleasant enough in the alpine coolness. In the 1860s, as described by W. Williams, the routine went something like this:

> Those determined to make the most of the invigorating climate rise with the sun, and take a walk or ride on some of the good roads. On their return the rest are up, and then comes breakfast. Each spends the day as fancy directs, just as idle people do everywhere else, and very few at Mussoorie have anything to do but to kill time the best way they can. In the evening comes the walk or ride on the Mall, which lasts till dark; and as late hours are not the fashion, except perhaps at the club, where cards or billiards keep some up till the small hours, the domestic fireside closes the day.[5]

And the domestic fireside was pleasant indeed, especially compared to the searing heat of the plains. Accommodations tended to be modest, except for the 'exulted ones' of the civil and military services who lived a more lavish lifestyle, usually in the western and more fashionable side of the Station. Indeed, the western part of Mussoorie, including Happy Valley, remained the posh part of the Station until well after Independence, rather like the more wooded and less crowded upper Landour of today. Writing of her experiences as a student in the 1930s–1940s, author and former Woodstock student Marguerite Watkins recalled, 'We [Woodstock students and family] had never been in that part of Happy Valley. How civilized it was with houses next to each other on flat yards with trimmed grass; no langurs swung from the trees…we were ready for the picnic lunch and chose a lush place not too obviously part of someone's lawn.'[6]

The domestic fireplaces and stoves of Mussoorie were kept blazing with charcoal carried up by porters from the plains. More recently, conservation regulations have put paid to the large-scale use of charcoal, replaced by a reliable supply of LPG (liquefied petroleum gas). *(Courtesy of British Library)*

Wilson had this to say about the houses in Mussoorie in the 1860s:

> The houses are built on or near the crest of the ridge, and extend ten or twelve miles along it. Most are on the southern slope, or on the ridge itself, there being but few on the bleak northern side…There are many good trees about the place, chiefly oaks and rhododendron; but a great many have been cut down for firewood, and all would ere this have disappeared, but for an order not to fell any more within a certain distance. The houses are built much in the same fashion as in the plains, with a verandah on one or more sides, and with one or two exceptions, are all single-storied. Most of the old ones are thatched; but a great many, built of late years, have flat *pukkah* roofs…Nearly all the houses belong to officers in the civil or military service, and yield a very fair return for the capital invested in them. From Rs. 601 to Rs. 1,201 is the usual rent of a house for the six months it is occupied…The owners have, however, foolishly continued building new houses year after year, so that there

are now too many for the usual number of visitors, and consequently some must remain without tenants.[7]

Seasonal visitors often rented more modest bungalows than those to the west and later, boarding houses cropped up, although visitors who would come up to Mussoorie each year tended to buy a property if possible. Shorter term travellers sought out the hotels, once these became established. Missionaries in and around Landour often had facilities provided to them by their sponsoring societies.

THE STORY OF BASSETT HALL

Bassett Hall, located just above Christ Church, was certainly one of the largest and grandest houses in Mussoorie. It still is. Constructed in 1836, probably under the supervision of Captain Rennie Tailyour of the Bengal Engineers, who was also responsible for overseeing the construction of Christ Church in the same year, Bassett Hall has had a varied history, but happily it is still preserved in pristine condition.

In 1852, the Bassett Hall Estate changed hands when James Skinner, the eldest son of James Hercules Skinner, founder of Skinner's Horse, and a co-owner, Mrs N. Watkins, sold it off to Major Henry Christian Talbot of the 61st Native Infantry. Major Talbot owned Bassett Hall until 1861 but he obviously was not a full-time occupant, for it is known that Woodstock School—then called the Protestant Girls' School—was a temporary occupant. Woodstock had opened in 1854 in Caineville House, and 'a year later the school was moved to Bassett Hall near Christ Church, in order to allow some building work to be done at Caineville, and then moved back to the original site'.* After the Crimean War (1853–1856), invalided soldiers were put up at the Hall including, presumably, John A. Hindmarch, a Crimean veteran buried in Camel's Back Cemetery. Steel rings in the ceiling, from which ropes dangled to support injured appendages, can still be seen in some of the Bassett Hall rooms. In 1861, Talbot sold the Bassett property to Captain A.P.W. Orr. (Talbot died in Mussoorie some years later, on 22 November 1868; a plaque in his memory still remains in Christ Church.) Captain Orr, too, rented the property out. In 1870, Bassett Hall housed the

*Jones, Edith M., Caroline Wilkie and Mary I. McGee, *Woodstock School, The First Century, 1854-1954*, second printing, Dehra Dun: Vikalp Printers, 1999: 1.

Summer Home for Soldiers' Children, established that year with funds raised by General John Biddulph, the first British agent in Gilgit (1878–1881). The Summer Home was initially run by Reverend J.A. and Mrs (Charlotte) Stamper in Bassett Hall. But after one year, Glenburnie, located near the Municipal Gardens to the west, was purchased for the home from the estate of General Sir Charles Reid (see Chapter 5).

In 1871, also during the time of Orr's ownership and following the Summer Home occupancy, the Right Rev. Robert Milman, lord bishop of Calcutta and metropolitan of India, visited Mussoorie. 'The Bishop had taken Bassett Hall, at Mussoorie, for a few months, and he arrived there with his sister on the 22nd of April. The house had a fine view over the Dun, and the plains beyond. The season was unusually wet, and alternations of rain and cloudy mists of a dense and uncomfortable description hid most of the beauties of the place... Bassett Hall was situated very near the church, where there was daily service... His study of the languages was carried on with a Munshi, all the time he was at Mussoorie...The Bishop left Mussoorie on September 1, to continue his visitation of the Northwest Provinces.'[*]

In 1882, the late Captain Orr's executors sold Bassett Hall to Lionel Douglas Hearsey. This was the Hearsey who in 1870 had given the German-made tower bells to the nearby Christ Church (see Chapter 10). Hearsey held on to the pile until 1895 when it was sold to C.H.A. Twidale. However, Twidale obviously couldn't keep up with the mortgage payments and, almost exactly a year later (1896), he and the Delhi & London Bank sold Bassett Hall to the proprietors of the Modern School, Messrs Frederic Maurice Smith, Charles Edmund Freeman and Edwin Arthur Murphy.

The Modern School was intended to prepare boys for the English public schools '...at the age of fifteen or sixteen, so as to avoid the failures so often incurred as the result of sending boys home at too early an age...Those who are not destined to go home are carefully prepared for Indian careers...'[**] This school did not last far into the twentieth century and, in 1910, the property was sold

---

[*]Milman, Frances Maria, *Memoir of the Right Rev. Robert Milman, D.D., Lord Bishop of Calcutta & Metropolitan of India, with a Selection from His Correspondence and Journals*, London: John Murray, 1879: 181-189.
[**]Bodycot, F. ('compiler'), *Guide to Mussoorie with Notes on Adjacent Districts and Routes into the Interior, Mussoorie:* Mafasilite Printing Works, 1907: 154.

by Frederic Smith and Jane Essex Sinclair (who in 1897 had acquired Freeman's share) to Major (Dr) Gordon Travers Birdwood of the Indian Medical Service.

Birdwood was a Cambridge (Peterhouse College) and Guy's Hospital (London) graduate who had gained second place in the Indian Medical Service examination. He served with the Abor Expedition (in what is now Arunachal Pradesh state), as well as in the Waziristan and Chitral campaigns, and most significantly in his career, he was the principal of the Agra Medical School from 1903–1910. Later, he worked at Lucknow Medical College. A fellow of Allahabad University, he wrote what was at the time a very popular book, *Practical Bazaar Medicines*. He also authored *Clinical Methods in Tropical Diseases*.

Dr Birdwood was the last English proprietor of Bassett Hall. In 1915, before his retirement back to Deal in Kent on the English Channel, Birdwood sold the hall to Raja Suraj Baksh Singh of Sitapur. The raja changed the name of the estate from Bassett Hall to Kasmanda Palace, after his estate in Sitapur district (Uttar Pradesh state).

With its fabulous views and gleaming white presence, Kasmanda Palace is still one of the most beautiful buildings in Mussoorie. Today, it is owned by Rajkumar Dinraj Pratap Singh, great-grandson of Raja Bahadur Baksh. It is operated as a twenty-four-room luxury heritage hotel.

Most cottages were snug and, in consonance with the British Isles-like climate, house names too inclined wistfully towards 'Home'. The Victorian settlers gave nostalgic English, Scottish, Welsh or Irish names to their bungalows, including literary ones. Thus in Mussoorie and Landour houses were named Annandale, Alyndale, the Antlers and Abbotsford (the latter linked to Sir Walter Scott's home in Scotland); Dahlia Bank, Strawberry Bank, Sunny Bank and Bothwell Bank (the latter recently renovated by businessman and philanthropist, Sanjay Narang); Ockbrooke, Brooklands, Oakville and Oldville; Hazel Brae, Heather Brae and Briar Brae ('Brae' being a Scottish word for a hillside or slope); Glengowan, Glen Luce and Glenburnie, Rokeby, Kenilworth, Ivanhoe and Woodstock (all works by Sir Walter Scott).[8] And there was even Bleak House (Charles Dickens). Irish names were—and still are—particularly prevalent, names such as Mullingar and Trim (the latter very likely named after the castle and small town in County Meath to the northwest of Dublin, near where Arthur Wellesley, the first duke of Wellington, was born). While Logarithm Lodge to the west in Hathipaon cannot be considered 'inclining towards Home', it clearly does

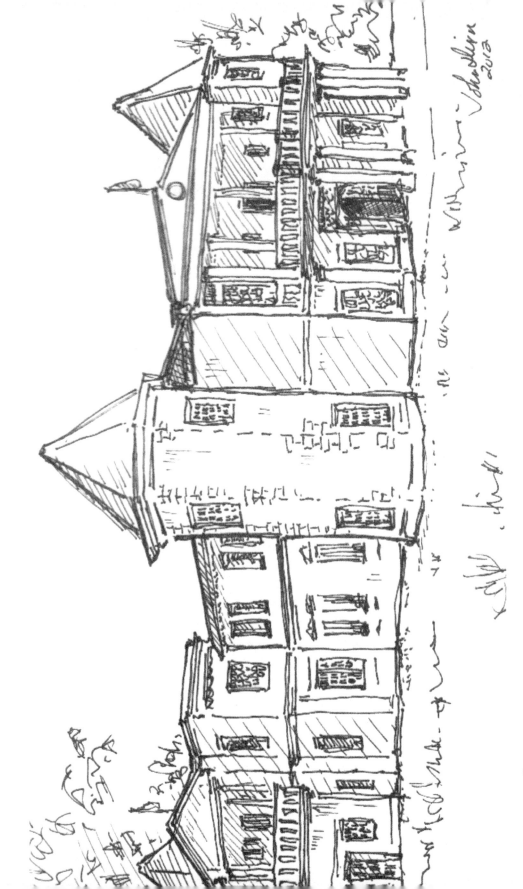

Bassett Hall, now named Kasmanda Palace, was constructed in 1836 and is one of the oldest, largest and grandest houses in Mussoorie. The hall has had a varied history, including serving host to invalids of the Crimean War. Happily, it is still preserved in pristine condition today.

(Sketch courtesy of John Dixon, Hawaii, USA)

reflect the important presence of the Survey of India in Mussoorie. And Bodycot comments in his 1907 guidebook that the residents in the west of Mussoorie must have been '…particularly pious', for there was the Deanery, the Vicarage, the Rectory (transformed by 1907 into Plaisance⁹), the Priory and the Monastery, topped off with the 'Nunnery' crowning Waverley Hill.¹⁰ Some of these names have changed with Indian ownership, but many are still retained to this day.

Whatever their names, these houses were maintained by an impressive staff of khansamahs (cooks), khitmatgars (butlers), malis (gardeners), dhobis (washermen), bhishtis (water carriers), jhampanis (coolies), mehtars (sweepers) and ayahs (nannies), the latter attending to children and memsahibs alike.

The Rectory was typical of the grand homes that graced the western and most fashionable part of the Station. This lovely house was renamed 'Plaisance' in the middle of the nineteenth century, when Mr Thomas Theophilus Forbes's wife, who had French connections, occupied the estate. Later, Plaisance was purchased by Ranjit Singh (OBE). Today, the Hotel Carlton Plaisance is run as a guest house by his descendants. It is well-stocked with eye-catching ephemera from earlier days.
(Courtesy of Alkazi Collection of Photography, New Delhi)

A Mr Lawrence opened the first shop in Mussoorie in 1829, selling general goods. This is said to have been the first business started in Mussoorie but, as we've seen, the Old

Brewery undertaking was quick to follow in 1830. And it wasn't long before Landour and Mussoorie had shops aplenty, most of them located in Landour's Sadar Bazaar.

Fanny Parkes noted in 1838 when she was in Landour that '…everything is to be had there—pâtée [sic] foie gras, bécasses truffées, shola hats covered with the skin of the pelican, champagne, Bareilly couches, shoes, Chinese books, pickles, long poles for climbing the mountains, and various incongruous articles.'[11]

By 1884, Northam reported:

> Here [at the police post located at the lower end of Landour] are the large native merchant's shops, the clothe merchants, and the native grain merchants, &c., &c... A nerik, or price current, for all kinds of commodities is published weekly. This Bazaar is frequently crowded by Europeans in the evening, and a good deal of business is done… Many of the native merchants purchase their goods through agents in England, France, America, and other countries, so that goods of nearly all descriptions can always be obtained in Landour.[12]

Today, the Landour shops still cater to residents for all basic commodities, since many shops on the Mall in Mussoorie are largely for modern-day tourists. However, one would look in vain for such 'incongruous' articles as pâté de foie gras and bécasses truffées (the latter is woodcock—*Scolopax indicus,* a species found in the Himalayas—prepared with truffles).

From Mussoorie's earliest days through to almost the middle of the twentieth century, the lady of the house (the 'memsahib') would generally confine her shopping in the bazaar to the stores selling European goods, leaving the day-to-day purchases to cooks and, perhaps, other household staff; that is, if basic household requirements were not brought right to the door, a service that was commonly provided well into the twentieth century. Speaking in 2004, long-term Landour resident Reverend Bob Alter described home delivery this way:

> It was still the days, in the [19]30s and [19]40s, when almost everything you needed was brought to your door—the milk-man, the egg-man, the bread-man, the meat-man, the vegetable-man, the cloth-man, the jam and pickle-man, the kabari wallah [collector of cast-off goods], the barber, the lace-man, Doma with her Tibetan wares, the box-wallah with buttons and thread and yarn and other household items including soap and toothpaste, the cloth-man, the mochi or shoemaker, and even the darzi, or tailor, who would come and sew on your

verandah. Apart from the milk-man and the bread-man, all the rest are gone. Now you have to send to the market for most of what you need, though one can phone in orders to shops like Prakash's in Sisters' Bazaar, or Ram Chander, in town, who will make deliveries for you.[13]

As one of the premier hill stations in northern India, Mussoorie was a good business home for European establishments. In 1860, the Station had three European shops, 'besides millinery and clothing establishments.'[14] By 1900, there were many other European-run shops, a number of them commented upon in some detail in *Echo's* 1908 guide to the Station. By the early-1930s, most of the European-owned shops had been taken over by Indian merchants.

Among the best known of the early European shops was Fitch & Co. Ltd, who were chemists and also wine, spirits and general goods merchants. Started in 1862 by Mr J.L. Lyell under the name Lyell & Co., it was taken over in 1882 by Mr T.W. Fitch who continued it as Fitch & Co. Ltd. Fitch & Co. Ltd did have competition as chemists in Mr P.A. Keogh's business which, after his death, was taken over in 1906 by M.R.B. Hamer. 'By careful management and strict

Price Current

	Srs.	Chs.
WHEAT, 1st quality … …	14	0
DITTO, 2nd ditto … …	15	0
FLOUR, 1st quality … …	13	0
DITTO, 2nd ditto … …	14	0
RICE, 1st quality … …	7	0
DITTO, 2nd ditto … …	15	4
GRAM, old … …	14	8
DITTO, new … …	13	4
BARLEY … …	15	0
URDAWA … …	12	12
MOONGH (DAL) … …	15	0
MUSSOOR (DITTO) … …	11	0
OORUD (DITTO) … …	16	0
GHEE (PLAINS) … …	1	14
DITTO (HILLS) … …	2	2
OIL (SWEET) … …	4	0
DITTO (COMMON) … …	4	4
SUGAR, 1st quality … …	2	8
DITTO, 2nd ditto … …	3	12
SALT (LAHORE) … …	7	0
DITTO, SAMBUR … …	6	8

This 'price current' list appeared in *The Hill*, Mussoorie's first-ever newspaper, on 12 December 1861. This price list would have helped the memsahib keep track of bills brought to her by servants, as she probably would have very rarely gone to the bazaar to purchase items such as these, preferring herself to frequent the so-called 'European shops'.

(Courtesy of British Library)

attention to business, the status of the [Hamer] firm has been considerably raised, and it is now one of the most successful businesses in Mussoorie.' Hamer's is still in business in Mussoorie and is now owned by Mr V. P. Hari and his son, Atul Hari. Besides the traditional dry goods store in Kulri, the company runs a nearby lodge. Hamer's is unique in that it is the only shop from the colonial period that has kept its original name. In the early 1900s, there was also the J.B. & E Samuel chemist shop in West End House, which was a successor company to D. Cartner Chemists (carried on by J.H. Clarke & Co. for a time before Samuel took over the company).

(L) In 1906, R.B. Hamer took over the chemist and general merchandise shop in the Kulri section of the Station. Hamer's is still in business, operated by V.P. and Atul Hari, and is unique in that it is the only shop from the colonial period that has kept its original name.

(Courtesy of British Library)

(R) Fitch & Co. Ltd was one of the premier shops in Mussoorie for nearly one hundred years. As this 1907 advertisement shows, it was a purveyor of medicines and many other goods, including wines and spirits. During the First World War, Fitch even rented and ran the Rink entertainment centre and was said to have realized considerable profit from it.

(Courtesy of British Library; advertisement from Bodycot, F. ['compiler'], Guide to Mussoorie with Notes on Adjacent Districts and Routes into the Interior, *Mussoorie: Mafasilite Printing Works, 1907)*

FITCH & COMPANY, LTD*

Messrs Fitch & Co., Ltd., General Merchants, Auctioneers, Chemists, Wine and Spirit Merchants, Mussoorie, carry on a business in the providing of the necessities and luxuries of life, which for variety and extent is unequalled in Northern India. In fact they well deserve the designation of the "Local Whiteley's." In Mussoorie, the firm holds an undisputed position as the foremost trading firm with a connection which extends universally among residents and visitors. Their position in the Station is the outcome of the many years that the Company in its present and former form has carried on business. It began with the early days of Mussoorie in the year 1862 and has kept pace with what has become now the most important hill station in Northern India, growing with the growth of Mussoorie. The Company's dealings range over a wide variety of business. Amongst the many departments are the following:—wines and spirits;

★from *Cyclopedia of India*, Calcutta, Cyclopedia Publishing Company, 1908: 296–298 in vol. 1.

English, Continental and American canned stores of all descriptions; hardware and ironmongery, electro-plated and silver goods, cigars, cigarettes, pipes, tobaccos, [and] fancy goods of every kind. They are well known as the original sole agents in India for Nester Gianaclis cigarettes, and also at the present time for the famous Evangele Christou's Egyptian cigarettes. The Company also carries on a large business as dispensing chemists, and supplies the Station with aerated waters from their aerated water factory, in which two large machines of the most modern pattern are constantly at work. Another department is devoted to house furnishing and they also possess a large clientele as valuers and auctioneers. The enterprise of the Directors puts the firm ahead in the matter of novelties of all kinds of which they are large importers from England, the Continent, America and Japan.

Being in a favourable financial position, they are able to buy in the cheapest market for cash of which circumstances their constituents reap the full advantage in moderate prices based on small profits. They are exporters of Indian indigenous drugs to some of the largest manufacturing chemists in England. The enterprise of Fitch & Co. caused them to be first in the field in the introduction of acetylene gas to Mussoorie when that illuminant first came into notice. They are now equally active with electricity and are making arrangements to have all their buildings electrically lighted.

The origin of Fitch & Co. as stated dates back to 1862 when it was established by Mr. J.L. Lyell under the style of Lyell & Co. Under this designation it was carried on for some twenty years till in the year 1882 the whole going concern was taken over by Mr. T.W. Fitch who, upon acquiring the business, continued it under the style of Fitch & Co. Mr. T.W. Fitch remained the sole managing proprietor of the firm till 1888 when Mr. C.F. Fitch who had joined the firm in 1885 became a partner. Mr. T.W. Fitch dying in 1899, Mr. C.F. Fitch conducted the affairs of the firm as managing proprietor until 1895 when he took Mr. S.V. Jolliffe into partnership. For the next seven years Messrs Fitch and Jolliffe carried on the business jointly, but in the year 1902 the advantages of converting the business into a limited liability company strongly presented themselves and the Company as at present constituted came into existence with Messrs Fitch and Jolliffe as Directors. Since then the financial side as well as every other aspect of the business has flourished exceedingly as is testified by the fact that a dividend of ten per cent has been paid yearly since the Company's formation. The Directors of the Company have been very active in extending the scope and conveniences of the business. Since the formation of the Company they have purchased a considerable property adjoining their own premises and have just completed new show rooms and store and a wine *godown* (warehouse), besides buildings for the accommodation of their numerous native staff. They have also opened a branch at Dehra Dun which on a smaller scale contains as varied a stock as their Mussoorie establishment. The equipment of the offices is well up to date. All the departments have telephonic communication with the Directors' offices, and the latter are also connected by telephone with all the principal places of business and Government offices in the Station. Each department is under the supervision of an European Assistant, with Mr. C. F. Fitch as General Manager, and Mr. S.V. Jolliffe In-Charge of the Financial Department. Both the Directors had special training for their respective duties, and before coming to India having obtained valuable experience with leading business Houses in London, Manchester and Bradford. Mr. Fitch and Mr. Jolliffe hail from the west of England, were educated in Plymouth, are now both 46 years of age, and have every prospect before they reach the meridian of life of seeing the business of Fitch & Co., Ltd become by far the largest and most important in Northern India. They personally superintend every detail of the daily work, so as to keep thoroughly in touch with the pulse of the business, thus ensuring a very satisfactory working both from a shareholder's point of view, as well as from that of their numerous constituents. The result of this directly personal control is known by the yearly increasing volume of the Company's turnover, and is emphasized by the fact that none of their shares are at present obtainable (even at a premium) on the market.

The Company have the honour of an appointment as chemists and general merchants to H.E. The Earl of Minto, Viceroy and Governor-General of India, and have held similar appointments from every successive Viceroy from the time of Lord Lytton and also from H.R.H. the Duke of Connaught, when H.R.H. was in command of the Meerut Division.

The London Agents of the Company are Messrs Ledger Sons & Co.; Muller Maclean & Co.; and for Paris, Messrs Constant Mertens & Coo. The telegraphic address of the Company is "Fitch," and their Telegraphic Code is A.B.C.5.

(L) C.F. Fitch joined Fitch & Co. in 1888 in partnership with T.W. Fitch. In 1895, C.F. Fitch partnered with S.V. Jolliffe (R) and, together, they managed the company well into the twentieth century, by which time it had become a limited liability company. Fitch & Co. was Mussoorie's largest business house, importing many goods from England, the Europe continent, America and Japan while exporting indigenous medicinal drugs around the world. The only comparable company in the Station, in terms of reach beyond the local area, was the Himalaya Feed Stores in Barlowganj (below the Mall), which produced and exported high-quality vegetable and flower seeds.

(Courtesy of British Library)

It seems, from the European companies discussed in *Echo,* that the residents and visitors to Mussoorie had plenty of interest, time and money to indulge in embellishing their personal appearance. J.C. Bechtler Son & Co. sold fine jewellery. Dill & Co. were also jewellers as well as noted watchmakers. H Clark & Co., established in 1879 and with their own building on the Mall (Mall View House), specialized in tailoring, making shirts for men and dresses for women. It was 'the shrine of Mussoorie fashion' and, as highlighted in their advertisement in *Echo's* guide, 'shirt makers to His Majesty the Amir of Afghanistan and Baron Curzon of Kedleston, and many other distinguished patrons.' Trevillion & Clark, established in 1896 near 'Windy Corner', also made a specialty of millinery and dressmaking, with European assistants to manage their departments. Mrs Draper made hats. 'Mrs Draper's whole training has been in millinery. She learnt the art of hat-making in Kensington, and has held the position of head milliner to several West End firms. In her showrooms, clients can select in comfort from a stock imported direct from Paris and London.' Not to be outdone by Mrs Draper, Mr Hakman was a specialist in wigs and perfumery and a make-up artist, which came in handy for performances of the Mussoorie Amateur Dramatic Club. M.S. Hathaway and Co. was '…one of the finest shops to be seen in these Provinces and where the latest styles and fashions may always be found. Their dressmaking and millinery departments are always in the hands of experienced English assistants and can be relied on for quality, fit and style at moderate price.' Open in Mussoorie for the Season and in Lucknow for the winter, the Cash Boot Stores in Southend House stocked footwear from England but also had bespoke, repairing and manufacturing departments. The latter featured the 'Beet-aul' brand.[15]

And amazing as it may seem in today's India, pianos were at one time actually manufactured in Mussoorie. In 1899, Mr A. Liebchen, piano tuner and maker, was set up in business by Fitch & Co. in the Criterion Restaurant building near the library. Four years later, the entity was given over by Fitch and Co. to Mr Liebchen himself. In 1907, another local music business that had been operated by Mr J.D. Bevan in Mussoorie for the previous twenty years was added to Messrs A. Liebchen & Co. Operating by this time from Mall View House, Liebchen dealt 'in all kinds of musical instruments. Imported pianos are by first class makers only. As a speciality, pianos are made on the premises… A large music room is available for practicing, rehearsing, etc. at moderate rates. Professor Rampezzotti, DRCM [Doctor of the Royal College of Music], a well-known teacher for piano, violin, and singing, attends daily.'[16]

There was also the famous Rust photography shop, whose originals today sell for a 'small fortune' in the upscale antiquarian shops of New Delhi and London. This business was started in Mussoorie in 1872 by Mr Thomas Alfred (T.A.) Rust and carried on from 1893 to 1914 by his son Julian Rust out of Regent House on the hill in Kulri.[17] Later, there came the Kinsey Brothers and several other studios.

But it was not just the European shops that prospered, for the Station required a huge amount of food. These consumables—vegetables, rice, spices—came from the hills surrounding Mussoorie or from the plains. The schools, of course, were major consumers for the local grocers and wholesalers. In 1936, C. Williams wrote:

Apart from the benefit to the younger generation that our many schools are providing, have you ever thought on how much the prosperity of Mussoorie, or its trades people at least, depends on these institutions? Taking only the question of food, estimated on a conservative basis with one of our poorest schools as a

(Above) Mr J.D. Bevan operated a music business for twenty years (1887–1907) out of the thatched building in the foreground, which is now where Mela Ram & Sons photography shop is located. In 1907, Mr Bevan sold out to Messrs A. Liebchen & Co.

(Photo by Mr and Mrs S.A. Hill from the Ballade of Photographs, 1888, captioned by Rudyard Kipling, Rare Book and Special Collections Division, Library of Congress)

(L) Kinsey Brothers was one of Mussoorie's premier photography studios in the first half of the twentieth century. This Kinsey photo is of the debonair Leslie George Payne. Mr Payne worked in Mussoorie for Messrs Fitch & Co. as a pharmacist 1928–1934.

(Photo kind courtesy of John and Sonia née Payne Harriyott, England)

criterion, the domiciled schools in the station consume in their nine months' term: loaves of bread 11,88,000; rice lbs. 1,18,800, milk seers 1,18,800; meat seers 91,800; vegetables lbs. 1,62,000; fuel seers 1,62,000; and sugar lbs. 86,400. God bless the schools![18]

Consider what these figures must be today.

So, in short, Mussoorie was well-provisioned in terms of European and European-style commodities and in locally grown staples for the table. And there was plenty of domestic help available to add further to one's comfort. It was a blending of goods and services that added greatly to the Station's attractiveness.

Well-cared for in these respects, the comfortable and homely householders in the Station could turn their attention to that great Victorian passion, gardening. The period during which Mussoorie and Landour were being established—beginning in the late 1820s—coincided with a growing interest in gardening in England, an interest that quickly extended to the pleasant climate of the hill stations where familiar European varieties thrived and made the landscape less alien to the colonialists. Many of the European houses in the Station had very good gardens, with violets, dahlias, buttercups, sweet peas, blue gentians, blue bonnets, tulips, climbing roses, geraniums, clematis, honeysuckle and hollyhock, all familiar and pleasing to the sentimental English eye and, hopefully, to the judges at the Annual Flower Show held each August. Wild strawberries, raspberries and blackberries were plentiful and familiar vegetables such as cabbages, cauliflowers and turnips were also grown. Fruit trees were planted too; plums, pears and apples.[19] And of course, there was the ever-helpful mali (gardener), an essential member of the domestic staff, who could do so much of the heavy work. When needed, one could also rely on the expertise of the staff at the Municipal Gardens (Company Bagh). Quality seeds were available from the Himalaya Seed Stores in Barlowganj, a company that surely was one of the Station's most successful.

The Himalaya Seed Stores was a remarkable establishment. It was begun in 1889 by Mr R. Barton-West, the husband of Mrs E.C. Barton-West who started what became Wynberg Allen School. The operation moved to Barlowganj in 1894, from whence it expanded into an enormous business, filling orders 'from every province in India, from Burma, Ceylon, Aden, Zanzibar, East Africa, Japan, China Johannesburg, Cape Town, Afghanistan, Siam [Thailand], Malay States and even from the Channel Isles and Great Britain... With an establishment like the Himalaya Seed Stores in the country, there is now no need for garden lovers to send to England or America for their seeds, &c., as the firm under notice can handle orders from the smallest to the largest quite as satisfactorily as any of the well-known seed establishments at Home.' Upon Barton's death in 1893, the company was taken over by Mr W. W. Johnston, a fellow of the Royal Horticultural Society and a prolific writer on matters connected with horticulture. His book—*Gardening, a Guide for Amateurs in India*—was 'perhaps the most largely read book in India on the subject.'[20]

The Himalaya Seed Stores in Barlowganj provided the Station's gardeners with all they might need in the way of flower and vegetable seeds; manures including guano; and books on gardening. In time, the seed company went far beyond supplying local demand and became widely known around the world for providing high-quality vegetable and flower seeds. *(Logo from advertisement in Bodycot, F. ['compiler'],* Guide to Mussoorie with Notes on Adjacent Districts and Routes into the Interior, *Mussoorie: Mafasilite Printing Works, 1907)*

In these pleasant bungalow settings amidst gardens that reminded owners of Home, memsahibs, with help from ayahs, looked after their small children. There may have been English nannies but, more often, childcare was entrusted to an Indian woman. Older children, particularly sons, were often home in Britain, studying in boarding schools or residing with relatives. But the younger ones would come to Mussoorie for the Season with their mothers, for the comforts of a mild climate and 'to preserve life and breath'. These were much pampered children who, in the early years particularly, still fell victim to disease.[21] The hill climate was meant to prevent such a dreadful outcome. Apparently, the results were successful. Said Fanny Parkes as early as 1838, 'The children! It is charming to see their rosy faces; they look as well and as strong as any children in England. The climate of the hills, however, is certainly far superior to that of England.'[22]

To amuse the little ones, various outings were often planned. There were perambulators on the Mall, attended by ayahs and bearers, trips to the Municipal Gardens and picnics at the more accessible of Mussoorie's waterfalls. But no event was more successful than the quintessential fancy-dress party. All in all, Station life was pleasant for the children, whose sallow complexions when coming from the plains changed to ruddy cheeks in the hills. It was gratifying for parents who were anxious about their children's health and, indeed, for their very lives.

From the earliest days of the Station, children and adults alike enjoyed the many waterfalls around Mussoorie. A prime spot for tea parties was Kempty Falls on the Ringal Nadi which, up to recent times, was isolated and uninhabited. Now, it is five easy miles from the library, situated on the Mussoorie–Chakrata Road. A high waterfall—or, rather, a series of five waterfalls all within the horizontal distance of a few hundred yards and aggregating to a total fall of about 600 vertical feet (183 metres)—cascades into a stream through a succession of pools surrounded by rocks and vegetation. This idyllic spot now has become overrun with tatty tea stalls and 'dress-up-in-local-costume' photo studios, catering to crowds of tourists during the Season. The name Kempty is said to be derived from 'camp tea', in tribute to the tea parties held here. Lake Mist is a pleasure spot en route to Kempty Falls.

Bhatta Falls, near the villages of Bhatta and Kyarkuli, was also used for picnics and, later, these falls were harnessed to power the hydro-electric scheme. Hardy Falls, approached by the southwestern spurs of Vincent Hill, was deemed unfit for children and memsahibs; it was '…only visited by men and boys out for a day's constitutional or for sport…the distance from Mussoorie form[ing] a bar to their being visited except on rare occasions.' And why the name 'Hardy Falls'?

> Because when the boys of Mr Maddock's school 'discovered' the falls Mr Hardy was Principal of the institution and had accompanied his charges on the ramble that led them to the spot. And lest the world would not accept the students' christening, they labouriously carved the name in a rock by the fall and time has not effaced it.[23]

Murray Falls, located below Dhobi Ghat, was also difficult to approach:

> Murray Falls and [nearby sulphur] springs were discovered by Dr Murray more than thirty years ago [in the early 1850s]. Dr Murray had some huts built near these springs, and sent a number of ailing soldiers from the Landour Depôt to benefit by what he considered the healing powers of these waters; but the experiment was not pursued.[24]

Later the water from the springs at Murray Falls was bottled and sold[25] but apparently, that experiment also failed.

Mossy Falls and Hearsey Falls in Barlowganj (lower Mussoorie), where the

A 1941 fancy-dress party for British children at the Charleville Hotel. The young girl in the centre standing to the right of the young Beefeater is Verena Rybicki née Morgan. Mrs Rybicki's father, William Stanley Morgan, was a British doctor in the Indian Medical Service, stationed on the North West Frontier while his family remained in Mussoorie.
(Photo kind courtesy of Verena Morgan Rybicki, Massachusetts, USA)

Hearsey and Skinner families were prominent, were also popular picnic sites. Mossy Falls, which still provides water to Oak Grove School, was said to have been named after a Mr Moss.

> Picnicking by this water, on their own estate, the Hearsey family had as guest Mr Moss of the Himalaya Bank, who was affectionately known as "Mossy" by his associates. Scrambling over some rocks the guest slipped and fell to anchor well midstream, to a chorus of guffaws, and thus supplied the long elusive name—"Mossy Falls"![26]

Kempty Falls was a popular picnic spot for the Station. Picnickers were sometimes followed by their cooks and bearers, who would provide hot meals. The name 'Kempty' is said to be derived from 'camp tea', in tribute to these elaborate tea parties. Kempty was at one point considered for a scheme to provide water and electricity to the Station; however, negotiations with the raja of Tehri fell through and the Bhatta Falls site in British territory was finally chosen. Although now far from pristine, Kempty Falls is still a popular site with visitors to the Station.

(Kind courtesy of the late H. Michael Stokes, Kent, United Kingdom)

Mossy Falls in Barlowganj was a popular picnic site. It still is the water source for Oak Grove School. As noted in the message on the back of this picture postcard message, Mussoorie was a favourite honeymoon spot even in 1919.

(Postcard photo from the private collection of the late H. Michael Stokes, United Kingdom)

Landour Depot   *April 1900*

The 'spring at home' in Landour in April 1900. It was uncommon, but not unheard of, for NCOs to be accompanied to India by their wives. However, many of these officers married while in India.

(Courtesy of the National Army Museum, London)

So, for the 'at home-away-from-Home' part of life, everything was in good order in the Station. Servants were taking care of household chores and the children. Memsahibs could shop in European-like stores. There were early morning rides (or walks) for active adults, and many outings for children and adults alike. For the adults, there were other sources of entertainment in the form of balls, private evening parties, archery meetings, polo meets, theatricals, a run for a few days to Deyrah for the races and then the Season was over.

Notes

1. 'May', *Mussoorie Portraits in Rhyme, Taken during the Season,* Mussoorie: Beacon Press, 1888. During the 1888 Season, such doggerel by 'May' (a nom de plume) appeared in *The Beacon,* a local newspaper, and was later compiled into a small booklet. (British Library)

2. The Cossipore Arsenal in Calcutta—originally called the Gun Carriage Agency—was opened in 1801 by the East India Company for the repair and manufacture of gun carriages. Much transformed by technology, the facility is now called the Gun and Shell Factory. Today, it manufactures state-of-the-art ammunition and ordnance for the Indian military services.

3. Williams, C. ('The Rambler'), *A Mussoorie Miscellany,* Mussoorie: Mafasilite Press, 1936: 47-48. Today, no one in the Station seems to know where the Mussoorie cannon ended up.

4. Blucher's Hill is 7,205 feet above sea level (2,196 metres). Gun Hill is 7,029 feet (2,143 metres). These are the two highest points in Mussoorie proper (not including Landour or even the Benog Hill located to the west).

5. Wilson, W. ('Mountaineer') *A Summer Ramble in the Himalayas with Sporting Adventures in the Vale of Cashmere*, London: Hurst and Blackett, 1860: 22-23.

6. Watkins, Marguerite Thoburn, *Two Taproots: Growing up in the Forties in India and America,* USA: Xlibris Corporation, 2004: 165.

7. Wilson, Ibid, pp. 14-15.

8. Sir Walter Scott did not publicly acknowledge authorship of his novels, beginning with *Waverley* (1814) until 1827, exactly the time when Mussoorie and Landour were first being developed. Before this time, he was popularly referred to as 'The Great Unknown'.

9. Originally called the Rectory, the Plaisance was owned for many years by Mr Thomas Theophilus Forbes of the East India Company. Following the First War of Independence in 1857, the nawab of Oudh was temporarily exiled with his family to an encampment in Bengal. It was here that Mr Forbes met and married Eileen, the nawab's daughter from his French–Belgian wife. Eventually, Mr Forbes set Eileen up at the Plaisance Estate in Mussoorie, which he purchased on 13 December 1897. Eileen's French connections account for the fact that the estate was given a French name, while other colonial properties in Mussoorie generally had English, Scottish, Irish or Welsh names. Eileen Forbes continued to live at Plaisance long after her husband passed away. Shortly before her own demise in the 1930s, Eileen retired to England and sold the Plaisance estate fully decorated and furnished to Mr Ranjit Singh (OBE), whose family has steadfastly preserved the architectural and decorative integrity of the premises (information from various sources, as well as from current Plaisance owners, Ajit and Anu Singh).

10. Bodycot, F. ('compiler'), *Guide to Mussoorie with Notes on Adjacent Districts and Routes into the Interior,* Mussoorie: Mafasilite Printing Works, 1907: 52-53. There is no indication of a house called the 'Vicarage' on the 1929 map of the Station.

11. Parkes, Fanny, *Wanderings of a Pilgrim, in Search of the Picturesque, during Four-and-Twenty Years*

in the East; with Revelations of Life in the Zenana, London: Pelham Richardson, 1850: 230 in vol. 2.

12. Northam, John, *Guide to Masuri, Landaur, Dehra Dun and the Hills North of Dehra*, Calcutta: Thacker, Spink and Company, 1884: 48.

13. Alter, Bob, *Mussoorie Then and Now*, Reverend Alter speaking to a group of visiting Woodstock School Alumni, Oakville, Landour, Mussoorie, Uttarakhand, India, 24 October 2004 (unpublished).

14. Wilson, Ibid, p. 13.

15. Kinney, T., *The Echo Guide to Mussoorie*, Mussoorie: Echo Press, 1908: 96-107.

16. Kinney, Ibid, p. 104.

17. The first record of Thomas Rust as a photographer is in 1869 when he worked as an assistant to F.W. Baker in Calcutta. A year later he was running the Calcutta Photographic Company with W.T. Burgess and did so until 1874, so one can assume that he was already an experienced professional photographer before joining Baker. In the 1870s, Rust opened five of his own studios in Allahabad, Mussoorie, Murree, Landour and Meerut. Thomas Rust's landscapes are considered very artistic and he may well have had some formal training in this area. His son Julian joined the firm in the 1890s and continued until 1914. (British Library)

18. Williams, Ibid, p. 65.

19. Kennedy writes, 'It has been claimed that the first English apple tree to be transplanted into Indian soil was nurtured in Mussoorie' (Kennedy, Dane, *The Magic Mountains, Hill Stations and the British Raj*, Delhi: Oxford University Press, 1996: 47). Credit for bringing apples to the region may go to Frederick Young and, possibly, Frederick 'Pahari' Wilson.

20. Kinney, Ibid, p. 103-104.

21. A major anxiety for British families in India was the high rate of infant mortality. In the Bengal Presidency—of which Mussoorie was a part—between 1860 and 1869, the average death rate was about 148 per thousand among British children under the age of five, while in England during the same period the mortality rate was about sixty-seven per thousand. The grief of losing children was expressed time and again by British mothers. Maria Amelia Vansittart, the wife of Henry Vansittart—Bengal Civil Service, superintendent of Dehra Dun in the 1840s, and property owner in Mussoorie—noted in her diary on 26 March 1846, that between eight and nine in the evening a little girl was born, and in the entry of 13 April she described her daughter's burial. The rate of infant mortality decreased as the century progressed, but it was still high enough to create anxiety and helplessness among British mothers (adapted from Fass, Paula [editor], *Encyclopedia of Children and Childhood in History and Society*, New York: MacMillan Reference Books, 2003).

22. Parkes, Fanny, Ibid, p. 229-230 in vol. 2.

23. Williams, Ibid, p. 95.

24. Northam, Ibid, p. 38.

25. Kinney, T., *The Echo Guide to Mussoorie*, Mussoorie: Echo Press, 1908: 37.

26. Ibid.

Completed in 1903, the summer home of the Maharaja of Kapurthala, Chateau de Kapurthala, still dominates the western end of the Mall. The compiler of *The Gazetteer of Dehra Dun*, H.G. Walton, wrote in 1911, 'The only building with any pretension to architectural beauty [in the Station] is the Chateau de Kapurthala...[it] is solidly built in the French style and presents a great and pleasing contract to the adjacent houses.'[1] *(Kind courtesy of Ajay Mark, Landour)*

9

ROYALS OF THE HIMALAYAS

Mussoorie seems from the first to have been deemed
an eligible residence for native princes.
~ *From the Guide to Mussoorie, 1907*[2] ~

It is an anomaly that the most imposing and one of the most beautiful structures in all of Mussoorie should have been inspired by French rather than British architectural styles for, after all, the Station was a sort of 'little England' for its first one hundred years. Yet it is so and, even today, the Chateau de Kapurthala, with its turreted rooftops and coat of arms emblazoned on the central masonry, reigns over the Mall in glorious tribute to an elegant but less egalitarian era.

The chateau is beautifully situated at the west end of the Mall above the library and the Savoy Hotel. It was built during 1900–1903 by the widely travelled Maharaja Jagatjit Singh of Kapurthala (thirteen-gun salute[3]), the Europhile head of the eponymous princely state in northern India.[4] His Highness was married six times (twice to European women, Spanish and Czech), was decorated numerous times by the British, served as one of India's representatives to the League of Nations, and was rajpramukh (head) of PEPSU[5] until his death. His nearby bolthole, of course, was his chateau in Mussoorie, which is still home during the Season to his heir, Brigadier His Highness Sri Sukhjit Singh.

During the Second World War, when Mussoorie was more crowded than usual with Indian princes who could no longer travel to Europe for their holidays, the chateau became a centre of entertainment, the highlight being an annual garden party on the grounds, followed by a ball on the sprung wooden dance floor inside. 'Guest seldom went home before two in the morning.'[6] And to add to the festivities in the Station, it is said that the Maharaja Rana Sahib of Porbander (thirteen-gun) wrote and recorded Western dance music, including numbers called 'Mussoorie Mists' and 'Russian Roubles'.[7]

But while none could compare in grandeur to the chateau, there were many other royal homes in Mussoorie, some owned and some rented, but all enjoyed by

An early postcard showing the equipage of the royal family of Kapurthala. Members of the Kapurthala family were for many years central to the social life of the Station.
(Postcard photo kind courtesy of the late H. Michael Stokes, Kent, United Kingdom)

princes of India as retreats during the Season. Besides the Chateau de Kapurthala, the 1929 Survey of India map of Mussoorie shows several other royal properties including Ranbir Villa, near the Sylverton Estate, His Highness Kalsia; Airfield Estate above Barlowganj, HH Bhopal; Summerville near the kutchery (courts), HH Tehri Garwhal; Padmani Niwas on the Mall below Christ Church, HH Rajpipla; Eric's Own near the Carlton's Plaisance Hotel, HH Tikari; and Dunseverick, where the Dunsvirk Court Hotel is now located, HH the Gaekwad of Baroda. As M.S. Kalyanasundaram has noted, 'Mussoorie flourished and grew under the lavish patronage of the Indian rajas.'[8]

Like the British, Indian royalty were attracted to Mussoorie by the salubrious climate, relatively easy access and informal atmosphere. But there were other reasons why Mussoorie appealed to them. Most importantly, Indian royals were readily given permission by the colonial government to establish themselves in Mussoorie, something that was often difficult to obtain at official hill stations, particularly Shimla.

And on the Station's social scene, no one outranked them in terms of the order of precedence, since the Station was without high-level British officials, the only 'official residents' during the Season being district officers, military men in the cantonment and field parties of the Trigonometrical Survey of India. In addition, there was a critical mass of royalty during the Season, which allowed these princes to meet their equals without formality, protocol or the distraction of the burdens of state.

However, the royal retreats of Mussoorie did not extend to Landour—if one discounts Castle Hill, where Maharaja Duleep Singh was confined in 1852 and 1853—since the cantonment area was subject to military restrictions. In any case, in the early days, Mussoorie and particularly its western side was considered the posh and more desirable area of the Station.

Besides Kapurthala, there were three other of the eight Punjabi princely states that had retreats in Mussoorie, namely, Jind (thirteen-gun), Nabha (thirteen-gun), and Kalsia.

Located on the road down to St George's School, the Jind estate was appropriately  named Oakless, for the lack of oak trees on the property. Today, it is owned and maintained by friends of the family. HRH Rajmata Prithvi Bir Kaur, the second wife of the maharaja of Jind, Sri Tikka Sahib Rajbir Singh, was known by the children in her family as 'Aunt Pretty', not only because of the phonetic similarity to 'Prithvi' but also due to her stunning good looks, purportedly from her Romanian grandmother. In the Station, Aunt Pretty was well-known for exercising her horses and terriers on the Mall.

The royal house of Nabha settled into the Barlowganj area in what today is the Claridge's Hotel. Ranbir Villa, located near the Sylverton Estate, was the summer home of His Highness Kalsia.

The stunningly beautiful princess, Niloufer Khanum Sultana of Hyderabad, added considerably to the social scene in Mussoorie during the Second World War period. *(Courtesy of Library of Congress)*

However, there were some 'bigger guns' than the Punjabi princes in Mussoorie.

Baroda (twenty-one-gun) was a leading princely state, and His Highness the Gaekwad (maharaja) and his family travelled to Mussoorie to make their seasonal home at Dunseverick, which was located where the Hotel Dunsvirk Court now stands, near the Bellevue Estate. Although the conditions have changed, the site remains the same.[9] The 7,200 feet (2,195 metres) site commands a wonderful view of the Dun Valley to the south and the far off snows to the north.

The nizam of Hyderabad (twenty-one-gun) did not have a seasonal residence in Mussoorie but his daughter-in-law, the stunningly beautiful Princess Niloufer Khanum Sultana of Hyderabad (b.1916–d.1989), made an impressive showing in the Station during the war years. She spent much holiday time in Mussoorie as she—like other Indian royalty—was unable to travel on holiday to Europe during the Second World War. Her Highness Niloufer was one of the last princesses of the Ottoman Empire and was married to the seventh nizam's second son, Prince Moazzam Jah Bahadur. She added impressively to the attractions at the annual flower show by presenting the prizes during the years of the Second World War.[10]

Members of the royal house of Jaipur (seventeen-gun) also spent the Season in Mussoorie at their summer residence. Their house—a wedding gift to Maharani (Rajmata) Gayatri Devi from her grandmother—is located on the road up to Manava Bharati School (formerly, Dumbarnie).

Rushbrooke Estate was the Mussoorie summer home of the maharaja of Rajpipla (thirteen-gun). The maharaja gifted the estate to his wife, Maharani Padmini, and today, it is the Hotel Padmini Niwas, a beautifully situated 'old-world' inn on the Mall set amongst majestic deodar, cypress and oak trees and with lovely gardens. The life of the maharaja of Rajpipla, who ascended the gadi (throne) in 1915, was interesting and unusual. Lieutenant Colonel His Highness Maharana Shri Sir Vijaysinhji Chhatrasinhji Sahib, KCSI,[11] proved to be an excellent administrator, promoting education, building hospitals and undertaking various other public works and, as a result, he was the first Rajpipla ruler to win the hereditary title of 'maharaja'. Vijaysinhji was also a great horseman, and is still the only Indian owner to have a horse win the famed Epsom Derby (1934). His stud went on to win many other races in India and in Europe. Despite being known for his long sojourns in Europe and his loyalty to the British crown, Maharaja Vijaysinhji started a nationalist movement in Rajpipla in the 1940s and remained active in promoting independence. Today, the major part of the former princely state of Rajpipla forms the Narmada district in Gujarat, with Rajpipla town as its headquarters.

The local 'host' of Mussoorie was the raja of Tehri-Garhwal (eleven-gun), who had given up—or had taken from him—the real estate on which Mussoorie was built. On the termination of the Nepal War in 1815, that portion of the hereditary possessions which lay to the west of the Alakananda River was restored in 1820 to Raja Sudershan Shah, while the parganas—a group of neighboring villages—of the Dun and Raingarh were retained by the British government, although Hyder Young Hearsey claimed ownership of the Dun (see Chapter 10).

But not all the royals who resided in Mussoorie were there by their own choice. For some reason, Mussoorie, more than any other hill station, was used by the British as a retreat-in-exile—house arrest, in fact—for deposed royalty. This may have come about because Mussoorie was a more politically out-of-the-way station for high-profile prisoners, unlike other major stations that were summer capitals. Yet, at the same time, Mussoorie was quite accessible.

These circumstances led to a unique relationship between Afghanistan and Mussoorie, for the Station played host to events that played out in the aftermath of the First Anglo–Afghan War (1839–1842), the Second Anglo–Afghan War (1878–1880) and the Third Anglo–Afghan War (1919).

The first Afghan royal to fetch up in Mussoorie was Amir Dost Mohammad Khan (b.1793–d.1863). Dost Mohammad had come to power in Kabul in 1826 and, by the late 1830s, was facing off against the British in the First Anglo–Afghan War (1839–1842), having allegedly made overtures to the Russians. This conflict was said to be a 'Great Game' manoevre by the East India Company to ensure the safety of India against Russian attack by installing a trustworthy ally—Shah Shuja—on its western frontier. The cold-blooded murder of British officers Alexander Burnes and William Macnaghten and the horrific retreat of General William Elphinstone's army and its camp followers have provided grist for serious historical analysis, as well as for novels and movies, for over one hundred years.

But before their final defeat, the British had enjoyed a battle victory at Ghazni, and it was at this time, on 2 November 1840 to be precise, that Dost Mohammad surrendered to the British. Thereupon, he was hustled off to Mussoorie.

Dost Mohammad was kept as a political prisoner on a hilltop site—now part of the campus of Wynberg Allen School—in what was called Bala Hissar by the Mussoorie locals, after the historic palace fortress in Kabul ('Bala Hissar' means 'high fortress' in Persian). Ultimately, good fortune returned to Dost Mohammad when the Afghans finally defeated the British, and he returned to Afghanistan and his throne. Dost Mohammad continued to rule as amir of Afghanistan until his death in 1863.

A British rendering of the surrender of Amir Dost Mohammad Khan during the First Anglo–Afghan War (1839–1842). Dost Mohammad spent almost two years in Mussoorie at 'Bala Hissar' on a hilltop that is now part of the campus of Wynberg Allen School. *(Courtesy of Library of Congress)*

It was during the Second Anglo–Afghan War (1878–1880) that Amir Mohammad Yaqub Khan (b.1849–d.1923) was captured and sent to the Station. Yaqub Khan was amir of Afghanistan for a very short period from February to October 1879, after his father Sher Ali fled from the British during a conflict precipitated by Sher Ali's refusal to accept a British diplomatic mission while welcoming a Russian one. This was, of course, more of the Great Game. In May 1879, with British forces occupying much of the country, Yaqub signed the Treaty of Gandamak, relinquishing control of Afghanistan's foreign affairs to the British, allowing for a British Residency in Kabul and giving up some territory along the eastern border with India...but gaining a £60,000 sterling per annum subsidy. An uprising against this agreement, in which Yaqub was implicated and in which the British Representative Sir Louis Cavagnari and his staff were killed, resulted in an avenging expedition led by Sir Frederick Roberts and Yaqub's abdication (or perhaps, his outright ouster). Some time after

Amir Mohammad Yaqub Khan at Gandamak with Afghan and British officers, May 1879 (L to R: Mr William Jenkyns, secretary to Cavagnari and lead negotiator, later assassinated; Major Cavagnari, British resident in Kabul, later assassinated; Amir Yakub Khan; Daoud Shah, Yakub Khan's commander-in-chief; and Habibullah Khan, Yakub Khan's prime minister). At Gandamak, Yakub Khan signed a controversial treaty with the British, a treaty that neither ended the Second Anglo–Afghan War, nor assured him of his throne. Yakub Khan spent forty-three years in Mussoorie and died in Dehra Dun in 1923. This photo was taken by the well-known nineteenth-century photographer, John Burke, who accompanied British forces into Afghanistan and covered the events of the Second Anglo–Afghan War (1878–80), becoming in the process the first significant photographer of the country and its people.

(Courtesy of Library of Congress)

Yaqub's exist, the British installed his cousin, Abdur Rahman Khan, on the throne. Abdur Rahman had confirmed the Treaty of Gandamak, leaving the British in control of the territories ceded by Yaqub Khan[12] and ensuring British control of Afghanistan's foreign policy in exchange for protection and a subsidy. The British did abandon their provocative policy of maintaining a British resident in Kabul, but having achieved their other objectives, they withdrew and the bloody war ended. In the meantime, Yaqub had been bundled off to Mussoorie, escorted there by the Northumberland Fusiliers. Feeling that he had led a wretched life as amir, he is famously quoted as saying that he would rather be a grass cutter in a British camp than ruler of Afghanistan, so it was probably better all round that he put up at

The ruins of Bellevue '...on a fine site on the southern spur of Vincent Hill' where Amir Mohammad Yaqub Khan was put up for forty-three years after his exile from Afghanistan in the wake of events during the Second Anglo–Afghan War (1878–1880). Bellevue, now renamed 'Radha Bhawan', is disputed property, thus accounting perhaps for its dilapidated condition. *(Kind courtesy of Corrie Maya Daurio, USA)*

Bellevue '...on a fine site on the southern spur of Vincent Hill.'[13]

It was said that, '...At Bellevue he [Yakub Khan] has a large retinue to minister to his wants and his pleasures, and as he is permitted to ride about the Station at will—a privilege of which he takes abundant advantage—the fetters which bind him to Mussoorie and Dehra must be loose and easy.'[14] Nonetheless, Yaqub was understandably not entirely pleased with his perceived Elysium circumstances, which allowed him 'free access' to all parts of the Station and surroundings, as the 'The Rambler' makes clear in his 1936 guidebook:

> Ex-Amir Yaqub Khan was invariably accompanied by a British Political Officer, who on the many rides around the Station could never understand the prisoner's habit of suddenly spurring his pony into a fast gallop, without a word of warning to his companions. These bursts of speed became more and more frequent and

the officer eventually put it down to mere whim, till one day the full meaning of it was borne to him in a most discomforting manner. The officer had stopped to converse with a friend while the rest of the cavalcade ambled on till a bifurcation of the road was reached, near the Library, whereupon the prisoner spurred hard for his pony to shoot forward down the road to Rajpore—and perhaps, to freedom. That, at least, was what the officer concluded the dash was maneuvered for, and his only chance of intercepting the run-away was to urge his own pony to leap down the steep drop to the road below, which is what he did. The Governor-General was informed of the incident by telegram and orders were sought in the event of further similarities. The reply was 'Don't hurt one hair of his head'.[15]

The ex-amir—later styled only as 'sardar' by the British—died at the age of seventy-four in Dehra Dun on 15 November 1923 (see Appendix D for Amir Yakub's obituary in *The Times*). Decendants of Amir Yakub Khan still live in Dehra Dun and surrounding areas.

The very lengthy negotiations that followed the Third Anglo–Afghan War (1919) again brought Mussoorie into the vortex of Anglo–Afghanistan affairs. The end of the last war in 1880 had ushered in almost forty years of reasonably good relations between Britain and Afghanistan. But still, the British were deeply involved in managing Afghanistan's foreign policy which, despite a large subsidy, was of course an irritant to the Afghanis. Thus, shortly after Amir Amanullah came to the throne in February 1919 upon the murder of his father, he proclaimed a jihad (holy war) against Britain. On 3 May 1919, Amanullah's troops crossed into India, but British Indian troops quickly pushed them back and they in turn entered Afghanistan. Amanullah sued for peace. The subsequent Treaty of Rawalpindi (8 August 1919) ended the fighting but was just the start of protracted negotiations. This treaty—a tentative victory for Afghanistan, in that it made clear that Afghanistan controlled its own foreign policy, even though the British subsidy was ended—called for a return to fully normal relations between the two states, contingent on successful negotiations which were to start after a six-month cooling off period.[16] In the meantime, Amanullah complicated these follow-on negotiations for the British by quickly acting upon his right to establish diplomatic relations with foreign powers, including the Soviet Union and the United States, while Britain continued to consider Afghanistan within its sphere of influence and thus, was strongly desirous of an exclusive alliance.

The first three months of negotiations following the Third Anglo–Afghan War (1919) took place in Mussoorie during the summer of 1920. Unfortunately, results were minimal and negotiations to achieve normal relations continued in Kabul during almost all of 1921. The final Treaty of Kabul returned British India and Afghanistan to more tranquil relations, at least for a time.

Indo–Afghan Conference, Mussoorie, 1920,
British and Afghan delegates. Standing (L–R): Sardar Abdul Wahhab, Colonel Pir Muhammad (Afghan delegate), Lieutenant Colonel S.F. Muspratt, DSO (British delegate), Sardar Abdul Hadi Khan (Afghan delegate), Mr J.G. Acheson (officer-in-charge of arrangements).

Seated (L–R): Diwan Narinjan Das (Afghan delegate), Mr S.E. Pears, CIE (British delegate), SardariI-Ala Mahmud Beg Khan Tarzi (chief Afghan representative), Hon'ble Mr H.R.C. Dobbs, CSI, CIE (chief British representative), Nazir Ghulam Muhammad (Afghan delegate), Nawab Sahibzada Sir Abdul Qaiyum, KCIE (British delegate). *(Courtesy of British Library)*

Photograph taken at a diplomatic dinner party at the Savoy Hotel, hosted by the Afghan delegates during the three months of negotiations held in Mussoorie after the Third Anglo–Afghan War. Note that while ex-amir, Yakub Khan, must have been in the Station, he was apparently not to be seen at these meetings, even at the dinner. *(Courtesy of British Library)*

This, then, was the state of play when negotiations between Afghanistan and the British were opened in Mussoorie on 17 April 1920, with a phalanx of Afghani representatives facing off against British officials. Unfortunately, even though these talks continued for three months (till 18 July 1920), they did not produce any concrete results, and it took yet another conference in Kabul, phased over eleven months during 1921, to achieve normal relations. In the end, the Treaty of Kabul assured mutual respect with regard to internal and external independence (that is, Britain did not get an exclusive alliance with Afghanistan). Afghanistan reluctantly reaffirmed its acceptance of the boundary west of the Khyber Pass, subject to minor realignments (which later resulted in the Durand Line). Legations were to be opened in London and Kabul, consulates established in various Indian and Afghan towns, and Afghanistan was to be permitted to import arms and munitions through India. No customs duties were to be charged for goods in transit to Afghanistan, and each party agreed to inform the other of major military operations in the frontier belt. Representatives of both states were to meet in the near future to discuss conclusion of a trade convention, which was signed in June 1923.

The third royal-in-exile in Mussoorie was from the Punjab. Well before the arrival of Yaqub Khan at Bellevue and a few years after Dost Mohammad had been pent up at Bala Hissar, the British installed Duleep Singh, the deposed Sikh child-king, on Castle Hill in Landour.

The story of His Highness Maharaja Duleep Singh (b.4 September 1838–d.22 October 1893) is well-known and often considered tragic, given the tug-and-pull of two cultures and religions that characterized his life.

After the death in 1839 of Ranjit Singh, the 'Lion of the Punjab', the Sikh kingdom fell into anarchy, leading to two Anglo–Sikh Wars and finally, the annexation of the Punjab by the East India Company on 29 March 1849. During this period of chaos, Duleep Singh had been put on the throne at the age of five years, with his mother Rani Jinda Kaur as regent. After annexation, Duleep was deposed at the age of ten by the East India Company's Governor General Hardinge and sent to Futtehghur, to the east of Agra in what was then the North West Province (now, Fatehgarh, the headquarters of Farrukhabad district in Uttar Pradesh state). Under the care of Sir John Login, MD, of the Medical Service, the young maharaja was given a tutor, Mr Walter F. Guise, the brother of a company doctor. Influenced by Guise as well as by Bhajun Lal, a young Hindu Brahmin sympathetic to the Christian faith who had been assigned as a companion, Duleep was baptized a Christian on 8 March 1853 at the age of fourteen by Reverend W.J. Jay, the chaplain at Futtehghur. However, later in life, Duleep returned to the Sikh faith, at a Khande di Pahul (Amrit) ceremony that took place on 25 May 1886 in Aden on his way to India, a trip he was not allowed by the British to complete.

During the Seasons of 1852 and 1853, Duleep was sent from Futtehghur to Landour for comfort and convalescence. At that time, Mussoorie was about four days' journey from Futtehghur. He remained for weeks at a time at the 'Castle' in Landour, so named because of his presence. The Castle, which had been the property of George Bladen Taylor and later of Henry Vansittart, was said to have been lavishly refurbished and furnished by the government to accommodate him (see Chapter 4 for details on the Castle Hill Estate).

In the summer of 1852, while in Mussoorie, the well-known artist George Beechey painted Duleep in oils.[17] One of the paintings was later given as a parting gift to the governor general, Lord Dalhousie, in exchange for which Duleep received a Bible from Dalhousie.[18] In Mussoorie, Duleep Singh saw a good bit of European life and learned to play cricket with English boys. He also became fond of shooting, which became a lifelong passion. But none of his influential Sikh countrymen were permitted to approach him, nor was he permitted to correspond with his mother. In fact, he was cut off from all his old associations.[19]

Duleep's Futtehghur and Mussoorie days ended when he was sent to Britain in 1854[20], where he became one of Queen Victoria's favourite courtiers, although he later resented her—'Mrs Fagin'—for not returning the Koh-i-noor that he had worn as a child and for what he considered miserly and unfair treatment by the government that had stolen his kingdom. On a trip to Egypt, en route back from an 1860–1861 visit to India to reunite with his mother, Duleep met and married a German/Egyptian Coptic girl from Cairo, Bamba Muller. They had six children, who were raised in London and at his beloved Elveden Hall, near Thetford on the Norfolk–Suffolk border.[21] Duleep married again, this time Ada Douglas Wetherill, a former domestic worker. They had two children.[22] All eight children died without issue, ending the direct line of Sikh royalty.

Eventually disillusioned with the British government for its refusal to compensate him in any significant way for having taken his kingdom, Maharaja Duleep Singh attempted late in life to collude with the Russian tsar to return to the Punjab. But the tsar would have none of it. Duleep left Moscow and returned to Paris with no intention of returning to England. In fact, he never did. He died in Paris in

Maharaja Duleep Singh as he was in his youth in Landour and, shortly thereafter, in England.
(L) This portrait of the maharaja was painted by the well-known nineteenth-century artist George Beechey at Castle Hill Estate in Landour in 1852, when the young maharaja was a shy fourteen-year-old. He spent the Seasons of 1852 and 1853 at Castle Hill, the estate so named because of his residing there. *(Courtesy of Thetford Museum, England)*
(R) This photograph of the debonair maharaja was taken by his German teacher Dr Ernest Becker on 23 August 1854 at Queen Victoria and Prince Albert's holiday home, Osborne House, on the Isle of Wright. The maharaja had arrived in England just three months previously in May 1854, at the age of about sixteen years. He very soon became a favorite of Queen Victoria's; however, later in life, he became disillusioned with the treatment meted out to him by the governments in London and Calcutta.
(Photograph from Peter Bance's book, The Duleep Singhs, The Photograph Album of Queen Victoria's Maharajah, *Phoenix Mill: Sutton Publishing Limited, 2004: 31)*

The Maharaja Duleep Singh equestrian statue on Butten Island in Thetford, England. The Elveden Estate near Thetford was the maharaja's home in England. This statue was unveiled in 1999 by Charles, Prince of Wales. The town of Thetford benefited greatly from the generosity of the Duleep Singh family, particularly that of Prince Frederick, who supported many local endeavours including the founding of the Thetford Museum. *(Carl Palmer Photography, courtesy of the Thetford Tourist Information Centre, England)*

1893 at the age of fifty-five. He had, by then, made two brief, tightly-controlled visits to India, once in 1860–1861 (to bring his mother to England) and in 1863 (to scatter his mother's ashes). His request to have his body returned to India was declined for fear of unrest, given the symbolic value the funeral of the son of 'the Lion of the Punjab' may have caused in the light of growing resentment toward British rule. Rather, Duleep Singh was buried, under the supervision of the India Office, in St Andrew's Church on his beloved Elveden hunting estate, beside the grave of his first wife, Maharani Bamba, and his son Prince Edward Albert Alexander Duleep Singh.

Encouraged by Dr Login, Duleep had for many years supported ten missionary schools for boys in and near Futtehghur and in England too, he and his children supported various worthy charities. Interestingly, as recently as 1999, a life-size bronze statue of Maharaja Duleep Singh showing him on a horse was unveiled by Charles, prince of Wales, at Butten Island in Thetford, an English town close by his Elveden Estate.[23]

With the annexation of the Punjab in the spring of 1849, the child-king Duleep Singh was dethroned and put under the care of Dr John Spencer Login, an Orkneyman in the employ of the East India Company's medical service. Throughout the hot season of that year, the ten-year-old Duleep was kept in the Citadel of Lahore—Ranjit Singh's palace—with Dr Login as his 'jailer' (Login was referred to as Killah-ki-Malik or Lord of the Lahore Citadel). Missing his own son who was in England, Dr Login quickly developed a sympathetic fondness for the 'remarkably intelligent' boy and many years later when Dr Login died in England, it was the Maharaja Duleep Singh who had inscribed on his tomb, '...in grateful remembrance of the tender care and solicitude with which Sir John Login watched over [my] early years.'

In the early days of annexation, the Calcutta government was keen to remove Duleep from the Punjab, fearing that anti-British Sikh sardars (noblemen) would rally around the deposed maharaja in an attempt to restore the Khalsa army and the Sikh dynasty. Having caused the British much trouble, Duleep's mother, Rani Jinda Kaur, had already been scuttled off to various jails, finally ending up at Fort Chunar (in what is now Uttar Pradesh state). From there, she escaped to Kathmandu, Nepal, only to become a virtual prisoner of Maharaja Jung Bahadur Rana and kept under the supervision of the British resident of Nepal. Years later, Duleep brought his mother to England and she died there.

During the hot season of 1849, with Duleep in the citadel, Governor General Lord Dalhousie considered various options for his removal. In a letter to his wife dated 5 September 1849, Dr Login noted that the Doon Valley had been suggested:

'I shall be truly glad when it is settled what is to be the future destination of Duleep Singh. Sir Henry [Henry Lawrence, president of the board of administration of the annexed Punjab] and Mansel [Charles G. Mansel, member of the board] both advise his being sent to England at once; but Lord Dalhousie [governor general] is not fond of suggestions, so we all wait for his decision. Sir Henry says that the Doon, with a large estate or jagheer, might not be a bad thing.'

Later, in November (22 November 1849), Login again wrote: 'I am told it is not unlikely that the old Begum Sumru's palace near Meerut (Sirdanah [Sardana]) may be fixed upon.'

But, in the event, Futtehghur was agreed upon as a residence for the young prince, far from the political machinations of Lahore. Login wrote on 28 November 1849:

'I have just returned from him [Lord Dalhousie, who was on tour to Lahore]. He told me that, after much consideration, it had been determined to remove the little Maharaja to Futtehghur, and that he wished much that I should continue in charge of him there on my present allowances, and do all that I could to make him comfortable and happy.'

Thus, the Futtehghur Park, 'befitting his rank and station', became Duleep's home from shortly after his eleventh birthday (celebrated at a grand fete arranged by Dr Login in Lahore on 4th September 1849), until he left for England in April of 1854 at the age of sixteen.*

Except, that is, for the summers of 1852 and 1853, when the maharaja was ensconced in the Castle in Landour.

In August 1851, Dr Login had noted in a letter to Lord Dalhousie:

'Having requested the Maharaja to state fully all his wishes to your Lordship, he has not omitted the opportunity of making known his anxiety to go to the hills next hot season...the reasons he assigns for his wish to go to the hills are, that he can apply more steadily to his studies in a cooler climate, and can have more English boys for playfellows.'

The maharaja had his desire fulfilled the next hot season (1852). Mrs Login writes:

'As the object of Duleep Singh's temporary residence in the hills was to enable him to pursue his studies more effectually, Login did not consider it advisable that he should have his mind distracted by the gaieties usually going on there. He therefore turned a deaf ear to the numerous applications for aid in getting up races, theatricals, balls, etc. But feeling it right to do all he could for the social enjoyment and pleasure of the community, he endeavored to promote pleasant outdoor meetings, such as picnics, cricket matches, and archery meetings,

---

*Futtehghur Park was sacked and burnt during the Mutiny of 1857, Duleep Singh's servants killed and all of his valuable possessions plundered (they had been left behind under guard, as it was thought at the time that he would return from England to live there). Duleep was never compensated.

by giving handsome prizes on the latter occasions, providing a good band to play on the Mall, giving frequent musical parties, prizes to the boys' school, getting up a museum of natural history, etc. During the second visit of His Highness to Mussoorie [1853] he also arranged a series of twenty lectures on various subjects, to be given by qualified lecturers (many of them officers in the service). The small fee for each (fifty rupees), given by His Highness was almost invariably applied by the lecturer to some useful object, such as enlargement of the church*, library, or dispensary, thus benefiting the stations generally. These lectures were much enjoyed by Duleep Singh.'

The lectures that Dr Login arranged were indeed impressive. They were on the subjects of astronomy, fine arts, meteorology, philosophy, natural history, theology, the habits of bees, comets, chemistry, electricity, ancient history of India, zoology of the Himalayas, peculiarities of the English language, literature of the present day and botany.

Login noted in a letter to Lord Dalhousie:

'I am glad to say that the Maharaja continues to enjoy his residence in the hills greatly. I have availed myself of the opportunity of getting a drawing-master and music master to give him lessons, and he really makes good progress. He now speaks English with fluency, and much more correctly, and with better pronunciation, than natives of Central India generally. He takes great pleasure in the society of English boys, of whom a few come every Saturday from Mr. Maddock's school [see Chapter 5] to join him at play, and I have also been able to secure him constant companions in the two sons [Frank and Charles] of Major Boileau, of the Artillery, who come to study Urdu with him....As His Highness's residence is at some distance from Mussoorie, he lives as quiet and retired a life as he did at Futtehghur, enjoying, however, all the advantages of the delightful climate, and the active outdoor exercise which it enables him to take. I have been able to clear a sufficient level space for a playground on the Manor House Estate, so as to admit of his playing cricket, in which he takes great delight.'

Besides cricket, the young maharaja also enjoyed hawking (although discouraged by Dr Login, as it was already considered an unbecoming blood sport), shooting

---

*This would have been Christ Church, which was enlarged in 1853 while Duleep Singh was in the Station, by the addition of transepts, chancel area and a Gothic-style roof, paid for by private gifts, including from the young maharaja (see Chapter 6).

and coursing (hunting with dogs), and the new art of photography.

Duleep's studies were reported as going on well in Mussoorie, his progress on the flute and cornopean (cornet) progressing to the extent that he became a part of a band of eight or nine men. 'This band is a great pleasure to the community at Mussoorie, as they play on the Mall on stated evenings, where their appearance is hailed with delight.'

George Beechey's oil painting of Duleep, done in Landour, arrived in July 1852 at Government House. Lord Dalhousie wrote:

'At last, after a long delay upon the river, your Highness's portrait has arrived. It is in excellent condition, not at all injured by the weather. It is very like you, and does great credit to Mr. Beechey as an artist. Your highness [sic] has done me really a great favour in offering to me this likeness of yourself.'

Maharaja Duleep Singh left Landour in October 1853 at the end of his second season there, never to return to the hill station.*

*All quotations from Login, Lady Lena, *Sir John Login and Duleep Singh*, New Delhi: Nirmal Publishers and Distributors, 1986 [reprint of 1889 publication].

There was one other royal figure exiled to Mussoorie; however, in this case it was not an exile forced by the British overlords. Dev Shamsher Jang Bahadur Rana (b.1862–d.1914) was maharaja of Nepal for a short period (144 days) in 1901. After being ousted from the throne in an internecine feud, he was sent briefly to eastern Nepal. But shortly thereafter, Dev Shamsher removed himself and moved to Mussoorie with his family. With his extensive entourage, he lived the rest of his life at his Fairlawn Palace estate in Jharipani (lower Mussoorie). Dev Shamsher named one of his sons Mussoorie Shamsher Jang Bahadur Rana.

Russian royalty also found its way to Mussoorie. In the spring of 1842, Prince Alexis Dmitrievich Soltykoff (Saltykov) (b.1806–d.1859) visited the Station briefly, but vividly recorded his time there as part of his published travel memoir, *Voyages dans L'Inde* (Travels in India), illustrated with lithographs based on his own drawings. After spending time in Dehra Dun, Prince Soltykoff journeyed up the hillside to Mussoorie where he spent a month 'improving under the influence of favourable weather'. Soltykoff's notes reflect his impressions of Mussoorie's atmosphere: 'the air is light, dry, and fresh. All things said, it is a superb climate'.[24]

A few years ago, there was a small article in *The Times of India* noting that members

Maharaja Dev Shamsher Jang Bahadur Rana ruled as a hereditary prime minister in Nepal for only four months in the year 1901, whereupon he went to India in self-imposed exile and took up permanent residence in Mussoorie. He named one of his sons 'Mussoorie'. *(Photo kind courtesy of Purusottam S.J.B. Rana, Kathmandu, Nepal)*

of Christ Church had formally hoisted the tiranga (national flag of India) atop the church tower in an Independence Day ceremony (the event also marked the repair of the flagstaff that hadn't featured a flag since the days of the Union Jack). Much to the amusement of local townspeople and churchgoers, the article went on to say, 'During the British rule, only members of the royal family used to worship at this church.'[25] Nothing could be further from the truth, since British royalty rarely visited Mussoorie and certainly no member of the British royal family ever lived in the Station. To hopefully avoid such a mistake in the future, the padre found it expedient to leave a short history of the church lying about the building for the edification and education of curious reporters![26]

Yet, while no English royal ever lived in Mussoorie—and thus had no need to build a church—the Station did occasionally entertain English royalty. But these visits were few and far between; there were only three such visits, in fact, since one cannot easily elevate governors general and viceroys to 'royal' status.[27]

The first member of the English royal family ever to visit Mussoorie was HRH Alfred, the duke of Edinburgh, in 1870. He was the third child and second son of Queen Victoria and Prince Albert. HRH Alfred was on an official two-month tour of India that began in Calcutta and ended in Bombay. His visit to Mussoorie and Landour lasted just one day. Dr J. Fayrer was a medical attendant in the duke's party and later recorded his memories of the tour. Dr Fayrer does not specifically mention that the duke planted a memorial deodar tree in the Landour Cemetery, but there is still a plaque there noting the event. In any case, the record in clear regarding HRH's stop in Landour.

February 15th [1870].—H.R.H. was received at Deyrah by Mr. Roos, C.S. [Civil Service], Superintendent of the Dhoon, Colonel Macpherson, C.B. [Companion of the Bath], Commanding the Sirmoor Battalion, and several other gentlemen, residents of Deyrah. This morning after breakfast, H.R.H. received several gentlemen residing at Dehrah, and inspected the Sirmoor Battalion, and then, accompanied by Mr. Williams, C.S.I. [Companion of the Star of India], Mr. Ross, Colonel Macpherson, and Mr. Thomas, Superintendent of Police, drove to Rajpore at the foot of the hills, and then, mounting on ponies, rode up to Mussoorie and Landour, where they were received by Colonel Chippendale and Dr. Kellett, the officers of the Convalescent Depôt. After ascending to the highest point of Landour—the Lalterba [sic, Lal Tiba]—about 7,500 feet [2,286 meters] above the sea, whence a magnificent view of the snows was obtained, H.R.H. and suite rode to the Club, where they were entertained at tiffin by the officers of the Depôt. They then rode down the hill again to Rajpore, and then drove back to Deyrah in time for dinner. The day was most favorable. The recent rain had so completely cleared the atmosphere, that a beautifully distinct view of the distant snowy range was obtained. The peaks of Duri Nauth, Bunder Ponch, Keddarkanta, and Gungootri and Jummootri were visible. The air was dry and bracing, but not unpleasantly cold; indeed, the sun's rays were such as to make it rather inconveniently warm in ascending and descending the hill. The thermometer at Landour never falls below 26° Fahrenheit [-3.3 celsius] and at 2 p.m. it was pleasantly warm on the highest peak. The expedition was a most agreeable one, and HRH was much pleased, not only with the magnificent scenery of the Himalayahs, but also with the rich and prosperous appearance of the Dhoon and the charming station of Deyrah.[28]

And that is about all we know about the duke of Edinburgh's visit to the area, except that the bag during a subsequent shikar in the 'Oude Terai' totalled 303 jungle inhabitants, including five tigers.[29]

The second English royal visit to Mussoorie was made in 1884 by Prince Arthur, the first duke of Connaught and Strathearn and earl of Sussex (b.1850–d.1942), and the duchess of Connaught (Princess Louise Margaret of Prussia), while they were hunting in the area. Prince Arthur was the seventh child and third son of Queen Victoria and Prince Albert, and a friend from childhood of Maharaja Duleep Singh.

…in April [we] find Mussoorie being hurriedly tidied; brooms, paint, spit and polish everywhere, with the greatest bustle and expense centred in Tivoli Garden for the reception of the Duke and Duchess of Connaught, who arrived on April 17 for shikar which was followed by a memorable lunch and much merry-making in the…palatial …Tivoli Garden."[30]

There is still a Connaught Castle in Mussoorie, located in the area between the State Bank of India and the post office that functions as a small hotel. Connaught Circus in New Delhi was also named after the first duke.[31]

The third and most recent time that Mussoorie hosted English royalty was in 1906 when Mary, Princess of Wales, paid a rather unexpected three-day visit. The 1905–1906 official visit to India by the Prince and Princess of Wales—later King George V and Queen Mary—had brought Their Royal Highnesses to Lucknow in February 1906 but, from this point, their tour had to be entirely rearranged. The plan had been to proceed to a shooting camp in Nepal but a cholera outbreak there made it necessary to drop that part of the programme altogether.[32] Instead, a shooting expedition in the princely state of Gwalior was arranged for His Royal Highness, and a separate programme was quickly arranged for Her Royal Highness, which included visits to Lucknow, Cawnpore (Kanpur), Agra, Dehra Dun and Mussoorie.[33]

Mary, Princess of Wales, and later Queen Mary (wife of King George V), made an unexpected visit to Mussoorie in March 1906, when an outbreak of cholera in Nepal disrupted hunting plans. She was the last member of the British royal house to visit the Station.
(Courtesy of Library of Congress)

The royal chronicler reported:

From Benares His Royal Highness railed to Gwalior, with one short halt for a few hours at Cawnpore. The Princess commenced an informal little tour, which brought her into very close touch indeed with phases of Indian life which she has lost no opportunity of studying.

Dehra Dun was reached on March the 1st, and in this lovely little station, hidden amongst the forests of the lower Himalayas, several restful days were spent. The Princess stayed in the cottage home of Major Watson, C.I.E. [Companion of the Indian Empire], Commandant of the Imperial Cadet Corps. Her Royal Highness visited the Mess of the 2nd Gurkhas, taking tea with the officers, and was much interested in the Mess trophies and plate; she inspected the Lines, and conversed with the Native Officers. Another excursion was to Mokampur by motor, where lunch was served in the heart of the forest.

On March 2nd the Princess motored to Rajpur and was carried in a dandy—the Indian equivalent for a sedan chair—to Mussoorie, the loveliest hill station in the North. The weather during the three days' stay there was magnificent, and the view of the snow-clad hills superb. Advantage was taken of these favouring conditions to see as many places of interest as possible. Luncheon was taken at the Himalaya Club, whence Her Royal Highness climbed to the still higher military sanitarium at Landour. Landour was covered with more than a foot of snow, and some of the roads were impassable. However a path was dug to the cemetery where the tree planted by the Duke of Edinburgh [in 1870] was seen to be flourishing exceedingly.

Amongst other places honoured by a visit were the Mussoorie Convent and the Soldiers' Home at Landour. The Princess took a keen interest in all she saw, down to the manufacture of walking sticks—a trade that is greatly encouraged in these parts. Some walking sticks were bought by the Princess from an exceedingly poor craftsman. "Lo!" cried the admiring onlookers. "Now is our brother's shop made. And he was of the poorest. How did the Rani know it?"

On Sunday, March 4th, after service at Christ Church, the Princess returned to Dehra Dun. [From there, HRH went by motor car over the Mohan Pass, visiting the Hurbanswala Tea Estate, Haridwar, a section of the Ganges Canal, and a foundry and Thomson College at Rookee...] With visits to both of these [latter] establishments the private tour of the Princess closed. In this manner Her Royal Highness completed her acquaintance with a country in which, at every stage, she manifested a keen and informed interest.

The Prince from his shooting camp and Her Royal Highness from Haridwar....met at Hathras Junction and thence the Royal party travelled to Aligarh [on 8 March 1906 and then onwards, exiting India at Karachi on the H.M.S. Renown on 19 March 1906].[34]

While in Mussoorie, Her Royal Highness stayed at the Hotel Charleville. A hotel was an unusual accommodation during a royal tour and, indeed, it was the princess's only hotel stay during her travels in India. This was probably due to the impromptu nature of her visit to the Station. Her Royal Highness also attended a garden party in her honour on the Savoy Hotel grounds (in the area that was later named the 'Beer Garden').

A reminder of Princess Mary's visit still exists in Mussoorie. After worshipping on 4 March 1906, Her Royal Highness planted a deodar in the garden at Christ Church. Both the tree and the commemorative plaque can still be seen, as well as her picture that hangs in the north porch of the church.

Both the duke of Edinburgh in 1870 and Princess Mary in 1906 planted deodar trees during their visits to Mussoorie and Landour. The trees are still standing in the Landour Cemetery and in the gardens of Christ Church, each having a commemorative plaque. The Princess Mary plaque (R) reads, 'This tree was planted by HRH the Princess of Wales on Sunday March 4th 1906 after attending morning service at Christ Church.' The duke of Edinburgh plaque (L) reads rather more simply, 'Planted by HRH Duke of Edinburgh, Feb 1870.'

(Kind courtesy of Mela Ram & Sons, Mussoorie)

So, a tree here, a plaque there, a chateau, a maharaja summer residence-turned-hotel, a 'castle' with bureaucrats comfortably settled in, and even a few erstwhile Indian princes still here and there during the Season—all lingering reminders of an earlier era, when royalty merged with the Raj in this most 'eligible' of places.

Notes

1. Walton, H.G., *The Gazetteer of Dehra Dun,* first published 1911, Dehra Dun: Natraj Publishers (reprint), 2007: 245.
2. Bodycot, F. ('compiler'), *Guide to Mussoorie with Notes on Adjacent Districts and Routes into the Interior,* Mussoorie: Mafasilite Printing Works, 1907: 34.
3. For all of the royal houses discussed in this chapter, that is, those which had connections to Mussoorie, the gun salute number is given according to 'The Indian Salute States in 1931', taken from Farwell, Byron, *Armies of the Raj, from the Great Indian Mutiny to Independence: 1858-1947,* London: W.W. Norton & Company, 1989, Appendix B. This formal hierarchical system—the Order of Precedence in British India—classified the rulers of princely states by the number of guns used when paying honours to them, signifying their prestige and importance in the eyes of the British. The highest of the so-called 'salute states' enjoyed twenty-one guns and the lowest three guns, although as a practical rule most salute states enjoyed at least nine guns. However, there were many 'minor' rulers who were not deemed entitled to any gun salutes.
4. Kapurthala was a Sikh princely state in the Punjab (with almost half the population being Muslim), between the Sutlej and Beas rivers. The Royal House of Kapurthala traces its family history back some 900 years, when the foundations of the state were laid by Rana Kapur, a member of the Rajput ruling dynasty of Jaisalmer.
5. The Patiala and East Punjab States Union (PEPSU) was a state of India, created in 1948 by amalgamating eight Punjabi princely states, namely, Kapurthala, Patiala, Jind, Nabha, Faridkot, Kalsia, Malerkotla and Nalagarh. In 1956, PEPSU was merged into the Indian state of Punjab. Part of the former PEPSU is now in the state of Haryana.
6. Pillai, K.K., *A Gathering of Princes,* from the brochure of the Mussoorie Winter Festival, Millennium Carnival 24 December 1999–1 January 2000: 7.
7. Pillai, Ibid, p. 8.
8. Kalyanasundaram, M.S., *Indian Hill Stations,* Madras: Tamil Puthakalayam, 1961: 16.
9. Dunseverick in Mussoorie was named after Dunseverick Castle in County Antrim in Northern Ireland. When the estate became a hotel, the name apparently was changed to 'Dunsvirk'.
10. Pillai, Ibid, p. 10.
11. Knight Commander of the Star of India. No further appointments were made to this Order after Indian Independence. The motto of the Order, suggested by Lady Canning, was 'heaven's light our guide'. The 'Star of India', the emblem of the Order, also appeared on the flag of the Viceroy of India.
12. British control was extended up to the Khyber Pass, and Afghanistan ceded various frontier

areas and Quetta to the British.

13. Williams, C. ('The Rambler'), *A Mussoorie Miscellany*, Mussoorie: Mafasilite Press, 1936: 42-43.

14. Northam, John, *Guide to Masuri, Landaur, Dehra Dun and the Hills North of Dehra*, Calcutta:Thacker, Spink and Company, 1884, Bath: Pagoda Tree Press reprint, 2007: 26-27.

15. Williams, Ibid, p. 42-43.

16. Other terms of this initial treaty—the 1919 Treaty of Rawalpindi—denied Afghanistan the right to import arms and ammunition through India, ended the payment of a subsidy, and confiscated the arrears in payments. Finally, undefined portions of the Khyber were to be demarcated by a British commission and Afghanistan was to accept the Indo–Afghan frontier as marked (this became the Durand Line).

17. George Beechey, son of the royal academician Sir William Beechey, was at the time the portrait painter at the court of the King of Oude.

18. The large and elaborately tooled, leather-covered Bible may still be seen in the Thetford museum.

19. Bance, Peter, *The Duleep Singhs, The Photograph Album of Queen Victoria's Maharajah*, Phoenix Mill: Sutton Publishing Limited, 2004: 20.

20. Maharaja Duleep Singh and his party sailed for England on 19 April 1854 and reached Southampton a month later.

21. (In order of birth) Prince Victor Duleep Singh, Prince Frederick Victor Jay Duleep Singh, Princess Bamba Sofia Jindan Duleep Sutherland née Singh, Princess Catherine Hilda Duleep Singh, Princess Sophia Jindan Alexdrowna Duleep Singh and Prince Albert Edward Alexander Duleep Singh.

22. Princess Pauline Alexandra Duleep Singh and Princess Ada Irene Beryl Duleep Singh.

23. Information on the life of Maharaja Duleep Singh was taken from various sources. Details regarding his conversion to the Christian faith were taken from Allison, Walter Leslie, *One Hundred Years of Christian Work of the North India Mission of the Presbyterian Church, USA*, Mysore: Wesley Press and Publishing House, circa 1937 (no exact date of publication given), p. 28-30. (In this publication, Allison makes it clear that Duleep Singh was not directly involved with the Presbyterian missionaries in Futtehghur who, as it turned out, were all murdered during the First War of Independence.)

24. Soltykoff, A. *Voyages dans l'Inde*, Paris, Garnier Frères, Libraires—Editeurs, 1848: 266-267.

25. *The Times of India*, 18 August 2006.

26. This splendid effort on the part of the padre has apparently failed. A recent (October 2010) *Outlook Traveller* article noted that the State Bank of India building 'was built to house Queen Victoria on her visit to the hills'. Queen Victoria never visited India, let alone Mussoorie.

27. Louis Mountbatten, the twenty-fourth and last British ruler of India, was the first and only viceroy of royal lineage. He was born His Serene Highness Prince Louis of Battenberg, although his German styles and titles were dropped in 1917 when he was created marquess of Milford Haven. He never visited Mussoorie.

28. Fayrer, J., *H.R.H. The Duke of Edinburgh in India*, Calcutta: The 'Englishman' Press, 1870: 42-43.

29. Ibid, p. 65.

30. The Tivoli Garden was abandoned after the 1905 earthquake.

31. The first duke of Connaught's grandson, Alastair Windsor, became the second duke of Connaught upon his grandfather's death in 1942, but he too died only fifteen months after his grandfather's death. Upon Alastair's death, the dukedom became extinct.

32. However, when King George and Queen Mary came back to India for the 1911 Coronation Durbar, they were finally able to enjoy a Nepal hunting trip in the foothills of the Himalayas.

33. _____*Souvenir Album Descriptive of the Indian Tour of Their Royal Highnesses the Prince and Princess of Wales*, November 1905 to March 1906, Madras: Higginbotham & Co., 1906: 11.

34. Reed, Stanley, *The Royal Tour in India, A Record of the Tour of T.R.H. The Prince and Princess of Wales in India and Burma, from November 1905 to March 1906*, Bombay: Bennett, Coleman & Co. 1906: 410-413.

George Everest, the man made famous by a mountain, resided in Mussoorie from 1832 to 1943, having purchased the Park Estate, sight unseen. Today, the property west of the library is owned by the Uttarakhand government.

(Courtesy of Library of Congress)

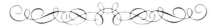

10
LEGENDS IN THEIR TIME AND OURS

Wood burns because it has the proper stuff in it;
and a man becomes famous because he has the proper stuff in him.
~ *Johann Wolfgang von Goethe, German philosopher and author of* Faust ~

Over the years, Mussoorie has been home to a number of fascinating and sometimes famous historical figures. Having been founded as a 'British' hill station, it is logical that these mostly nineteenth-century individuals hailed from Britain or had British ancestry. Most, but certainly not all!

Among these early residents, none has enjoyed the worldwide recognition accorded to Welsh surveyor and geographer Colonel Sir George Richard Everest, the surveyor general of India who made his home in Mussoorie from 1832 to 1843 while he was in charge of the Great Trigonometrical Survey.

Everest (b.4 July 1790–d.1 December 1866), the man made famous by a mountain, bought his Park Estate to the west of the library sight unseen and, apparently, at considerable cost. But nonetheless, he knew what he was getting and his surveyor sights were on the mountains that needed mapping. At the time, Mussoorie itself '...was already developing into [a] toffee-nosed township... one of British India's premier hill resorts.'

It was a long and interesting road that brought Everest to his sylvan and surveying outpost.

In 1799, a Yorkshireman, William Lambton, had persuaded Governor General Richard Wellesley—the great exponent of the 'Forward Policy'[1] and brother of Arthur Wellesley, later the duke of Wellington—that a trigonometrical survey of India should be undertaken. The decades-long, painstaking and meticulous triangulation process started at Madras (Chennai), then proceeded to Bangalore and Cape Cormorin (Kanya Kumari), and later north through the lands of the nizam of Hyderabad and beyond. Lambdon died on 7 January 1823, of heat exposure and exhaustion in Maharashtra and, thereupon, George Everest took acting charge of the Great Trigonometric Survey, a mission to map the entire subcontinent of India. For the next twenty years, Everest would make the Great Arc his personal affair.

By the time the Great Arc triangulation exercise reached Mussoorie in the winter of 1832, the demanding and dictatorial Surveyor General George Everest was fully in charge.

The journey [from Calcutta to Mussoorie] took five months. In a flotilla of boats, some of which had to be specially adapted to prevent their sinking under the weight of machinery [including the Great Theodolite, which made the mapping possible], the Survey's main establishment of men, instruments and horses sailed up the Ganges, then took to roads and hill tracks to trail up to Mussoorie, seven thousand feet [2,134 metres] above sea level on a ridge in the Himalayas.

There Everest had just purchased an estate [Park] which he had designated as his new headquarters and from which all operations would be conducted during his remaining years in India [for Survey historians, this was the so-called

'Everest Decade', 1832-1843]. The place, although he had never see it, never been near Mussoorie, never even seen the hills, was carefully chosen. From the ridge, to the north and to the west, there stretched, in a breathtaking panorama of sublime savagery, the snow-scarred peaks of the Great Himalaya. Everest had finally set his sights on the mountains.

At Hatipaon he would devote himself exclusive to the Great Trigonometrical Survey, 'my own darling profession' as he called it; and from this podium in the Himalayas he would conduct the Great Arc to its climax in what he reckoned to be 'as perfect a performance as mankind has yet seen'.[2]

Hathipaon[3]—Everest's own residence within the 600-acre Park Estate that he had purchased from General William Sampson Whish[4] 'at a very heavy cost'—still stands against the harsh elements on this windy and exposed ridge, although in a dilapidated state. But at the time, it was declared '...the finest estate in the hills'.[5] There are no longer any traces of the staff quarters, Logarithm Lodge and Bachelors' Hall, or the observatory, workshops and storage facilities. The property is now owned by the Uttarakhand government—successor government to Uttar Pradesh—but sadly neglected as a historic site where great scientific research was once undertaken. One can still get there on the road that Everest had constructed.

However, while Park Estate was Everest's personal 'headquarters', the head office of the Great Trigonometrical Survey and the recess quarters of all sorts of survey parties—scientific, topographical and revenue—were in Mussoorie itself. In 1907, Bodycot observed:

The G.T. [Great Trigonometrical] Survey had its office for a short time at Montrose House [on Evelyn Hall Road, above Christ Church], and thereafter, for a good many years, at Evelyn Hall, near the top of the Camel's Back; the highest point just above the office being utilized as an observatory. Many a survey officer who subsequently distinguished himself in geodetic work made his first acquaintance with a big thirty-six inch theodolite [the 'Great Theodolite'] in the little observatory on the top of Camel's Back under the paternal guidance of Mr. J.B.N. Hennessy, for many years in charge of the Headquarters offices, and afterwards Superintendent of the G.T. Branch of the Department. After the amalgamation of the three separate Survey Departments, Trigonometrical, Topographical and Revenue, into [the Survey of India in 1877, thirty-four years after Everest had left Mussoorie], the Headquarters of the Trigonometrical

Branch were retained in their 'winter quarters' at Dehra Dun, where they now are. Evelyn Hall is now known to fame as a Nursing Home; but several survey parties from Upper India and elsewhere, have always recessed in Mussoorie, and the number has considerably increased this year.[6]

Officers of the Trigonometrical Survey, 1860s. For many years, the survey had its offices at Montrose House on Evelyn Hall Road above Christ Church and thereafter, at Evelyn Hall itself, near the top of the Camel's Back. George Everest worked from his Park Estate, but this was not an official headquarters, even though much trigonometrical work was done there. *(Photo courtesy of British Library)*

In 1908, the government again purchased the Castle Hill Estate for Rs 300,000 (the British Indian government had sold it after Maharaja Duleep Singh's exile to England), with the intention that all survey parties recessing at Mussoorie in the summer should be housed on this estate, while some sections of the office would remain up in Mussoorie for the whole year.[7] The Survey of India continues at the Castle Hill Estate—one of the Station's premier locations and still very nicely wooded—while headquarters remain at Dehra Dun. The Great Theodolite, which was once installed at Evelyn Hall, now is preserved with pride at the Survey of India offices in Dehra Dun.[8]

And, as the world knows, Peak XV at Latitude North 27° 59' 16.7" and 29,002 feet (8,840 metres) above sea level—the highest mountain in the world—was named in 1865 in honour of Colonel Sir George Richard Everest, the eminent geodesist and former resident of Mussoorie. This recognition was bestowed upon the recommendation of Andrew Waugh, the surveyor general of British India at the time, and with the endorsement of the secretary of state for India and the Royal Geographical Society. Everest received this 'highest' honour just a year before he died and twenty-two years after he had left India.[9]

Other famous early nineteenth-century residents included Dr Hugh Falconer (b.1808–d.1865), who was in Mussoorie at almost the same time as Everest (both overlapping, of course, with Frederick Young himself). When Falconer was not working as the lead botanist at the Saharanpur Botanical Garden, he stayed at his Logie Estate near the Municipal Gardens, part of which is now a boutique hotel. Besides being a botanist, Falconer had a keen interest in palaeontology, an interest he shared with Sir Proby Thomas Cautley (b.1802–d.1871), the man behind conceiving and supervising the construction of the Ganges Canal during 1831–1843 that brought under irrigation over 767,000 acres of land (3,100 square kilometres). Cautley, who also became much

involved with the Roorkee (engineering) College, spent his Mussoorie days at his estate to the west (near Falconer), a property which later became Dumbarnie School and is now part of the residential and day Manava Bharati School (see Chapter 5). Together, Falconer and Cautley traipsed around in the Siwalik Hills on their fossil expeditions. Many of the specimens they found ended up in the British Museum and can still be seen there.

These four nineteenth-century men— Young, Everest, Falconer and Cautley— certainly are the most famous early residents of the Station, each exceptionally talented and well-regarded worldwide in his particular field.

Another famous—some would say infamous—nineteenth-century resident of Mussoorie was Frederick Wilson, also variously known as 'Hulson Sahib' or 'Pahari' Wilson (b.1816–d.1883).

His is a rag-to-riches story built of trees. During the latter part of the nineteenth

The Great Theodolite that made possible the Great Arc triangulation was literally carted across India and up to Mussoorie, where it was installed and used at the Survey's Evelyn Hall Estate offices. It now rests at the Survey of India offices in Dehra Dun. *(Courtesy of Library of Congress)*

century, the railway construction boom produced enormous demand for wood to be used as railway ties, as did the kilns producing bricks for construction of the Ganges Canal. Entire forests of deodar and other trees disappeared from the Himalayan foothills. And no one had more to do with or benefited more from this than Frederick Wilson.

Wilson, a Yorkshireman from Wakefield, had come to India in 1836 as a clerk with the rank of private in the East India Company's army (Queen's Eleventh Light Dragons). He soon fetched up at Meerut, the great army encampment, but in 1837 was invalided to Landour. This was his first introduction to the Garhwal hills. Due to continuing ill health (chronic dysentery), he was sent back to England and mustered out of the army in 1838.[10] Yet, intrigued by the possibilities in Garhwal and undeterred by any health concerns, Wilson returned to India—having got a berth as a ship's purser—determined to be a hunter (deer for musk pods, exotic wildlife for taxidermists and collectors) and shikari guide. His early Garhwal years were not without struggle and, at one point, he found himself in the lowly position of butler to the retinue of Prince Waldemar of Prussia, a far cry from 'hunter'. Nonetheless, in time, Wilson garnered contracts, rounded up Garhwali labourers, freely cut down the trees of the Garhwal hills, floated them downstream, sold them for use as railway ties and firewood, and banked a lot of money. At one point, he even minted his own coins or tokens. He married twice and both were Garhwali hill women. He befriended A.O. Hume, the famous nineteenth-century ornithologist, humanist and founder of the Indian National Congress and, despite his humble origins, Wilson became a leading figure in the status-conscious Station and in Dehra Dun. He died in Mussoorie and is buried in the Camel's Back Cemetery, next to his second wife, Gulabi (later called Ruth).

Besides his village property in Harsil, deep in the hills, Wilson owned houses and property in Dehra Dun, including Astley Hall which still exists by that name but in a much-altered state, and three houses in Mussoorie (Rokeby, Ivanhoe and Parade Point) which he left to his widow and sons, Charles and Henry. Rokeby (Rokeby Manor) is now a boutique hotel, Ivanhoe is an antique shop and Parade Point is an apartment building with a facade that is recognizable but without the turrets.[11] Wilson's relatives back in England also benefited from his largess. Upon his death, Wilson was extolled as having '...made his way to ample fortune by dint of thrift, tact, keen perception, rare intelligence and the exercise of those upright principals which governed his general conduct in life.' His burial was said to have been a 'spectacular farewell', with all the leading citizens of the Station and his colleagues in attendance.[12] Today, Wilson is sometimes perceived as more unworthy than his friends and colleagues thought him at the time, given that he amassed his wealth by harvesting public lands and denuding the hillsides.

Perhaps more justifiably noteworthy than Wilson is the Hearsey family, once the 'owners' of the Dun, who made their presence felt in the Valley even before the British defeat of the Gurkhas.

The first of the Hearsey family to come to India from England was Andrew Wilson Hearsey, junior, son of Captain Andrew Wilson Hearsey, senior (d.1778). Andrew (junior), who was born in 1752, became a loyal and faithful soldier of King George III and entered the service of the East India Company in 1765 at the age of thirteen, when he was appointed to an East India Company cadetship. In India, at the age of sixteen years, he saw action for the first time during the war against Hyder Ali of Mysore. After a lifetime of military service, Lieutenant Colonel Andrew Wilson Hearsey died at Allahabad on 10 July 1798 and was buried there.

But it was Hyder Young Hearsey (b.1782–d.1840) who entered most famously into nineteenth-century Indian history…and into the history of Dehra Dun (which, incredibly, he once owned) and Mussoorie. Born in India, some historical records indicate that Hyder Young was the son of Harry Thomas Hearsey, a brother of Andrew Wilson Hearsey (junior), and therefore nephew to Andrew. Other records indicate that he was Andrew's cousin. Still others indicate that Hyder Young was an illegitimate son of Andrew. While his exact paternal heritage is uncertain, what history does agree upon is that his mother was a Jat lady and, therefore, Hyder Young was an Anglo-Indian, and one destined to become rather well-known.

Hyder Young Hearsey was raised—as nephew, cousin or son—by Andrew Wilson Hearsey. In a rather exotic statement, Hyder Young had been given the name of Hyder Jung, even though Hyder Ali of Mysore was an enemy of England against whom Andrew had fought. Hyder later anglicized his second name 'Jung'—'which, combined with Hyder, was a truly warlike designation'—into 'Young'.[13]

Hyder Young was sent home to England and educated at the Royal Military Academy (RMA) at Woolwich in southeast London (the RMA was founded in 1741). After Woolwich and his return to his native India, he joined the service of the nawab of Oudh but finding that unsatisfactory, he became a cavalry captain in the army of one of the Maratha leaders, Daulatrao Scindia (whose army was headed by the Frenchman Pierre Cuillier-Perron). Later, Hyder Young became an officer under George Thomas, another adventurer with a small fiefdom centred around Hansi (now in Haryana state). By the age of twenty-one, Hyder Young had carved out for himself a small principality in Mewat (now part of both Haryana and Rajasthan states); married Zuhur al-Nissa, a princess from Cambay (Gujarat state); and established himself as a true soldier of fortune with an army of five thousand at his command '...to use in favour of the first power which might make a satisfactory bid for his alliance.'[14]. At the outbreak of the second English–Maratha War in 1803, Hyder Young and his troops joined the East India Company's army. Later, in 1808 and apart from his military career, Hyder Young was involved in surveying the Ganges from Haridwar to Gangotri, and in 1812, joined William Moorcroft[15]—in disguise!—up to Lake Manasarovar in forbidden Tibet. After his return from Tibet, Hyder Young continued in his service to the company, fighting in the Gurkha wars during which he was captured. He remained a prisoner of the Gurkhas in the hill town of Almora, located in Kumaon, until 27 April 1815 when that fortress surrendered.

However, before Hyder Young's capture and eventual release, he had become acquainted with the exiled raja of Garhwal, Sudarshan Shah. Raja Shah, who despaired whether he would ever regain his kingdom from the Gurkhas, sold off the parganas of the Dun and Chandee to Hearsey as he badly needed the money. The speculation seemed a rash one, as every indication pointed to the desire of the company to avoid war with the Gurkhas. Hyder Young, however, was of an enterprising character and was seized with the idea that sooner or later he might find a means to re-conquer Garhwal for the raja and himself. He concluded a bargain with the raja in a deed dated 22 June 1811. Hyder Young paid Rs 3,005 for the Dun and Chandee.

It turned out to be a good investment, but only with regard to Chandee. After the British had indeed pushed back the Gurkhas, Hyder Young's services were fully recognized and in the event, he sold Chandee to the East India Company for Rs 1,200 to be paid annually '...to me and my heirs and successors from generation to generation in perpetuity commencing from the first day of January 1812...' This agreement—signed on 28 October 1815—included a provision for the sale of the Dun pargana to the company, '...whenever the region in which it lay came into its possession.'[16]

However, when the East India Company did come into control of the Dun, it failed to complete the purchase from Hyder Young, '...for which Hyder Young Hearsey would have evidently accepted a moderate sum. Dehra Dun is now [1905] very valuable, and Hyder Hearsey's descendants have for many years endeavoured vainly to obtain a consideration of their claim for a completion of the purchase.'[17]

After an illustrious military career but without what he thought was proper compensation for the Dun, Hyder Young Hearsey died at Kareli (Bareilly district, Uttar Pradesh state) in 1840. His descendents, too, never received compensation for the Dun. However, they continued on there.

Hyder Young's eldest son was (Captain) William Moorcroft Hearsey. William Hearsey's son, Lionel Douglas Hearsey, inherited his grandfather Hyder Young's estates at the beginning of the twentieth century. It was this Lionel Douglas who in 1870 gave the German-made tower bells to Christ Church in Mussoorie. It was also he who built the Tivoli Garden in Barlowganj. When in Mussoorie, Lionel Douglas and his family resided on the Maryville Estate in Barlowganj, which he had inherited.

Both Lionel Douglas Hearsey and his younger brother, John Bennett Hearsey, had entered the nawab of Oudh's service in the 1830s, prior to annexation, in what amounted practically to the forcible collection of revenue. Later, they both served in the EIC's army, John Bennett Hearsey rising to the rank of lieutenant general and known for having disarmed Mangal Pandey during the March 1857 Barrackpore uprising. John Bennett returned to England in 1861 as Sir John, having been elevated by Queen Victoria to the Order of the Bath for his successful command at Barrackpore during the 'Mutiny'. He died at Boulogne, northern France, on 24 October 1865. Sir John's six sons all entered public service. Mr and Mrs Lionel Douglas Hearsey lived at Lakhimpur-Kheri (Uttar Pradesh state, near Nepal border), where they kept up the hospitable traditions of their family. 'Mr Lionel Hearsey [was] a far-famed *shikari*, whose knowledge of the craft of the jungle [was] acknowledged to be of the highest order.'[18]

General Sir John Bennett Hearsey (b.1793–d.1865) was the grandson of Hyder Young Hearsey, the one-time 'owner' of the Dun Valley. John Bennett fought during the 'Mutiny' or First War of Independence, and played a significant role in disarming Mangal Pandey during the March 1857 uprising at Barrackpore.

(Courtesy of the National Army Museum, London)

When Lionel Douglas Hearsey and his wife moved permanently to their main estate at Lakhimpur-Kheri, Lionel gave the Maryville Estate in Barlowganj to his sisters. The Tivoli Garden, where the duke and duchess of Connaught were entertained by the civil authorities in Mussoorie in 1884, had been carved out of the Maryville Estate, but the garden was destroyed in the 1905 earthquake.

Linked to the Hearseys as fellow soldiers, neighbours in Barlowganj and relatives through marriage, the Skinner family is still well-known in Mussoorie and beyond. James Hercules Skinner (b.1778–d.1841), founder of the Skinner's Horse Regiment, never lived in Mussoorie and perhaps never even visited. But Sikander Hall in Barlowganj is where many of his descendants eventually settled and, indeed, where some still live.

Foiled in his dream of becoming a British soldier because of his mixed blood (his mother was a Rajput and his father a Scotsman), James Skinner, at the age of sixteen, entered the Mahratta army under Benoit de Boigne, the French commander of Maharaja Scindia's forces. He remained in the same service until 1803 when, on the outbreak of the Second Anglo-Maratha War, all Anglo-Indians were dismissed from Mahratta service. Having shown great military skill, he thereupon joined the East India Company's army (as Hyder Young Hearsey did at the same time), raising on 23 February 1803 a regiment of irregular cavalry called 'Skinner's Horse', informally and variously known as the 'Yellow Boys', 'Yellow Devils' or 'Canaries' because of the colour of their uniform. Skinner's Horse still exists in the Indian Army as the Armoured Regiment of Skinner's Horse (1st Horse). For his service to the EIC, James was granted in 1818 the jagir (grant of land) of Hansi (now in Haryana state), which yielded him Rs 20,000 a year. In 1828, he was given the rank of lieutenant colonel in the British service, and his brother, Robert, became a major. Later, James became a colonel and was made commander of the Order of Bath (CB).

But it was Alice Skinner (b.5 November 1861–d.6 March 1923), James's granddaughter, who built Sikander Hall in 1920 in Barlowganj, so named because James Skinner's adoring soldiers had compared him to Alexander the Great by calling him 'Sikander Sahib'. Alice, who had married her cousin Stanley Skinner (son of Alexander Skinner), was famed for her generosity and kind spirit. Eager to provide for her poor relations, Alice used her own money to build Sikander Hall (despite the protestations of her rather miserly husband) and entertained her relations there during the summer months. She had purchased the land in 1916 from the Crown Brewery Estate, and built the hall in 1920. Alice died in 1923, only three years after

Sikander Hall was completed. Instead of leaving the house to her husband, Alice bequeathed it to two orphaned nephews, James and Hercules, sons of her late brother George Skinner. She did, however, leave the remainder of the Crown Brewery land, including the ruins, to her husband.

And it was at Sikander Hall that Michael Alexander Robert Skinner, the great-great-grandson of James, was born on 29 September 1920, one of nine children. Michael went on to become the last member of the Skinner family to command Skinner's Horse (1960–1963). He died in England on 17 March 1999, and his ashes were buried in the Skinner Family Cemetery on the grounds of St James' Church in Delhi (the church was built by James Skinner). A memorial to Michael exists in Mussoorie in the form of an inscription put up in his honour by the Indian Army at Christ Church, where he was a prominent member. Two of Michael's sisters, Lillian and Sylvia, and one brother, James ('Jimmie'), still live at Sikander Hall, Barlowganj.

(L) A portrait photo of the famously generous Alice Skinner, who built Sikander Hall for her poor relations. Alice (b.1861–d.1923) was the granddaughter of James Hercules Skinner, founder of Skinner's Horse. (R) Photo of Lieutenant Colonel Michael Alexander Robert Skinner, the great-great-grandson of James Skinner, founder of Skinner's Horse. Known as 'ramrod Skinner' by his regimental colleagues for his posture, principled dealings and straight talk, Michael Skinner saw action with his regiment during the Second World War in Persia and Italy. He went on to become the last of the Skinner family to Command Skinner's Horse (1960–1963). The Indian Army placed a memorial inscription to Michael Skinner in Mussoorie's Christ Church, where he was an active member.

(Kind courtesy of Lillian Skinner Singh, Mussoorie)

In the literary world, no Mussoorie resident of yore has become better known than John George Lang (b.1816–d.1864), who was 'rediscovered' in the 1960s by Ruskin Bond, himself a well-known writer and present-day resident of Landour. After being given a clue about the existence of John Lang by an Australian friend, Bond found John Lang's grave in the Camel's Back Cemetery, and there began the unravelling of a fascinating history of a colourful and complex man.

John Lang was the grandson of a Jewish convict who had been banished to Australia for stealing eight silver spoons. His father was a sea captain who died before Lang was born. His mother, Elizabeth Harris, was the daughter of two convicts. Born and raised in Australia, a good student, Lang went off to England where he earned a law degree, even after being expelled from Cambridge for engaging in 'Botany Bay tricks' such as writing blasphemous verses, putting chamber pots on the spires of Trinity College, fraternizing with girls, neglecting his studies, drinking too much and 'most scandalously of all'[19] for being seen on the stage!

After a short career as a barrister in Sydney, where he managed to alienate just about everybody who mattered, Lang opted to work in India, where his brother-in-law had a legal practice in Calcutta. Here, Lang reinvented himself as a successful lawyer by, for example, getting the East India Company to pay the money it owed to an Agra businessman named Jyoti Prasad. He is also remembered for defending the rani of Jhansi, albeit unsuccessfully, who had been deprived of her kingdom under the so-called 'Doctrine of Lapse'.

In Mussoorie, Lang translated Persian poetry, edited the local rag *The Mofasilite* and ended up at one point in jail for defaming an East India Company official. In 1954, Lang returned to England—possibly for health reasons—where he moved in literary circles and met Charles Dickens. Soon, he began writing about India for Dickens's *Household Words* and, in 1859, returned to Mussoorie with a retainer to keep writing on India for *Household Words*.

Lang's novels include *The Forger's Wife, Botany Bay, The Ex-Wife* and *The Weatherbys*.

When Lang died, the *Madras Times* called him, 'a melancholy example of wasted talents and degraded abilities' but in Mussoorie the newspaper was more laudatory. It noted that while he was dying, he refused to cancel a public ball being held in his Mussoorie house. 'God forbid', he said, 'that any human enjoyment should be put a stop to on my account.'[20]

One hundred and forty-one years after his death, a plaque was installed in Christ Church in memory of this local legend, inspired by admirers from Australia.[21]

Another writer, Patricia Wentworth, was born as Dora Amy Elles in Mussoorie in 1878. The daughter of a British army officer, Wentworth was educated in London, returned to India after her studies and was first published in the *Civil and Military Gazette*. During her career—spent mostly in the United Kingdom—Wentworth wrote over seventy novels, the most famous being the Miss Maud Silver detective series. This series was so popular in the United States during the 1940s that Lippincott of Philadelphia became Wentworth's primary publisher, and released the Miss Silver novels in the US before their release in England. Wentworth died in 1961.

A truly colourful nineteenth-century figure in Mussoorie, but largely a failure at whatever he turned his hand to, was Mauger (pronounced 'major') Fitzhugh Monk (b.1815–d.1849). Monk certainly doesn't qualify as 'famous' but he was a fascinating local character, one we know about today only because his letters were published in 2006, almost 160 years after his death.[22] Monk was born in England to an Irish father and a Guernsey Island mother. In 1836, he qualified as a solicitor. However, within a year, he was serving in the East India Company Artillery under the assumed name of Gunner Fitzhugh O'Reilly, having left England at the age of twenty-two under a very dark cloud, described many years later as '…getting into some trouble (cherchez la femme…)'. After serving at Dum Dum (Calcutta) and Meerut, Monk was discharged from the East India Company's army and found his way to Mussoorie, where he was hired in 1840—under his own name—as 'Principal Classical Assistant' at John Mackinnon's Mussoorie Seminary for boys below Benog Hill. He later became head assistant, and ended up teaching French, fencing and drawing.

He married Elizabeth ('Bessy'), an Anglo-Indian, whose father was a retired officer of the late Begum Sumru of Sardhana (near Meerut).

In 1842, Monk wrote:

> Thank providence, the seminary at Mussoorie is a flourishing establishment and your affectionate Mauger one of its thriving members, happy in the arms of a loving wife, in the training of a tolerably manageable set of young urchins, in the enjoyment of good health, a good climate and as many comforts as a moderate income can afford.[23]

But it was not to last. While still teaching, Monk attempted trading in borax, wax, turpentine and cedar oil; horse breeding; and dispatching natural history specimens to England (birds, butterflies, beetles, etc.). At the Seminary, he had his detractors among the other teachers—'maligners'—and he had difficulties with Mackinnon, whom he once described as '...self-willed, obstinate and passionate.' In 1843, he left the seminary ('...I have better prospects on my own...') and bought an estate in Rajpur ('...my life will be principally mercantile with a dash of the agricultural and timber dealer'). But it didn't work out, nor did purchasing and operating the Victoria Hotel at Rajpur. Saddled with debt, trailed by his creditors, and ever '...a burden on his [father's] liberality...', Monk moved back up the hill in 1844 and soon after opened the Landour Academy at Mullingar with his brother-in-law, Reverend Isaac Lewin.

Mauger and Bessy had three children in three years of marriage but only a son, Hugh, lived to adulthood, having been raised by his material uncle. Bessy herself died in 1846, after giving birth to a daughter, and is buried in an elaborate vault in the Landour cemetery. Monk married again on 9 August 1849 to a woman, '...his best friends would [not] have approved of, for the girl was of no family or

Henry Wutzler, the German-born owner of the Charleville Hotel and the Criterion Restaurant, and caterer to viceroys and royal personages. Wutzler served for twelve years on the Mussoorie municipal board.

(Photo courtesy of British Library)

education, and considerably younger'. Monk died in Meerut on 9 December 1849, while en route home to England. He had made the decision to leave India, '...when he suddenly found his liabilities press too heavily, and he was persuaded he could obtain no assistance from home.' His plan had been to leave India without the knowledge of his creditors, let them seize his property and make what they could of it!

A rather more worthy citizen of the Station was Mr Henry Wutzler, a Mussoorie resident with a worldwide reputation as a hotelier who famously attended to the comforts of royalty. The German-born Wutzler (b.1853) was owner and manager of the Charleville Hotel and the Criterion Restaurant in Mussoorie and the large Royal Hotel in Lucknow. But his influence extended well beyond local inn keeping. With worldwide hotel experience, he was called upon during his time in India to cater to a string of distinguished guests. No fewer than eight viceroys testified to his skill, and among the commanders-in-chief of the British Indian Army for whom he catered were Lord Roberts, Sir George White, Sir W. Lockhart, Sir P. Palmer and Lord Kitchener. He catered to the touring tsar of Russia (prior to the tsar coming to the throne), His Imperial and Royal Highness Franz Ferdinand (who would become the emperor of Austria), Prince Albert Victor (son of King Edward VII), and the duke of Connaught, from whom he received a decoration. He was also in charge of four months' worth of catering for the 1905–1906 tour of the Prince and Princess of Wales (during which the Princess Mary visited Mussoorie). In Mussoorie itself, he served for twelve years as a member of the municipal board, from which he retired in 1903.[24]

Mrs Maisie Gantzer (b.1912–d.1996) was a well-known and greatly respected

The spirited and hugely
successful social activist of
Mussoorie, Maisie Gantzer.
*(Photo kind courtesy of Hugh and
Colleen Gantzer, Mussoorie)*

resident of the Station, one of the most formidable and successful social activists that Mussoorie ever produced. The wife of Joseph Francis Gantzer who himself was a local leader, having been elected as chairman of the municipal board in 1941 and appointed administrator of Mussoorie from 1941 to 1943, Mrs Gantzer was hugely successful in advocating for popular local issues and on behalf of fellow citizens.

Although not a member of historic Christ Church, Mrs Gantzer took the lead in saving it from the clutches of would-be developers. According to her son, Mussoorie resident Hugh Gantzer, 'when she found out that the historic church was about to be sold to a Christian quarrier for a song, she intervened, successfully asserting that Christ Church was part of Mussoorie's heritage and, so, no one had the right to dispose of it.'

Mrs Gantzer is most remembered for the central role she played in the 1980s—along with Princess Sita Devi of the House of Kapurthala ('the iron hand in the velvet glove'[25]) and Miss 'May' Badhawar, daughter of an ICS officer—in the Save Mussoorie Society's fight to close down the area's limestone quarries, which were ruining the environment and the town's tourist potential.

Again, as recalled by Hugh Gantzer:

Forewarned by fellow sympathizers that a quarrier's lorry was heading up via Library Bazaar, Mum would stage a dharna [peaceful protest] by sitting on a chair placed for her in the middle of the road a little beyond the arch at the entrance to the Mall. Despite pleas to Lucknow [at the time, Mussoorie was part of Uttar Pradesh state], quarrier interests were unable to get such 'obstructions' removed, given strong local support for closing down the mines and Mum's own formidable presence.

The limestone mafia hated her and she received threatening calls at night, but when the civic authorities offered to provide armed guards round the clock at Ockbrook [her residence], Mum politely refused saying, "I have a gun and I'm a much better shot than any of them. If anyone tries to break into my house, I'll shoot and face the consequences." The hate calls, and the sloganeering on the road above our cottage, ceased quite abruptly! Mum was then in her late seventies and she did have a gun and she was a very good shot.

Mum could not get around very much because of her arthritis but she used her phone as a very effective weapon against bureaucratic apathy and political skulduggery. People from all walks of life would ring her with their complaints and she never hesitated to blast the high and mighty to even the balance of justice. That sounds rather over-the-top but I can't think of any other way of putting it.

In the limestone quarries dispute, both the Parliament and Supreme Court were approached for redress. The mines were closed. The Library Bazaar was closed too, as a mark of respect, on the day of Maisie Gantzer's funeral.

Of course, it was not just well-known residents who helped to put Mussoorie on the map. There were many famous visitors to Mussoorie as well. In the early post-Independence period, these included the 14th Dalai Lama and Lal Bahadur Shastri. Members of the Nehru family visited regularly, pre- and post-Independence.

Lal Bahadur Shastri (b.1904–d.1966), who had been active in the Independence movement—indeed, suffering jail several times—became India's second prime minister (1964–1966). Before that he had headed the ministry of railways and transport in the Central Cabinet (1951–1956), and it was during this time that Shastri visited Oak Grove, the railways school in Jharapani. His name continues to be closely associated with Mussoorie, with the IAS (Indian Administrative Service) training centre on the Charleville Estate being established in his honour as the Lal Bahadur Shastri National Academy of Administration.

Lal Bahadur Shastri (with cane), independent India's second prime minister, visiting Oak Grove School in Jharapani while he was minster of railways and transport (1951–1956).

(Photo courtesy of Oak Grove School, Mussoorie)

His Holiness the 14th Dalai Lama and Prime Minister Jawaharlal Nehru together at Birla House, Mussoorie, in 1959, the same year that the Dalai Lama came to India in exile from Tibet.

(Courtesy of Library of Congress)

The Dalai Lama may be considered to have been a temporary resident, since he stayed in Mussoorie during that period in the early 1960s before McLeodganj in Dharamsala (Himachal Pradesh state) became his home away from home. While he was in Mussoorie, His Holiness gave weekly audiences on the grounds of the Savoy Hotel and, of course, his impact and that of his followers is still strongly felt in the Station. With the departure of the British and the subsequent arrival of many Tibetan refugees, what had been the grounds of the Happy Valley Club became over time a Tibetan colony, complete with the Shedup Choephelling Temple and the Central School for Tibetans. The Dalai Lama still visits Mussoorie and its Tibetan population every few years, and while there, stays in his quarters at the temple (see Chapter 6).

Members of India's leading political family visited Mussoorie frequently in the 1920s, 1930s and 1940s, including Jawaharlal Nehru, India's first prime minister (1947–1964), Jawaharlal's father Motilal Nehru, and Jawaharlal's daughter Indira Gandhi (prime minister, 1966–1977 and 1980–1984). Motilal took a seasonal residence in Mussoorie and, later, the family stayed at the Savoy Hotel. They also spent much time in Dehra Dun, where Nehru's sister Vijayalakshmi Pandit settled full-time. There is a bust statue of India Gandhi on the Mall. Just before Motilal Nehru's death on 6 February 1931, he reportedly travelled to Mussoorie for 'a change and better treatment' and apparently did make a slight recovery. However he continued to deteriorate and returned to Allahabad.[26]

Returning to Mussoorie's earliest days, it was Lord Auckland who was the first governor general to visit Mussoorie. Lord Auckland (George Eden)—whom history generally regards as responsible for the debacle of the first Anglo–Afghan War—was the ruler of British India from 1835 to 1842. His short visit to the Station was part of an official tour of upper India that he made with his two sisters, Emily and Fanny, who served as his hostesses since he was unmarried. Lady Emily Eden later published letters she had written during this tour to another sister in England. While she comes across in her correspondence as rather waspish and conceited, Emily's early nineteenth-century account of her experiences as an indulged traveller with 12,000 people in her and her siblings' 'progress' makes for fascinating reading. These official travellers—the governor general and his two sisters—were in Mussoorie from 17 March to 19 March 1838. Years later (1866), in the preface to her published letters, Emily bemoaned the passing of an era. 'Now that India has fallen under the curse of railroads, and that life and property will soon become as insecure there as they are here [in England], the splendor of a Governor-General's progress is at an end.'

Emily found much to complain about—mostly regarding the discomfort of travel ('I have long named my tent "Misery Hall"')—yet she had praise for Mussoorie ('Such a view on all sides of it!').

The governor general's party worshipped at Christ Church. 'We went to the little Mussoorie church yesterday morning' [Sunday, 18 March 1838]. But obviously Emily found the travel to the church more memorable than the sermon. 'The bearers are steady men, I have no doubt, but still I wish they would not race with each other; for at the sharp corners where they try to pass, the outer *jonpaun* [*jampan*] hangs over the edge, and I don't altogether like it.'[27]

The next day, the official party hastened back to Rajpur and onwards to Nahan, where Emily had many good things to say about the handsome raja.

Charlotte Canning, the wife of Charles, Viscount Canning, who was governor general from 1856 to 1862, was sent by her husband from Shimla to Mussoorie in May–June 1860, when he was unavoidably required to return to Calcutta during the hot season. Canning chose a difficult route for his wife, via the central Himalayan range rather than the shorter, normal route to Mussoorie, so that she might see the high mountains as far as Tibet while, at the same time, avoid the heat. It was thirty-one days before Charlotte reached Mussoorie, where she penned a long letter to Queen Victoria, saying that for her exertions she had been 'well repaid by all I have seen'.[28] Mussoorie must have seemed very comfortable, indeed, after such strenuous travel. Sadly, Charlotte died a little over a year later, having come down with malaria while returning to Calcutta from Darjeeling.

When writing of her visit to Mussoorie in 1887, along with the viceroy and their children, the vicerine, Lady Dufferin, declared Mussoorie not so cut off from the world as Shimla, the summer capital that was often derisively referred to, especially by British soldiers, as the 'Abode of the Little Tin Gods', the 'Viceroy's Shooting Box' or 'Mount Olympus':[29]

[Saturday, 9 April 1887] We made a long and very pleasant expedition to Mussoorie, which is the hill station immediately over this [Dehra Dun]. It is much smaller than Shimla, but it has the inestimable advantage of being on an outside spur of the Himalayas, and instead of being buried behind range after range of mountains, it is situated at the extreme edge of them and looks down about the plains as upon a map. It is not cut off from the world, and a person there who might be bored by hill station society could mount his horse and descend in half an hour to the larger world below. You can't imagine what a delightful sense of freedom this gives, because you don't know what it is to be encaged in the very heart of the Himalayas for the greater part of the year.[30]

One gets the sense that Lady Dufferin was fed up with Shimla!

A portrait of the vicerine, Lady Dufferin, who preferred Mussoorie—with its proximity to Dehra Dun and the 'larger world below'—to Shimla, the summer capital of the British government.
(Photo kind courtesy of Hugh Ashley Rayner, Pagoda Tree Press, United Kingdom)

But more than the musings of these viceregal visitors, it is the intrepid Fanny Parkes whose writing about Mussoorie in the 1830s most entertains and informs us today. Fanny (née Frances Susannah Archer, b.1794–d.1875) was far from the typical memsahib of her day. Leaving her British officer husband behind, she mounted elephant, horse or donkey with equal ease and went touring. She was a keen observer of India and Indian ways. Fortunately, she was also a keen diarist and amateur artist, and so there are fascinating glimpses of her time in Mussoorie and Landour, just as these twin towns were being established. In 1838, she took her own house in Landour for Rs 1,200 for the entire season near the cantonment quarters of invalids from the 16th Lancers and The Buffs[31]. She moved about the Station and its environs and, indeed, around northern India, with a freedom that in those days was not generally condoned for British ladies, who were expected to keep themselves aloof from Indians and local culture. She even helped oversee the construction of Cloud End, which her cousin Captain Edmund Swetanham, the commandant of the Landour Depot, was building.[32] Emily and Fanny Eden, who had to share the Station with Fanny Parkes during a few days of the 1838 Season, were not fans[33], but that didn't seem to bother Fanny Parkes. The hill air made Fanny feel strong. She picnicked at the waterfalls and in the Municipal Gardens, danced at a ball given by the bachelors of Mussoorie and Landour, collected and remarked extensively on the flora and fauna (she pronounced deodar oil good for rheumatic pains) and all the while obviously enjoyed herself, despite a few close calls along the steep paths and during torrential downpours.[34]

The view in 1838 from the house that the intrepid Fanny Parkes had taken on rent for the Season in Landour for Rs 1,200 or, as she meticulously noted, £120 for seven months. '...a good house, well situated, but very far from supplies...directly beneath it is a precipice; opposite is that part of the Hill of Landowr [sic] on which stands the Lall Tība, and is covered with oak and rhododendron trees....in the distance, are the snow-covered mountains of the lower range of the Himalaya.'
(From Parkes, Fanny, Wanderings of a Pilgrim, in Search of the Picturesque, during Four-and-Twenty Years in the East, with Revelations of Life in the Zenana, *London: Pelham Richardson, 1850, quotes from p. 228 and 237 and sketch from facing p. 237 in vol. 2)*

Of course, there were many other notable visitors or short-term residents. In 1929, almost exactly one hundred years after Fanny Parkes roamed the hillsides, Idi Amin came to Mussoorie to participate in a boxing competition. He later became Uganda's heavyweight boxing champion and, later still, the infamous military dictator and president of Uganda (1971–1979).

Richard Tauber (b.1891–d.1948), the great Austrian tenor, entertained in Mussoorie during several seasons. Acclaimed as one of the greatest singers of the twentieth century, some critics commented that 'his heart felt every word he sang'. The White Russian and former ballet dancer, Boris Lissanevitch, also made an appearance on the Mussoorie entertainment circuit in the late 1940s, along with his cabaret troupe, the Danish Beauties. Boris married one of his beauties and later became famous as the manager of the 300 Club in Calcutta and, later still, of the Yak & Yeti Hotel in Kathmandu. During the Second World War, the Austrian mountain climber, Heinrich Harrer (b.1912–d.2006), escaped from prison camp in Dehra Dun and slipped quietly through Landour on his way to Tibet. He later wrote about his adventures in *Seven Years in Tibet* which, in 1997, was made into a popular movie.

As noted in the message of this Fitch & Co. postcard (R), Mussoorie hosted in 1929 an international boxing competition in which Idi Amin, who would become the infamous dictator of Uganda, participated.
(Photo kind courtesy of the late H. Michael Stokes, Kent, United Kingdom)

Children of missionary parents ('mish kids') also made their mark on the world stage. Among them was John Morrison Birch·(b.1918–d.1945), best known for the right-of-centre society in the United States that bears his name. Born in Landour to Baptist missionaries, he and his parents left Landour when he was only two years old. Years later, Birch was killed by Communists in the tumult in China immediately following the Second World War.

Then there are the present-day notables with ties to Mussoorie, some of whose lives have spanned the British and independent India periods. Ruskin Bond (writer and recipient of the Padma Shri [an Indian civilian honour award]), Victor Bannerjee (actor), Bill Aitkens (writer), Hugh and Colleen Gantzer (naval officer, and both writers), the late Sudhir Thapliyal (writer and naturalist), Lillian Skinner Singh (the Station's grand dame), Tom Alter (actor and also a Padma Shri recipient) and Stephen Alter (writer). And of course, on the world stage there is the famous novelist Anita Desai, who was born in Mussoorie.[35] The stories of these notables are still being written. But like the Station's colourful characters of old, all are legends of their own time.

Notes

1. The 'Forward Policy' is a term used to describe the British military-political goal of protecting its restive North West Frontier and ensuring its control over all of India.
2. Keay, John, *The Great Arc, the Dramatic Tale of How India was Mapped and Everest was Named*, New, York: HarperCollins Publishers, 2000: 109-112.
3. Hathipaon means 'elephant's foot', although whether this refers to the stumpy profile of one of the flanking hills or to the indentation left between them is unclear (Keay, Ibid, p. 112).
4. Sir William Sampson Whish (b.1787–d.1853), KCB, of the Bengal Artillery, had taken possession of the Park estate area in May 1829 and built the Park House in 1829–1830. The estate's boundaries were ill-defined, but Everest himself got the matter sorted out in November 1833, the property initially consisting of 283 acres and, later, surveyed at 355 acres. Everest sold the estate in the early 1860s—twenty years after his departure from Mussoorie—to Colonel Robert Thatcher of the Bengal Infantry. Subsequent owners were Colonel Alexander Skinner and, then, John Mackinnon, his sons Philip and Vincent Mackinnon, and '…In 1942 the Development Corporation sold the Park to some Kumaon paharis for a song. It was they who cleared much of the forest and replaced it with potato cultivation'. In 1988, the Uttar Pradesh state government started acquiring the property (information from Smith, M.R., *Everest: The Man and the Mountain*, Scotland: Caithness, 1999: 147-154).
5. Parkes, Fanny, *Wanderings of a Pilgrim, in Search of the Picturesque, during Four-and-Twenty Years in the East, with Revelations of Life in the Zenana*, London: Pelham Richardson, 1850: 275 in vol. 2.
6. Bodycot, F. ('compiler'), *Guide to Mussoorie with Notes on Adjacent Districts and Routes into the Interior*, Mussoorie: Mafasilite Printing Works, 1907: 39-40.
7. Walton, H.G., ICS, *The Gazetteer of Dehra Dun*, first print 1911, Dehra Dun: Natraj Publishers, 2007 (reprint): 248.
8. There was another Survey of India officer who was professionally well-known, but in history is remembered most often because of his mysterious death. In the early part of the twentieth century, Henry Morshead—soldier, surveyor, linguist, explorer and mountaineer—worked for the Survey of India in Dehra Dun and Mussoorie. In 1929, he was appointed as the survey's director, Burma Circle. In 1931, in Maymyo, Burma, he was most mysteriously murdered and the case was never solved. A fascinating account of this incident has been written by

his son (Morshead, Ian, *The Life and Murder of Henry Morshead, A True Story from the Days of the Raj*, Cambridge: The Oleander Press, 1982).

9. In fact, there were already local names for Peak XV. The Nepalese call it Sagarmatha (goddess of the sky), and Tibetans call it Chomolungma (mother goddess of the universe). But both Nepal and Tibet were closed to foreigners at the time (1865) and, so, these local names may have been unknown to the British.

10. In Robert Hutchison's fictional account of Frederick Wilson's life, Wilson is described as having deserted from the 'Army of the Indus' during the first Anglo–Afghan War fought during 1839–1842 (Hutchison, Robert, *The Raja of Harsil: The Legend of Frederick 'Pahari' Wilson*, New Delhi: Roli Books, 2010).

11. Rokeby probably was named after a long narrative poem written in 1812 by Sir Walter Scott, who was very popular during this period. The poetical events take place in 1644 in Rokeby, Yorkshire and concern happenings following the Battle of Marston Moor. Ivanhoe was also a Scott novel, set in twelfth-century England.

12. Kala, D.C., *Frederick Wilson of Garhwal 1816-1883*, Delhi: Ravi Dayal, 2006: 25-155.

13. Pearse, Hugh, *The Hearseys: Five Generations of an Anglo-Indian Family*, Edinburgh and London: William Blackwood and Sons, 1905: 38.

14. Pearse, Ibid, p. 50.

15. Moorcroft was manager of the stud farm at Pusa, Bihar which still exists—on a much-expanded basis—as the Indian Agricultural Research Institute, Regional Station.

16. Pearse, Ibid, p. 60-61.

17. Pearse, Ibid, p. 64. The contention of the Hearsey family was that by buying Chandee from Hyder Young Hearsey, whose title to it was the same as that to the ownership of Dehra Dun, the East India Company recognized the validity of his ownership to both properties. In the event, the argument didn't work!

18. Pearse, Ibid, p. 406.

19. Medcalf, Rory, 'John Lang, our forgotten Indian envoy', *The Spectator,* London, 2010.

20. Ibid.

21. The memorial inscription to John Lang was installed with support from Australian scholars. The plaque was unveiled on 15 August 2005 by John Fisher, first secretary at the Australian High Commission, New Delhi. The inscription reads:

In memory of

John George Lang

b. 19 December 1816

Parramatta, Australia

d. 24 [sic, 21] August 1864

Mussoorie, India

Barrister, writer, journalist,

Wanderer

Editor of "The Mofussilite"

First Australian-born novelist
A scholar and a friend of India
A brilliant and restless soul
At peace in his adopted country

This plaque was erected to
Commemorate his extraordinary life
by
Rory Medcalf and Victor Crittenden

22. Morgan, Andrew, ed., *Mussoorie Merchant, the Indian Letters of Mauger Fitzhugh Monk, 1828-1849*, Bath: Pagoda Tree Press, 2006.
23. Ibid, p. 71.
24. Information on Henry Wutzler from *Cyclopedia of India,* Calcutta: Cyclopedia Publishing Company, 1908: 301 in vol.2.
25. Thadhani, Prem K. *Chronicles of the Doon Valley, An Environmental Exposé*, New Delhi: Indus Publishing Company, 1993: 156.
26. Ghosh, Devaprasad, *Pandit Motilal Nehru: His Life and Work*, Calcutta: Modern Book Agency, 1931: 22.
27. Eden, Emily, *Up the Country, Letters Written to Her Sister from the Upper Provinces of India*, London: Richard Bentley, 1867: 37-117. Emily Eden's visit to the 'little church'—presumably with her brother the viceroy, George Eden (Lord Auckland) and her sister, Fanny Eden—had to be to Christ Church, since in 1838 it was the only church in the Station, and it was indeed much smaller then, as it was not extended to its present size until 1853.
28. Allen, Charles, *A Glimpse of the Burning Plain, Leaves from the Indian Journals of Charlotte Canning*, London: Michael Joseph, 1986: 136-143.
29. Farwell, Byron, *Armies of the Raj from the Great Indian Mutiny to Independence: 1858-1947*, London: W.W. Norton & Company, 1991: 134-135.
30. Blackwood, Harriot Georgina, marchioness of Dufferin & Ava, *Our Viceregal Life in India; Selections from My Journal, 1884-1888*, 2 vols., London: John Murray, 1889: 154-155, vol. 2.
31. 'The Buffs' was the Royal East Kent Regiment, formerly called the 3rd Regiment of Foot and today continued as the Prince of Wales' Royal Regiment.
32. It is said that Edmund Swetanham got the Cloud End Estate as dowry from a local landlord whose daughter he married. This was at a time when 'mixed marriages' were not frowned upon, as they were later. He and his wife, styled as 'My Fair Lady' by Fanny Parkes in her *Wonderings,* had six sons, all of whom ended up as army colonels (Kala, Ibid, p. 46). There is a memorial inscription to Swetenham (d. 6 March 1963) in Christ Church.
33. Fanny Eden wrote in Cawnpore (Kanpur) of Fanny Parkes, 'We are rather oppressed just now, by a lady, Mrs Parkes, who insists on belonging to our camp and has entirely succeeded in proving that the Governor-General's power is but a name. She has a husband who always

goes mad in the cold season, so she says it is due to herself to leave him and travel about. She has been a beauty and has the remains of it and is abundantly fat and lively. At Benares, where we fell in with her, she informed us she was an independent woman and was going to travel to Simla by herself—which sounded very independent indeed. Then she applied to Captain Codrington who manages the ground to let her pitch her tent among ours. Now the sacredness of the Governor-General's street of tents is such that…of course that was refused. The Magistrate of one station always travels on with us to the next. To each of these Magistrates she has severally attached herself, every one declaring they will have nothing to do with her, upon which George observes with much complacency, "Now we have got rid of our Mrs Parkes"—and the next morning there she is, the mawk, her fresh victim driving her in a tilbury—and her tent pitched close to his.'

Later, Fanny wrote while in Mussoorie, 'Captain MacGregor just came in looking pale and breathless, and said, "I have just seen Mrs Parkes—here! She has sent her remembrance to Lord Auckland and the Miss Edens, and is delighted to think she has fallen in with them again, and hopes soon to make her way to Simla". There is something very horrid and unearthly in all this—nobody ever had a fat attendant spirit before.' (Dunbar, Janet, ed., *Tigers, Durbars and Kings; Fanny Eden's Indian Journals, 1837-1838*, London: John Murray, 1988: 106, 151).

34. Parkes, Fanny, Ibid, p. 224-259 in vol. 2.
35. Anita Desai née Mazumdar was born in Mussoorie on 24 June 1937 of a German mother, Toni Nime, and a Bengali businessman, D.N. Mazumdar. One of Anita Desai's four children is the Man Booker Prize-winning novelist, Kiran Desai *(The Inheritance of Loss)*.

The past meets the present. Even to this day, descendants of (primarily) Britons who had connections to Mussoorie still visit the Station. This photograph, taken by Dorothy Durling in 2009, juxtaposes a 1932 photo of the Christ Church wedding of her grandparents, Reverend Joseph Vail Barrows (b.1886–d.1972) and Nora Doreen Searle (b.1902–d.1937), with a present-day view of the church itself.

(Composite photo and information kindly provided by Dorothy Durling, USA)

POSTSCRIPT

Every empire wanes in the end—'one with Nineveh and Tyre'—but all our lives have been affected, sometimes directed, by the long march of imperialism.
~ Jan Morris, Stones of Empire[1] ~

The British were in India for 340 years, from August 1608, when the *Hector*, the East India Company ship, arrived off Surat (Gujarat state) after a seventeen-month voyage, up to February 1948, when the men of the First Battalion, the Somerset Light Infantry, marched through the Gateway of India (they had stayed on after 15 August 1947 to oversee some of the transition, at a time of great instability). Much has been written about the cost of this company and, later, Imperial rule[2]—about the economic exploitation, political subjugation, social ostracism and racism. The cost was great indeed and ultimately, of course, colonialism was forced to give way to the legitimate demand for freedom from foreign domination.

Yet, much that was good was left behind, not least being the seeds of parliamentary democracy, an independent judiciary and a language that would help bind the country together and link it more closely to the world beyond. Physically, there were the railways, the post and telegraph offices, the irrigation canals, the schools and colleges, an industrial infrastructure and a worldwide trading base. Independent India successfully harnessed these assets, ultimately expanding and redefining them in ways that would have been unimaginable in the middle of the last century, when the British returned to their island home.

'Incredible India!' indeed.

The hill stations—scattered along the lower ridges of the great Himalayan chain and in the higher reaches of the Central Plateau—live on as footprints of a British past. And, like the English language and the post office, they are also a vital part of present-day India, despite many changes that have taken place.

In 1961, M.S. Kalyanasundaram wrote: 'There may be a difference of opinion regarding the other vaunted benefits of the British Rule, but the summer resort idea is worth being encouraged along practical lines.'[3]

And encouraged it has been in modern India, to the extent that India's 'summer resort idea' could have fallen victim to excessive popularity, with the attendant problems of congestion and pollution of every sort. Some say this 'fall' has already occurred. Certainly, these colonial-era sanitaria have been changed—sometimes for the better, sometimes not—and redefined almost beyond recognition. Yet, for many residents and visitors, their charm remains largely undiminished.

During that historic autumn of 1947, when jubilation mingled with tragedy, Mussoorie, alas, did not stand aloof from the chaos that ensued. In the wake of Partition, feelings ran high and there was a great deal of anxiety. Students and staff at the schools were concerned for family and friends in the plains, particularly in the Punjab. When rioting began, the schools went into lockdown. Muslim shopkeepers in Landour sought to escape to safer climes and, post their departure, some of their homes and shops were torched (a number of Muslim shopkeepers later returned). A small Muslim school in Landour was also burned. The road to the plains was closed and so, food was scarce for some time. The trouble lasted for a long three weeks. Yet, compared to many other places, Mussoorie had gotten off easily...as it had during the First War of Independence.

The prosperity that the war years had brought to the Station did not last. As the 1950s progressed, Mussoorie went into an economic decline. The free-spending soldiers on leave had departed; the British rulers and businessmen left too, as did many of the British retirees. The Indian middle class had not yet discovered the station's attractions. At the same time, there were some new arrivals, Sikhs and Hindus from Pakistan. And the schools continued to inject money into the local economy. Yet, Mussoorie didn't start coming out of this economically stagnant period until the 1970s, the turnaround fuelled by new and expanding schools, and by the arrival of domestic tourists in ever-growing numbers.

Today, Mussoorie seems, in some ways, to have become a victim of its own popularity. There are now more than 200 hotels in the Station, which greatly overstretch the available facilities. And many of these hotels have minimal facilities. Water and electricity are in short supply and the municipal sewerage system is antiquated, although the rebuilding of these systems is ongoing (adding its own complications to Mussoorie's already-strained infrastructure). Buildings often do not meet earthquake-resistant standards. Vehicular traffic is a serious problem; traffic jams are common on the narrow roadways in the Station and on the main road up from Dehra Dun.[4] The Mall itself often becomes crowded with pedestrians, tourists seeking out local amusements like the ropeway to Gun Hill that was built in 1970, or the newer, unlikely attraction of an escalator to a small aquarium. The

Season now seems to extend for most of the year, often creating an atmosphere that is distinctly carnivalesque. However, there is some concern, particularly amongst shopkeepers, that Mussoorie is becoming a destination mostly for day trippers—sometimes derisively referred to as 'chhola bhatura' visitors—who spend very little money but add considerably to traffic and pollution problems, even as they enjoy a street-side chhola bhatura[5] snack while (briefly) taking the air.

Yet parts of the Station, especially Landour, are much as they were in earlier times, thanks in no small measure to the Indian military and their well-protected forested lands. Building restrictions have also helped to somewhat limit congestion, and organizations such as the Eco-Task Force do much to protect the natural environment. Indeed, were the nineteenth-century residents able to return, there is still much that they would no doubt find familiar.

At the same time, throughout Mussoorie, the inevitable signs of modernization and rapid social change are evident. Teenage students—still traditionally kitted out in

(L) The Union Jack atop the tower of Christ Church, in celebration of the coronation of King George VI (12 May 1937). (R) The tiranga (tricolour) of the Republic of India now flies atop the tower each year on Independence Day (15 August).

(British-era photo kind courtesy of Gopal Bhardwaj, Mussoorie; present-day photo from the authors' collection)

blazers from Mussoorie's many schools and roguishly loud in the way of teenagers across the world—chatter away on their free days at the popular coffee shops that now dot the town. Cyber cafes keep everyone linked in and hooked up. Store-owners hawk the latest trinkets to tourists. Huge buses roar up the narrow road to the Mall, spewing fumes and adding greatly to the chaotic traffic. Labourers doggedly repaint railings or rip up roads (supposedly 'improving' them). Songs from the latest Bollywood musical blare away. Oversized hoardings pollute the landscape, often blocking from view the natural beauty of the place. At times, the downside of modernization seems to have overwhelmed—indeed, overtaken—Mussoorie. Yet for those who search, solitary reflection and quiet peace can be found.

Whatever be the attraction—the 'carnivalesque' Mall or the quieter nooks—it can be enjoyed in a cool climate, away from the heat of the plains. As one hotel operator commented, 'It is very hot in the plains, so business will be good.' Modern-day visitors come to enjoy the pleasant weather and scenery, to relax and to escape the demands of daily life, the same reasons that drew the British in the first place to this Himalayan 'place apart'.

As the ghosts of the past mingle with the energy and surge of the present, the charms of Mussoorie continue to capture the imagination and uplift the spirit of those who spend time amongst the deodars and mist of this 'most enviable' hill station.

Notes

1. Morris, Jan, *Stones of Empire, The Buildings of the Raj.* Oxford: Oxford University Press, 1983: 1.
2. The rule of the East India Company ceased from 2 August 1858, although it was not until 1 November 1858 that Queen Victoria's proclamation announcing that fact was issued in India by Lord Canning.
3. Kalyanasundaram, M.S. *Indian Hill Stations.* Madras: Tamil Puthakalayam, 1961: 10-11.
4. As early as 1911, there were two schemes put forward that might have prevented today's traffic problems, but neither of them was implemented, probably due to cost. One was the Rajpur–Landour Rope Tramway service and the other was the Dehra–Mussoorie Electric Tramway scheme (Walton, H.G., ICS, *The Gazetteer of Dehra Dun*, Dehra Dun, Natraj Publishers, 2007 reprint [first printed in 1911], p. 247).
5. 'Chhola bhatura' is a Punjabi snack of chickpea and fried dough, often sold cheaply as street food. The day visitors who come to Mussoorie are often visiting briefly after going to nearby Haridwar on pilgrimage.

Appendix A

Additional Details of Frederick Young's Life

The following extract from the minutes of Fort William, Calcutta, 'Political Consultations of 6 June 1833', record the approval of Frederick Young as political agent for Dehra Dun. This approval was granted on an exceptional basis, since generally the East India Company did not assign officers simultaneously to both military and civilian positions. (Courtesy of British Library)

The Governor-General is pleased to record the following minute…

No. 38   Political Deptt

It has, I am aware, been doubted whether his designation of Superintendent of Deyrah Doon rendered Lt. Col F. Young ineligible to hold his situations in his present ranks, and I must concede thus much upon the point that it was only by a constructive assimilation of his office to one of a different designation, that brought him within the disqualifying rule…the operation of this rule was however suspended for an assigned period that Government might not lose the benefits of his experience in the course of some efforts to improve the revenue administration, and the management generally of the affairs of this civil charge.

The assigned period is about to close and Lt. Col. Young now asks for the designation of Political Agent, the grant of which, his duties as the representative of the Government with the Rajah of Garhwal will probably justify as will also in some measure the recent extension of the same designation to Captains Wade and Kennedy who were before only assistants.

The propriety of acceding to Lt. Colonel Young's request is offered for consideration of Council….

Calcutta 31st May 1833   Wm. [William Henry Cavendish] Bentinck
                                                                     [Governor-General]

◆

I am for acceding to it.

4th June 1833   C.T. [Charles Theophilus] Metcalfe
[Member, Council of the Governor-General]

♦

I am not aware of any objection to acceding to Col. Young's request...

A. [Alexander] Ross
[Member, Council of the Governor-General]

♦

Ordered that the appointment of Lt. Co. F. Young 34th Regt. Of N.I. [Native Infantry] to be Political Agent in the Deyrah Doon be published in the *Calcutta Gazette* and notice thereof sent at the same time to that officer.

(true copies)
(signed) Asst. Secy to the Govt.

♦

In the 1920s, a retired Indian Army officer, Major V.C.P. Hodson, began the formidable task of alphabetically arranging a list detailing the careers of the officers of the Bengal Army who had served between 1758 and 1834. Hodson's four-volume magnum opus was completed only in 1946, and it stands as a wonderful example of well-recorded historical detail. Its usefulness, for anyone interested in this aspect of the history of the Raj, continues to this day.

The entry for Frederick Young is given here in full, with some explanatory notes, as contained in Hodson's *List of the Officers of the Bengal Army, 1758–1834, Part IV*, London, Phillimore & Co. Ltd, Genealogical Publishers & Record Searchers, 1947: 544-545.

YOUNG, FREDERICK (1786-1874). General. Colonel 66th or Gurkha Regt. (now 1st K.G.O. [King George's Own] Gurkha Rifles). b. Green Castle, Moville, co. Donegal, 30 Nov. 1786. Cadet 1801. Arrived in India 19 July 1802. Ensign 12 July 1802. Lieut. (17 July 1804) 18 Mar 1805 [latter date indicates London's confirmation of promotion]. Capt. 23 Sept. 1821. Major 21 July 1826. Lt. Col. 1 Nov. 1830. Col. 3 Oct. 1842. Maj. Gen. 20 June 1854. Lt. Gen. 18 Feb. 1856. Gen. 28 Mar. 1865.

d. at his residence, Albany, nr. Dublin, 22 May 1874.

bapt. Lower Moville 10 Dec. 1786. 2nd son of Rev. Gardiner Young and Catherine Richardson his wife. Brother of Gardiner Young, *q.v.* [*quod vide,* which see…] *m.* Meerut 20 Oct. 1825, Jeanette Jamesina, dau. of John Jenkins Bird, *q.v.* (*See also* Aynott Chitty.) (She died Dinapore 10 Apr. 1852.)

Services: Barasat C.C. 1802-3. Apptd. To 1st Vol. Bn. 7 Oct. 1803. Second Mahratta War 1803-5; reduction of Cuttack 1803-4; capture of Balasore; Ensign 1st Vol. Bn.; posted to 12th N.I. (Native Infantry] 1805; Bhurtpore; Lieut. 12th N.I. Transfd. To 13th N.I. 1806; Adjt. & Qmr. do. 8 May 1806 till 1 July 1814; Intr. [Interpreter] & Qmr. 2/13th N.I. 1 July 1814 till 1815. Nepal War 1814-15; Kalanga; Nahan; Jaithak; Lieut. 2/13th N.I. (India medal). Taken prisoner during Nepal War. Comdd. Newly-raised Sirmoor Bn. 26 Aug. 1815 till 2 Jan. 1843. Third Mahratta War 1817-18. Operations against the freebooter Kowar Singh in Saharanpur district 1824; assault of mud fort of Kunjawa (w. [wounded]); Capt. Comdg. a detachment of 350 of Sirmoor Bn. Transfd. To newly-raised 34th N.I. July 1823; to 68th N.I. (late 2/34th) May 1824. P.A. [Political Agent] at Dehra Dun 13 June 1833 till Nov. 1842. Posted Lt. Col. To 35th N.I. 10 Sept 1831; to 58th N.I. 22 July 1834. Bdr. 2 cl. To comd. 4th Bde. 2nd Inf. Div., Army of Reserve (for Afghanistan), 6 June 1842; to comd troops in Bundelkhand 14 Oct. 1842. Posted Col. To 74th N.I. 21 Jan. 1843; to 65th N.I. 17 Apr. 1845; 66th (Gurkha) Regt. (late Sirmoor Bn.) May 1855 till 1869. Fur. p.a. [Furlough private affairs] 17 Mar. 1844 till 1846. Bdr. Comdg. Ferozepore 5 Jan. 1847; Bdr. Gen. comdg. Dinapore Div. 20 Sept. 1849 till 10 Nov. 1854. Fur. p.a. 5 Jan. 1855 till death.

Refs.: Burke's *Landed Gentry of Ireland*, p. 784, *s.n.* [*sub nomine,* under the name of…] Young, of Culdaff House, co. Donegal. *Gen. Frederick Young,* by his dau., L. Hadow Jenkins, 1923 (portrait by J. Reynolds Gwatkin, 1839). Boase. *The Times,* 29 May 1874, p.5. (Information taken directly from Hodson, Major V.C.P., *List of the Officers of the Bengal Army, 1758-1834, Part IV.*, London, Phillimore & Co. Ltd., 1947, pp. 554-555).

◆

Frederick Young's obituary as it appeared in *The Times*, London, on 29 May 1874.

General Frederick Young, late colonel of the 66th Bengal (Goorkha) Light Infantry Regiment, died at his residence, the Albany, near Dublin, on the 22nd inst., in his 88th year. The deceased officer's commissions bear date as ensign 1802, lieutenant 1805, captain 1816, major 1826, lieutenant-colonel 1830, colonel 1842, major-general 1854, lieutenant-general 1856, and general 1865.

♦

Young was buried on 26 May 1874 in the Deansgrange Cemetery, which is a couple of miles northwest of Ballybrack, County Kildare, east of Dublin. The gravesite is still in excellent condition. The inscription reads as follows:

To the Memory of General Frederick Young, late Bengal Army.
Born November 30th, 1786. Died May 22nd. 1874.
Erected in affectionate remembrance of a dearly beloved father by his children.
He giveth his beloved sleep.

The family representative in charge of the interment was Dr Charles Hamilton Fasson, Young's son-in-law, husband of his eldest daughter Catherine Mary (b. 20 January 1827 in Dehra Dun). Probate of Frederick's will was granted in Dublin on 1 July 1874 to Dr Fasson. Probate was sealed in London on 14 July 1874, on effects in England valued at under £3,000.*

---

*Burial, gravesite and probate information provided by Adrian Stevenson, a 5x great-grandson of George Young, brother of Gardiner Young (Frederick's father); and by Justin Homan Martin, Dublin.

Appendix B

Listing of Houses in Mussoorie

(From The Guide Map Of Mussoorie And Landour Of 1929*)

A

Abbey, The Abbotsford, Survey
   of India
Abergeldie and Cot. [Cottage]
Acorns, The
A.F.I. Hd. Qrs., (Arcadia) [the
   Auxiliary Force (India)]
Airfield, (H.H. Bhopal)
Airfield Cot.
Airyland
Albany Lodge
Albert Lodge & Cot.
Alicemount
Allahābād Bank, (Tiverton)
Allen Meml. School, (Bala
   Hissar)
All Saints Church, (C. of E.)
   [Church of England]
Aloha
Alyndale
Amāwan Palace
Anand Kanān
Anglesey
Annandale
Annfield
Antlers Cot.
Antlers, The
Arcadia (A.F.I. Hd Qrs.)
Artaigne
Arundel Cot.
Arundel Ho. [House]
Ashton Cot. & Court
Ashton Dale
Astell & Cot.
Astell Lo.

Athenaeum Lo. [Lodge]
Aubrey Vil. [Villa]
Auchnagie Cot.
Auchnagie Ho.
Auchnagi Lo.
Avenel

B

Bāla Hissār, (Allen Meml. Sch.)
Bāla Hissār Cot.
Band Houses, The
Baring Inst., (Book Depot &
   Shops)
Beechwood
Beehive, The, & Cot.
   (Landour)
Beehive Cot. (Mussoorie)
Bellevue (Landour)
Bellevue (Musssoorie)
Bellevue Cot.
Belmont
Belvedere
Benmore
Berylden
Bhatta Cot.
Bickleigh Ho.
Bimala Kutir
Bleak Ho.
Bluebird
Book Depot, (Cronstadt)
Bothwell Bank
Brandlesome
Brentwood, (Glen Lyon)
Brewery Ho.
Briar Brae

Briarwood
Brightlands
Brooklands
Broom Hill, (Isolation Hospl.)
Budhi Ho.
Buona Vista
Burnside, (Deb Bhawan)

C

Caineville Sch.
Castle, The, Survey of India
Catherine Cot. & Vil.
Cedar Hall, (Wynberg Homes)
Cefn Coed
Central Post Office, Rockstone
   Ho.)
Central Tel. Office, Connaught
   Ho.)
Chālet, The
Chapelton
Charlemont
Charleroi
Charleston
Charleston Cot.
Charleville Hotel, The
Chāteau, The (H.H.
   Kapārthalā)
Childers Cas.
Childers Cot. & Lo.
Christabel Lo.
Christ Church, (C. of E.)
Church of the Resurrection
   (C. of E.)
Church View
Church View Cot. & Ter.

Chynoweth Cot.
Cinema, (Ellesmere)
Cinema, (Picture Palace)
City Hall & Office
Civil Hospital
Clairville
Claremount
Clarence Ho., (Fitch & Co.)
Cliff Cot.
Cliff Hall
Clifton Vil.
Clovelly & Cot.
Clover Bank
Clover Cot.
Club View
Combe Regis
Commercial Ho., (Shops)
Community Centre
Congleton
Connaught Cas.
Connaught Ho., (Govt. Tel.
    Office)
Connis Cliff
Constantia, (Whyberg Homes)
Convent, The, (Waverley)
Convent, (Hampton Court)
Corner Cot.
Cosy Nook & Cot. (Landour)
Cosy Nook & Cot.
    (Mussoorie)
Cot Grove
Crag Lo.
Crags, The
Craig Cot.
Craignish, Survey of India
Craig Top
Criterion,The, (Shops)
Cronstadt, (Baring Inst.),
    (Book Depot & Shops)
Crown Brewery, (disused)
Crystal Bank

D
Dahlia Bank

Dale Cot.
Dale View
Daulat Bandar
Deal Cot.
Deanery, The
Deb Bhawan
Delight Cot.
Delight, The
Dene Hollow
Deodars, The & Lo.
Devonshire Ho. & Cot.
Dhār Cot.
Dieudonnée
Dilārām & Cot.
Dilkusha
Dingle, The & Cot.
Dingle Vil.
Dispensary, Charitable
Douglas Dale & Cot.
Dove Cot.
Dreamlands, (Ruins)
Dulce Domum [Sweet Home]
Dumbarnie Homes &
    Orphanage
Dunedin & Cot., Survey of
    India
Dungarvan
Dunseverick, (H.H. Gaekwar
Baroda)
Dūn Side
Dūn View, (Landour)
Dūn View Cot.

E
Eagle's Cliff
Eagle's Nest & Cot.
Eagle's Nest Vil.
Eagle's Ridge
Eastwood, Cot. & Lo.
Edenfell
Edgehill & Vil.
Eglantine
Elcot Lo.
Electric Power Ho.

Electric Pumping Stn.
Ellangowan, & Cot.
Ellesmere, (Cinema & Shops)
Elspeth
Emporium, The, (Shops)
Eric's Own (Rāja Tikāri)
Erindale
Esme Cot. & Lo.
Essex Lo.
Evelyn Hall, Crt. Lo. & Vil.,
    (Nursing Home)
Exchange, The, (Trevillion &
    Clark)

F
Fairie Hall
Fair Lawn
Fair View & Cot.
Falcon's Nest
Fellfoot
Fenloe
Fern Lo.
Fernwith
Fir Clump
Firs Cot.
Firs, The
Florence Cot.
Fowl House, Survey of India
Frankfort
Frosty Hall

G
Garden Cot.
Garden Reach
Garden Reach Vil.
General Post Office,
    (Rockstone Ho.)
Gentian Hill
Glanmire
Glanvilla Cot.
Glanvilla Hall
Glanvilla Ho., (Shop)
Glen, The
Glenbrook

Glenburnie, (Summer Home)
Glen Cot.
Glenelg
Glengowan
Glen Hayes & Cot.
Glen Head
Glen Luce, (Hīra Niwās)
Glen Lyon, (Brentwood)
Glen Rannock
Glen Rannock Lo.
Glenroy
Glenthorne
G.H. School (Kincraig)
Gorge Head, (Kashmir Hotel)
Govt. Telegraph Office
Gowan Brae
Gracemount
Grand Hotel, The, & Palladium
Grange, The
Grant Cas.
Greenmount & Cot.
Greenview Cot.
Grey Cas.
Groomsbridge
Guthrie Lo.
Gymnasium, The, (Landour)

H
Halfway, Ho. The
Halīm Cas.
Hamilton Ho.
Hampton Court, (Convent)
Hampton Court Cot.
Happy Garden
Happy Valley Tennis Club
Harmony Cot.
Hatville, (Shop)
Haven
Hazel Brae
Hazel Dell
Hazeldene, Survey of India
Hazelmere & Cot.
Hazelwood
Heather Brae

Helvetia, (Shop)
Hendon Hall
Henry Vil.
Hermitage, The
Hermitage Cot. & Lo.
Herne Cliff, Dale, Hill, Lea
  & Lo.
Highlands
Hill Cottage
Hillside
Hillview Cot.
Himālaya Club, (Old)
Himālaya Cot.
Holland Ho. & Lo.
Hollow Oak
Hollymount
Hollywood
Holme Croft
Holmwood
Homestead
Hope Cot.
Hope Lo., (Dairy)
Hospital, Civil
Hospital, Isolation
Hospital, St. Mary's Cottage
Hospital, Station, (Landour)
Hospital, Veterinary
Hotel, Charleville
Hotel, Grand, & Palladium
Hotel, Kashmir, (Gorge Head)
Hotel, Savoy
Hotel, Union, (Oxford Ho.)
Hussain Ganj Cot.
Hymen Cot.

I
Ilbert Lo.
Ingleside
Imperial Bank, (Himālaya Ho.)
Inspection Bungalow,
(P.W.D.)
Inverneal
Iona Ho. & Cot.
Isla Ho.

Ivanhoe & Cot.
Ivy Bank
Ivy Cot., (Mussoorie)
Ivy Cot., (Landour)
Ivydene
Ivy Vil.

J
Jess Cot.
Jura Ho.

K
Kachahri, The, (Courts)
Kandi Lo.
Kashmir Hotel, (Gorge Head)
Kasmanda Lo., (Bassett Hall)
Kellog Memorial Church,
  Methodist
Kenilworth
Kennedy Lo.
Kenneth Lo., (Civil Surgeon)
Kennora
Kildare
Killarney
Kilmarnock
Kincraig (G.H. School)
Kirklands, (Soldiers
  Furlo' Home)
Knockane
Knutsford
Koh-i-Nūr, (P.O. & Bank)

L
Lāl Tibba Cot.
Lammermoor
Lancer Lo.
Landour Cot.
Landour View
Landour Vil.
Laurel Bank
Lauriston Lodge
Lawrence Terrace & Cot.
Leopard Lo.
Library, The (Mussoorie)

Limerick Vil.
Lind Cot.
Lindley Hall
Lion's Paw
Livelands
Lixmount & Cot.
Lochletter
Lodge Dalhousie No. 639 E.C.
Logie
London Ho., (Shops)
Longsight
Longview
Longwood
Lyndhurst
Lynndale
Lynnedin
Lynn Haze
Lynn Regis
Lynnwood

M

Mackinnon's Brewery (disused)
Macquarrie
Mādho Bilās
Mafasilite Printing Works,
  (Exchange)
Malakoff
Mall Bank
Mall View, (Shops)
Manor, The
Manor Ho.,
  (St. George's College)
Maple Hayes
Maple Wood
Maple Wood Lo.
Margaret Cot.
Marine Hall
Marion Vil.
Market Hill
Mar Lo.
Maryville
Maudville
May Cot.
Mayfield & Cot.

McAuley Cot.
Meakin Hall, (Wynberg
  Homes)
Melrose, Survey of India
M.E.C. Church, (Osborne
  Meml.)
Midlands & Cot., (Woodstock
  College)
Midstream
Midstream Cot.
Monastery, The
Mona Vil.
Mont Clair
Monte Cristo & Cot.
Montpellier
Montrose Ho. & Cot.
Montville
Morningside
Mostyn Lo.
Mountain View & Cot.
Mount George
Mount Hermon
Mount Pleasant
Mount View & Cot.
Mulberry Lo.,
  (Police Inspector)
Mullingar & Cot.
Mull Vil.
Municipal Bakery
Municipal Schools

N

Nālāpāni Ho.
Nārāyan Niwās
Newby
New Home & Cot.
New Place
Newāz Building
  (Stiffles & Shops)
Nook, The
North View & Lo.
North View Vil.
Norwood
Nut, The

O

Oak Bush
Oak Cot.
Oakdene
Oak Grove (E.I.R. Sch.)
Oaklands (Mussoorie)
Oaklands & Cot. (Landour)
Oak Leaf
Oakless
Oakley Cot.
Oak Lo.
Oak Openings
Oakroyd
Oaks, The
Oakshade Cot.
Oakville, & Cot.
Ockbrooke, & Cot.
Oldville
Osborne Ho.
Oxford Ho. (Shops & Union
  Hotel)

P

Padma Niwās & Cot. (H.H.
  Rājpipla)
Palmerston
Parade Point Ho., & Cot.
Parade Side
Parade View
Paris Ho., (Picture Palace)
Parish Room, (C. of E.)
Parish Room, (R.C.)
Parsonage, (R.C.) The,
  (Landour)
Parsonage, (C. of E.) The,
  (Mussoorie)
Pavilion, The
Petersfield
Pharmacy, The, (Shop)
Phoenix Lo.
Picture Palace, (Paris Ho.)
Pine Rock
Plaisance
Pleasure View

Plevna Ho. & Cot. (Tilak
    Meml. Institute)
Police Stations & Outposts
Post & Telegraph Offices
Powys Cot.
Priory, The
Prospect Lo.
Prospect Point
Pumping Stations

R
Raghu Niwās
Rahmat Manzil
Ralston Cot.
Ralston Manor
Rām Newās Cot.
Rāmpriya Ho.
Ranbīr Villa
    (H.H. Kalsia)
Raspberry Bank
Ravensbourne
Rectory, The (Landour)
Rectory Lo.
Redburn, Cot., Lo. & Vil.
Redwood Cot.
Regent Ho., (Shops)
Reelick
Restaurant, (Grand Hotel (&
    Paladium)
Restaurant, (Stiffles)
Retreat, The, (Landour)
Retreat, The, (Mussoorie) &
    Cot.
Rink, The
River View
Roanoke
Rockcliff & Cot.
Rockdale
Rockford
Rock Haven
Rockstone Ho., (G.P.O.)
Rockville & Cot.
Rockwood
Rokeby

Rose Bank & Cot.
Roseleigh
Rose Lynn
Rosemary Cot.
Rose Vil.
Rughbir Nīwās (Guilford Ho.)

S
St. Andrews
St. Asaph
St. Bernards
St. Clair
St. Emilian's Ch. (R.C.)
St. Fidelis High Sch. &
    Orphanage, (R.C.)
St. George's Coll. (Manor Ho.)
St. Goar & Cot.
St. Helens
St. Marys Cottage Hospital
St. Pauls Church, (C. of E.),
    (Landour)
St. Peters Ch., (R.C.),
    (Landour)
St. Roque, Survey of India
Saiyid Manzil
Saiyid Manzil Cot.
Sanford Hall
Santi Kunja
Saplings, The
Saplings Cot.
Savoy Hotel, The
Saxon Vil. & Cot.
Scottsburn
Seafield
Seaforth Lo.
Sedborough & Cot.
Sedborough Lo.
Sebastopol
Sevenoaks
Sevenoaks Annexe
Shamrock Ho. & Lo.
Shamrock Cot.
Shanty, The
Shawfield

Silverwood
Sisters, The
Slateville
Snowdon
Snow View
Soldiers Furlo' Home,
    (Kirklands & Westonel)
Somerford Ho.
Southend Ho. (Shops)
South Hill
Southwood
Springfield
Spring View
Srī Nivās
Stainton Cot.& Lo.
Stapleton
Station Hospital, The
    (Landour)
Stella Cot.
Stone Ledge
Stoneleigh
Strawberry Bank & Cot.
Stuart Ville
Studio, The Summerville,
    (H.H. Tehri-Garhwāl)
Sunny Bank
Sunny Cot.
Sunny Lo.
Sunny View
Sunny View Vil.
Sussex Ho. & Cot.
Swanmore
Swiss Cot.
Sylvan Home
Sylverton & Cot.

T
Tafton
Tara Hall
Tara Hall Cot.
Tehri View
Telegraph Offices
Telephone Exchange,
    (Connaught Ho.)

Terence Hall
Terrace Cot.
Thanet Lo.
Theodore Cot. & Lo.
Thespic Lo.
Thistle Bank
Tilak Meml. Institute, (Plevna Cot.)
Timoleague
Tiverton Ho., Allahābād Bank)
Tranby Croft
Trim Cot., Lo. & Vil.
Tullahmore
Tullahmore Cot. & Lo.
Tulliemet

U
Undercliff
Undercliff Lo.
Union Church, (Interdenominational)
Upper Woodstock
V
Vaid Newās
Vale Head
Vale Ridge

Vale View
Verdun
Vermont
Vincent Hill School, (S.D.A.)
Violet Bank

W
Wakefield, & Cot.
Walnut Grove
Waverly Bank
Waverly Cot.
Waverly Dene & View
Waverly Lo.
Waverly Villa
Wayside, Cot. & Lo.
Wee House
West End Ho., (Shops)
West Lynn
Westonel, (Soldiers Furlo' Home)
Westward Ho.
Wharf, The
Whitby
Whitefield Cot. & Hall
White Ho.
Whytbank Cas.

Wild Wood
Willow Bank, (Landour)
Willow Bank, (Mussoorie)
Willow Lo.
Wimbledon
Windermere, & Cot.
Winscottie
Wisteria
Wolfsburn
Wolfscraig
Wolverdene
Woodlands Schools
Woodside
Woodstock School
Woodville & Cot.
Wycliffe
Wynberg High School & Homes

Y, Z
Y.W.C.A. (Dūn View)
Zephyr Hall & Cot.
Zephyr Hill Ho.
Zephyr Lo. & Cot.
Zigzag Cot.

*Published in 1922 under the direction of Colonel C.H.D. Ryder, CIE, DSO, RE, surveyor general of India, reprinted (no changes in map) in 1926, new second edition (slight alternations) published in 1929.

Appendix C

Details of Mussoorie Hydro-Electric Scheme*

Up to 1909 the water supply of Mussoorie was provided partly by gravitation from the Chalmer Khad and Khattapani springs and partly by steam pumping from the Mackinnon spring below the Library. Of late years however it has been recognized that the supply was quite inadequate to the demand, and in 1900 the question of the provision of a further supply was seriously taken up. In October 1902 the Sanitary Engineer, Mr. Aikman, presented a preliminary report and estimate for improving the Mussoorie and Landour water supply, coupled with a scheme for lighting both places by electricity. The general plan of the scheme was that power should be derived from the Kempty Falls and utilized firstly to drive electric pumps, which would pump up water from the Murray springs for the supply of Mussoorie, with subsidiary pumps for Landour, and secondly to light the streets, public institutions, hotels and private houses in Mussoorie. The cost was tentatively estimated at Rs.6,50,000 and a detailed scheme was actually worked out and approved; but unfortunately the negotiations with the Tehri Raja for the use of the Kempty Falls fell though, and the board chose as a substitute the Bhatta Falls on the south face of the Mussoorie Ridge, which had the advantage of being situated both in British Territory and also nearer the rail head at Dehra. Some further modifications were introduced into the scheme, on the recommendation of Major DeLotbiniere, who was called in to advise in September 1904. The final estimates as sanctioned by the Government in March 1905 come to Rs.7,29,560 for Mussoorie and Landour. The Landour portion of the scheme was however subsequently dropped as the cantonment authorities withdrew from participation in the scheme shortly after the final estimates had been passed. The general plan of the scheme is as follows:—

About two miles below the Mall and to the south of Mussoorie, near Bhatta village, two mountains streams join forces. Just below this junction are constructed the necessary head works, which control the flow of water from these streams into the steel pipes through which the water will flow to the generating station. The latter is situated at Galogi, approximately one mile below the head works. The generating station comprises three generating sets of 150 kilowatts each, the generators being alternating 3 phase, 50 cycle, 6,600 volt machines direct coupled to Pelton wheels, each set being controlled by a Lombard governor. These

*From Walton, H.G. *The Gazetteer of Dehra Dun*, first published in 1911 and reprinted by Natraj Publishers, Dehra Dun, in 2007, p. 253–256. Minor editorial modifications have been made to the quoted text.

machines are connected to the necessary switching apparatus fixed on the switchboard, whence two sets of high tension lines issue forth on their way to the pumping station, the one running over Vincent's Hill, feeding two sub-stations. Several springs situated in the Murray estate have been impounded for the supply of water which is led through pipes to a reservoir hard by the pumping station. The latter is situated about 1 ½ miles below the Old Brewery and contains two three-throw pumps rope-driven by two motors of 150 horse power each. The water is lifted, at the rate of 180 gallons a minute, some 1,700 feet to the topmost point of Mussoorie, Vincent's Hill, where are situated two reservoirs of 50,000 gallons capacity each. Thence the water flows by gravitation to all parts of the Station.

The secondary portion of the scheme provides for the lighting of all roads in the Station. The Mall is to be lighted by means of 2,000 candle power arc lamps and other roads by means of 32 candle power incandescent lamps. The Station has been divided into twelve approximately equal areas. At the centre of each area is fixed a transformer station, or sub-station. In each of these suitable apparatus transform the high tension pressure of generation to low tension pressure of 220 volves, suitable for a supply to the public, and from each sub-station issues a net work of wires, some of which convey the current to the public lamps while others will convey it to private houses. Electric energy is sold at the rate of four annas per B.T.U. (Board of Trade Unit), while the water is obtainable through a meter at the rate of Rs.2 per 1,000 gallons if supplied through house connections; at the public stand posts the supply is free.

The scheme is in many ways unique. The lift of 1,700 feet is certainly the highest lift in Asia and one of the highest in the world. The laying of the power pipe line is an exceptionally fine bit of work. The line, instead of running straight as most large power pipe lines do in Europe, has to follow the contour of the hills. The suvey of this line and the calculations involved so as to make sure of getting the right angles in the bends were of a most difficult nature. Great credit is due to Mr. [J.S.] Pitkeathly, the contractors' chief engineer, who almost sacrificed his life in his endeavours to complete this pipe line in time for the scheme to be opened in 1909. The actual cost of the scheme has far exceeded the final estimate of 1905. In 1908 the revised estimate for the completion of the scheme had risen to Rs.9,72,000 for Mussoorie alone—an increase of some 40 per cent on the original estimate. In the end the Government granted a subvention of Rs.25,000 for six years to the municipal finances, in order to assist the Board in defraying the charges due for interest and sinking fund on the loans incurred, until the scheme commenced to pay its way.

Commenced in January 1906, the scheme was practically ready for working by May 1909. The new hydrants were opened for public use on the 15th of that month. On the 24th—Empire Day—the electric light was switched on with some éclat for the first time. Since then the lighting and water services have been conducted with but few hitches. Experience has, however, shown that arc lamps are ill-suited to road lighting in a hill station, and they are being replaced by incandescent lamps on the Waverley Road between the Library and

Charleville Hotel. The only serious interruption which occurred was that caused by the heavy floods of the 11ᵗʰ August 1909. These breached the paved pipe line in two places and damaged the terre plein [level ground] on which the power house is situated. Temporary repairs were effected within a fortnight, but the permanent repairs are still under construction and are estimated at Rs.75,000. By the time therefore that the scheme is finally completed the total cost will probably have amounted to not less than 11 lakhs and may possibly come to more. Even to repay the interest and sinking fund charges on this sum at six per cent, an income of Rs.66,000 per annum would be required—which is scarcely within the bounds of proximate probability. The anticipations of speedy profit which were entertained at the time of the launching of the scheme are therefore never likely to be realized. At the same time the Board is taking active steps to promote light and water connections, and expects to have a hundred houses at least on its mains when the 1910 season opens. The income from these connections will be considerable. While therefore it is improbable that the scheme will, at any rate for many years to come, be a commercial success, it is quite possible that in the near future, the net cost of the scheme to the rates, will, after deducting the income derived from house connections not exceed the amount paid by the Board for the vastly inferior lighting and water supply which prevailed prior to 1909.

The Mussoorie pumping station, located about two miles (3.2 kms) below the Mall and to the south of Mussoorie near Bhatta village. *(Courtesy of Library of Congress)*

Appendix D

Details from the Lives of Mussoorie Personages

EX-AMEER's DEATH
A Link with Lord Roberts
[The Obituary of Amir Yakub Khan from *The Times*, London,
16 November 1923, p. 13]

Delhi, Nov. 15.—Sardar Mohammad Yakub Khan, a former Ameer of Afghanistan, died at Dehra Dun this morning.—Reuter.

Mohammad Yakub Khan, born in 1849, was the son of Shere Ali, who was Ameer of Afghanistan *from 1863 to 1866 (when he was deposed by his brothers) and again from 1868 to 1879. In* 1870 Yakub rebelled against his father and seized Herat, where he ruled as an independent prince until Lord Mayo, the Viceroy of India, effected a brief reconciliation in July, 1871. This only lasted until the following August, when Yakub again rebelled and was captured and imprisoned in Kabul. He was released, and when, after the outbreak of the second Afghan War, his father fled from Kabul (December, 1878) he seized the city and himself became Ameer on his father's death I February, 1879.

In May of that year he signed the Treaty of Gandamak, by which he gained an annual subsidy of £60,000. In September, however, mutinous Afghan troops massacred Sir Louis Cavagnari, the British Envoy, and his staff at Kabul, and Lord—then Sir Frederick—Roberts started at once, at the invitation of the powerless Ameer, to suppress the mutiny and avenge the massacre. Evidence, however, accumulated that the Ameer was stirring up the tribes against him, and, after the Afghans had lost Kabul and been defeated at Charasia, the Ameer Yakub Khan came to Sir Frederick's tent and there abdicated (October, 1879), after explaining that he had led a wretched life as Ameer and would rather be a grass-cutter in the British camp than ruler of Afghanistan. Yakub Khan was escorted down into India. Various suggestions made for his restoration came to nothing, and his son, Musa Khan, appears to have had a purely nominal reign (December, 1879-March, 1880) until Abdur Rahman, the grandfather of the present Ameer, was called back from his exile in Samarkand and made Ameer by the British in Kabul in July, 1880.

OBITUARY: LT-COL MICHAEL SKINNER

[The obituary of Michael Alexander Robert Skinner, written by Kuldip Singh, from *The Independent*, London, 17 May 1999, p. 7]

MICHAEL SKINNER, a scion of India's oldest military family, commanded the dashing cavalry regiment of Skinner's Horse more than 150 years after it was raised by his legendary ancestor James Skinner in 1803.

Known as "ramrod Skinner" by his regimental colleagues for his principled dealings and straight talk, he saw action with his regiment during the Second World War in Persia and Italy. On returning home in 1945 he was despatched to the turbulent North West Frontier Province (now in Pakistan) to battle feisty tribesmen constantly at war with the colonial government.

Shortly after Independence in 1947 Skinner's regiment, now armed with Churchill tanks, was despatched along with other Indian army units to "annex" the southern Muslim principality of Hyderabad, until then ruled by the Nizam, one of the world's richest men, who had refused to join the Indian Union of States.

After varied assignments including a stint as instructor at the Indian Military Academy in Dehra Dun in the northern foothills, and as a member of the three-nation International Control Commission in Vietnam, in 1960 Skinner took command of Skinner's Horse, founded by his great-great-grandfather. He was the first Skinner to command the regiment since its founder had died in 1842.

Skinner's Horse is the Indian army's fourth oldest cavalry regiment. It was raised by James Skinner in 1803 at Hansi, 80 miles north of Delhi, as an "irregular horse" following the grant of over 200 villages by the British East India Company that then controlled most of India. The rapidly expanding company, desperately short of British troops to help it annex territory and consolidate control, resorted to the old Mughal system of raising "irregular" units by committing *jagirs* or land endowments to military commanders—mostly enterprising adventurers who used the income from them to subsidise cavalry or infantry regiments.

James Skinner and his brother Robert were two such beneficiaries. Sons of a Scottish soldier and a high-caste Rajput mother who was part of his "war loot", they were brought up in army camps across India and became skilled horsemen. Around 1780 both applied to join the company's army, but were rejected on the grounds of being Eurasian and hence considered untrustworthy. Peeved by narrow British attitudes the two brothers joined the army of Scindia, the Maratha warlord who then ruled over central India with his headquarters at Gwalior, 180 miles west of Delhi, and opposed the expansionist company.

Scindia employed a host of brilliant French generals like the Count de Boigne and General Perron who had organised their chieftain's force along the lines of a European army. The Skinner brothers, especially James, performed admirably in numerous campaigns, frequently defeating superior British forces with their small, swift and well-knit band of committed horsemen. After several campaigns the Marathas, by now plagued by internecine rivalries, were convincingly defeated by the British general Lord Lake and hordes of Scindia's men flocked to join the company's army in 1802. The Skinner brothers and their risala (horse cavalry) were amongst them.

But the cavalrymen came with two conditions: first, that they never be asked to fight their former employer Scindia or his descendants and second that they be permitted to choose their own leader. Because of their awesome reputation Lord Lake agreed and the men unanimously chose Burra Sikandar—the older brother, James Skinner—as their leader. He was given some 200 villages around Hansi and Skinner's Horse came into being on 23 February 1803.

While choosing the regimental uniform Skinner was inspired by his mother's Rajput heritage, whereby a prince riding out to battle would vow to return victorious or die. They would anoint their faces with saffron, the colour of martyrdom, and don yellow robes over their armour which was tied with a yellow sash. Skinner chose yellow tunics as the regimental colour and every horseman recruited swore never to return from battle unless victorious. Through numerous campaigns in Afghanistan, and France and Flanders in the First World War, the Yellow Devils covered themselves with glory.

Till the early 1840s Skinner was the head of a group of aristocratic Eurasians living in Delhi. He owned an impressive town mansion near the old city's Kashmir gate area, built in classic style with high columns and colonnades. He entertained lavishly, and maintained an impressive harem. He also built St James's Church—where services are still held regularly, as a smaller copy of St. Paul's Cathedral—and he was buried beside the altar so that people could trample over him and help him atone for his sins. The grounds of the Anglican church are the Skinner family burial ground.

Michael Skinner was born in 1920 at Sikandar Hall, a baronial family mansion built by his ancestors as their summer home in Mussoorie, a picturesque hill town in the Himalayas 250 miles north of Delhi. His father James Skinner was a *zamindar* or landlord and Myrtle, his mother, was descended from the distinguished Hearsey military family. He was initially educated in England but completed his schooling at St George's in Mussorie in 1939 where he not only lost his pukka British accent but became an accomplished athlete and heavyweight boxer.

He joined the army and was commissioned into Skinner's Horse in 1942. Soon afterwards the German army launched its Russian campaign and the regiment was despatched to guard the Iranian oil fields. In 1943, as part of the 10th and 4th Indian Division they advanced to Italy where they came under sustained fire for long periods, successfully holding the Gothic Line against the German onslaught.

Returning home after the war, Skinner was assigned to the North West Frontier and after several exciting postings achieved his life's ambition in July 1960 when he took command of Skinner's Horse for three years. In 1950 he had married Margaret Skinner, a cousin, at St. James's Church. And though posted elsewhere, when India went to war with Pakistan for the second time in 1965, Skinner rushed to his regiment which was deployed on the northern Punjab front and offered his services, which were regretfully declined.

Michael Skinner left the army in 1966 to farm his ancestral lands at Hansi and was made an honorary brigadier in the 1990s by India's army chief for helping out ex-servicemen. A no-nonsense soldier, he was always fair in his dealings and outspoken to a fault to senior and junior officers alike.

Kuldip Singh

Michael Alexander Robert Skinner, cavalry officer: born Mussoorie, India 29 September 1920; married 1950 Myrtle Skinner (three daughters); died Epsom, Surrey, 17th March 1999.

GLOSSARY

Abdar	waiter.
Amir or Emir	commander, general, prince; a high title of nobility or office, used throughout the Arab world, as well as historically in nineteenth-century Afghanistan and in the medieval Muslim world.
Anna	an Indian coin worth one-sixteenth of a rupee.
Ayah	a nanny who usually attends children, but sometimes serves as a personal maid to a lady.
Bhishti	a water-carrier.
Bistar	bedding used during travel.
Chowk	a traffic-crossing or intersection.
Chowkidhar	a guard.
Dacoits	bands of roaming outlaws.
Dak	post or mail; also, the mail or postal arrangements; sometimes spelt dawk or dauk.
Dak Bungalow	a travellers' rest house at the end of a dak or mail stage. To travel by dak meant travelling by relays of palanquins or other carriage, as fast as the post would travel along a road.
Dandy or Dandi	a light litter of wooden frame covered with canvas and wax cloth and borne by bearers.
Dharna	a peaceful protest.
Dhajji	a type of building construction, consisting of a patchwork of timber and stone, with mud mortar.
Dhobi	a washerman.
Doli	strong cloth slung like a hammock to a bamboo staff, in which a passenger would ride carried by two or more men.
Gadi	throne.
Gharry or Gharri	a horse-drawn cab of sorts, often in the style of a wheeled palanquin (palki).
Jampan	an armchair-like mode of conveyance, carried by bearers.
Jampani	a coolie who carries a jampan or pulls a rickshaw.
Phaltoo	coolie; literally, someone lounging about, usually with little or nothing to do.
Jihad	a campaign waged by Muslims in defense of the Islamic faith against people, organizations or countries regarded as hostile to Islam.

Kala	black.
Khande Di Pahul	Sikh ceremony of initiation into the faith.
Kundy or Kandy	a woven basket that was strapped to the back of a coolie and used for carrying children or the sick.
Khansamah	a cook.
Khitmatgar	a butler or head waiter.
Kutchery	court.
Mahant	a headman or priest.
Maidan	an open garden, park or square.
Mali	a gardener.
Mazar	an Islamic, often Sufi, tomb of a religious mystic or pir.
Mehtar	a sweeper.
Memsahib	originally a term of respect for a married European woman, now including any married woman of rank.
Minar	column.
Munshi	teacher, often used to refer to an instructor of Urdu or Hindi.
Nerik	a tariff, rate or price-current, especially one established by authorities for the benefit of customers.
Palki	a litter, usually used to carry high-level or well-to-do persons, borne by four bearers.
Parganna	a group of neighbouring villages.
Pice	smallest of Indian coins.
Pukkah or Pukka	certain, reliable, authentic, true, proper, socially acceptable; of food, it may mean cooked, ripe, substantial.
Rajpramukh	head or head of state.
Sardar	leader.
Shaheed	martyr.
Shikar	hunting.
Tat	a hill pony.
Tiba	hill or peak, in the local Garhwali language.
Tonga	a hooded carriage, a kind of light and small, two-wheeled vehicle pulled by one or two horses.
Zamindar	landlord.

INDEX

Ramsey, Henry *see*
Mussoorie Seminary
Rana, Dev Shamsher Jang
Bahadur (Raja of
Nepal), 35, 246-247,
109
Krishna Kumari Devi
(wife), 35;
Rawdon-Hastings, Francis,
(Lord Moira) 4
Redemption, Church of the,
139-140
Reforestation, 79
Reid, Charles (General), 114,
129-130n[68]
Religious of Jesus and
Mary *see also* Waverley
Convent School, 88-94,
124n[17]
at Hampton Court School,
107, 108, 118
Rink, the, 55, 168-170, 197
Rosary Church, 146
Rust, Julian (photographer),
34, 37, 51, 217
Rust, Thomas Alfred
(photographer), 46, 165,
169, 185, 217
Sacred Heart Church (St
Emilian's Church), 146
Sahasradhara Road (Sulphur
Springs Road), 4
Sai Baba Temple, 150
Sanatan Dharam Temple,
150
Scandal Point, 58
Shastri, Lal Bahadur (Prime
Minister), 270-271
Shedup Choephelling
Temple, 150-151, 272
Shepherd, Charles

(photographer), 74
Shikar (hunting), 2, 48
Shops, 209-219
Shore, Frederick John, 7, 25,
48, 52, 64n[11]
Shri Digambar Jain Temple,
150
Sikkim, raja of, 16
Singh, Dinraj Pratap
(Rajkumar), 207
Singh, Duleep (Maharaja),
75, 230, 239-246
Singh, Jagajit (Maharaja of
Kapurthala), 228
Singh, Sukhjit (His Highness
Brigadier, Maharaja of
Kapurthala), 41-42, 228
Sirmur Battalion, raising of,
6, 7, 22n[24]
Sisters' Bazaar, 77
Skinner, Alexander, 87
sons of, 124n[12], 264
Skinner, Alice, 264-265
Skinner, George, 265
sons of, 265
Skinner, James Hercules
(Colonel, founder of
Skinner's Horse), 205,
264
Skinner, James (son of J.H.
Skinner), 205
Skinner, Lillian, 277
Skinner, Michael Alexander
Robert ('Mike',
Brigadier), 136, 265
siblings of, at Sikander
Hall, 265
Skinner, Robert (Major), 264
Skinner, Stanley, 264
Skinner, Thomas (Captain),
69-70, 159n[28]

Solaroli, Paolo (Marquis of
Briona), 88, 90
Soltykoff, Alexis Dmitrievich
(Prince), 246
Somber, David Ochterlony
Dyce, 88
St George's College ('Manor
House'), 104-107
cadets at, 171
cemeteries at 156,
founding of by
Capuchians, 104
Patrician management of,
105
military connections, 106
Nirmala Inter-College,
105 St Fidelis' School
and Military Orphanage
('St Fids'), 105
well-known graduates of,
106-107
St Michael's Parish Church,
146, 147, 156
St Paul's Church, 73, 77, 137
St Peter's Church, 77, 145-
146
Stiffle's Restaurant and
Ballroom (Garhwal
Terrace Hotel), 186,
scuffles at, 186-188
Stokes, Arthur, 85-87, *see
also Mussoorie Seminary*
son of, 123n[7]
Sultana, Niloufer Khanum
(Princess), 230-231
Summer Home for Soldiers'
Children, 114-117
at Bassett Hall, 206
Sumru, Begum of Sardhana,
88, 124-125n[18], 267
Surkhunda Devi Temple, 150

Printed in Great Britain
by Amazon

45832023R00194